# THE AUTHOR AND THE BOOK

David Northcroft spent the earlier part of his boyhood in Worcestershire and Sussex. However, when his father became exciseman at Cragganmore Distillery, Ballindalloch, Banffshire, he moved up to the North-East. He has seen no reason to live anywhere else ever since.

He attended Aberlour High School, followed by degrees at the Universities of Aberdeen, Cambridge and a doctorate at Stirling. His career has been in education, firstly as a teacher of English at Aberdeen Grammar School, then a member of staff at Aberdeen College of Education (later Northern College). By the time of his early retirement he was Vice Principal.

He has divided the happy years since then between helping to look after granddaughters and researching in, first, Scottish school education and latterly in oral history, where he has concentrated on building up an archive of personal reminisce from North-East folk. He is responsible for two earlier books: *Scots at School* (Edinburgh University Press, 2003) and *North-East Identities and Scottish Schooling* (Aberdeen University Press, 2005).

He has lived in Muchalls for over 40 years. He is married to Kathleen and they have two sons: Jonathan, who as Football Correspondent to the *Sunday Times* is forced to watch Man U and Chelsea rather than the Dons, and Matt, who is both a teacher and a Grade 1 referee. Matt, Elaine and his three granddaughters also live round the corner in Muchalls and are a constant source of wonderment and delight.

*Grampian Lives* purports to offer a collective portrait of the shape and texture of daily life in the North-East of Scotland, as experienced by the folk who have spent their formative years there. The personal recollections which appear in this book are extracted from the recorded words of the 250 people David Northcroft has interviewed and recorded during the last 10 years. Invariably the interviews have been made in the subjects' own homes and been conducted in an informal conversational style. The selection of witnesses – usually based on word-of-mouth recommendation or newspaper letters and stories – has been guided by the wish to cover a representative range of places, occupational backgrounds and ages.

The present volume focuses on the older generations, those who have been able to recall life in the first half of the last century. It is hoped that this volume will be followed by two more: *Grampian Lives 1950-2000* and *City Lives 1900-2000*. The latter will draw upon the reminiscences of those who were brought up in Aberdeen itself, as opposed to the country, coastal and small town people of the first two books.

Readers are invited to get in touch with observations and also recommendations of further interviewees. (35 Nethermains Road, Muchalls, AB39 3RN or 01569730621 or David@davidnorthcroft.wanadoo.co.uk)

Published in November, 2010
Second impression: August, 2011

Copyright © David Northcroft

A catalogue record for this book is available from the British Library

ISBN 978-0-9534534-6-7

Design and typesetting by Leopard magazine
www.leopardmag.co.uk

Printed and bound in Scotland by
Robertson, of Forfar

Published by Leopard Press
Auld Logie, Pitcaple, Inverurie, Aberdeenshire AB51 5EE

# GRAMPIAN LIVES

## Living through the twentieth century in the small towns and settlements of North-East Scotland

Volume 1: Early Century Lives and Memories: 1900–1950

## David Northcroft

Leopard
PRESS

# DEDICATION

To Abby, Erin and Rachael – three young Grampian lives in the making.

# ACKNOWLEDGMENTS

No book can ever be produced without the help of others: in the case of *Grampian Lives* that has been especially so.

While the great majority of the photographs which illustrate the reminiscences in the pages that follow have been provided by the speakers themselves – people who have trustingly allowed me access to precious family collections – I must also thank a number of other helpers. Brian Watt has generously opened up his extraordinary collection of old postcards for me to plunder. He is also author of two Richard Stenlake works: *Old Stonehaven,* 2000, and *Old Newtonhill and Muchalls,* 2005. Similarly, the two marvellous on-line libraries of images run by the Alford Image Library and the Glenbuchat Heritage Archive have been most helpful and forthcoming. In this latter connection I must mention Peter Duffus. The Buckie Fishing Heritage Museum has been similarly generous.

On a more specific basis, Brenda Ogilvie of Muchalls has tracked down and handed over the photographs of Mary Geddes which appear in the chapter, 'Going to School'. Ken Cruickshank has kindly given permission to take copies from his unrivalled collection of Glenbuchat artefacts. A number of other people have also furnished pictures. They are: Mark l'Anson (author of *The Scottish East Coast Fishing Industry*: Richard Stenlake Publishing, 2008); Stewart Wilson (author of *Old Midmar and Cromar*, Richard Stenlake Publishing, 2006); Andy Thompson and his 'Picture Reprints'; Dorothy Sutherland for the photographs of her mother Dorothy Stuart; Enid Nicol for those of her mother-in-law, Marigold Nicol; Sally Crumplin for those of her mother, Isabella Wilson; Muriel Sinclair for those of her aunt, Alexina Fleming.

A number of people have been helpful in other ways, either by facilitating contacts with likely speakers or by readily answering specific queries. They are: Davie and Evie Alexander; Shona Barclay; Andrew and Wendy Christie; David and Barbara Denoon; Jim and Mary Ewen; Kirsty Devaney; John Duncan; George and Margurita Esson; James Gordon; David Hartley; Heather Hopkins; Alastair Johnstone; Ian Law; Joe McDowall; Dorothy Maitland; Donald Mitchell; Fiona Squires; Jack Webster; Ian Russell and Alison Sharman, both of the Elphinstone Institute, University of Aberdeen.

I must also offer up heartfelt thanks to Lindy Cheyne and Ian Hamilton of Leopard Press, whose enthusiastic and inspiring co-operation has exceeded the normal bounds of professional assistance. Not only have they performed a highly skilled and creative task in editing and laying out the presentation of *Grampian Lives*, they have been very fine folk to have worked with.

I would dearly like to thank my family for being just that – my family, a constant source of life-giving support. The names of this incomparable set of North-East people are Kathleen, Jonathan, Matt, Elaine and young Erin, Abby and Rachael.

But above all else, my gratitude belongs to all the people who have opened up their memories to me. Once I had exhausted the circle of my own relatives and friends I became dependent upon the willingness of complete strangers to welcome me into both their homes and their lives, there to ply me with fly cups, home bakes and their own very human stories. The names which appear in this book confirm the truth that the North-East of Scotland contains some of the finest folk you could hope to meet anywhere. I hope they will accept *Grampian Lives* as my tribute to them.

# Front Cover

The picture is of a group of children gathering around a conjurer who has just been entertaining them. It was taken at Ballogie in the 1920s. It was supplied by Mrs Mary Campbell of Dingwall whose mother, Nell Baird, is the tall girl to the extreme right of the group. Her aunt, Alna, is at the other side, second left. Mary Campbell is also the granddaughter of Helen Singer, the teacher who appears in the photograph with her charges at Balloch School, 1904, on page 129.

# Notes

The words which appear in this book are taken from transcriptions of recordings of the recollections offered by the contributors. In each case scripts were sent back to the speakers for their amendments before an agreed version was arrived at. The accounts set out in *Grampian Lives* are selected extracts; the typical interview lasted 90 minutes and generated over 4,000 words. Editing has been kept to the minimum necessary to smooth out repetitions and hesitations.

Witnesses spoke in their own accents and dialect. As these ranged along a continuum of usage rather than falling into any distinct 'Standard English/ Doric' category – often within the one interview – the decision has been made to render their words in the one Standard form, excepting reported instances of direct speech. Here a more immediate, localised form has seemed to be more appropriate.

'Grampian' refers to the former Grampian Region as it was composed before the local government re-organisation of the 1990s. That is, the historical counties of Aberdeenshire, Banffshire, Moray and Kincardineshire.

The place names which appear after each speaker's name refer to the locations focussed on in their specific recollections, not their birth places.

Many more interviewees have given of themselves than I have been able to squeeze into this present volume. I hope that they will not take their omission as being enforced by anything other than exigencies of space. My great discovery in researching this book is that everyone – especially in the North-East – has a worthwhile story to tell, whether I have managed to find room for it or not.

Sadly, but inevitably given their ages, some of my witnesses have subsequently died. As, however, it has been difficult to ascertain exact dates and occurrences, the decision has been made to give the year of birth only. I can, however, report that at the time of writing, Alexina Fleming – the first person to appear in *Grampian Lives* – is still with us, at the age of 105.

# Contents

## Going to the kirk

## EARLY CENTURY LIVES: 3

## Life was hard

## EARLY CENTURY LIVES: 5

# Into work                                                                                             250

## EARLY CENTURY LIVES: 6

TWO WIDOWS' SONS

# GRAMPIAN LIVES: THE NORTH-EAST IN MEMORY AND IN LIFE

'The people are somewhat shy and reticent. When you meet them the speech is first of the weather. They hide themselves, as every real man does, in their ordinary intercourse. It is only in their confidential moments that they drop the mask and show the soul'.

**– W. S. Bruce.** *The Nor'east, Aberdeen,* 1922.

I have spent the first ten years of the present century gathering in the recollections of those who grew up in the earlier half of the last one. Since 2000 I have, with tape recorder to hand and, yes, pleasantries concerning the day's weather at the ready, travelled all over the North-East in order to interview a range of folk in the hope that, by giving an account of the formative circumstances of their own Grampian lives, they would reveal something of the stuff which makes up the character of an age and of a region.

In that time, I have gathered in some million and a half words of oral transcript, taken from 250 assorted individual witnesses. The pages which follow represent an edited selection of their accounts, arranged under those headings which stand for the common experiences of their time and of their communities: family, school, war, occupation, pleasures and hardships, the kirk, social events and going to work.

The interviewees come from a range of background and of circumstance. Their childhood homes stretch from Findhorn in the north, to Glenlivet and Ballater in the west, to Laurencekirk in the south. The oldest among them were already into adulthood by the time that Bruce published his book; the youngest have been born into the age of broadband, multi-channel TV and the mobile phone. Their domestic environments might be the cottar hoose, the rural council house, the fisherman's terraced two-rooms, the suburban bungalow – or the cold, roomy manse, the laird's mansion or a mediaeval castle.

The present volume confines itself to those who did their growing up in the period 1900 to 1950 and did so, not in the city of Aberdeen, but spread over its vast hinterland of rural settlements, small towns and fishing ports. Although each of the speakers lived on into the 21st century, the era they evoke has slipped into a history as remote from us now as the premiership of Lord Aberdeen and the Crimean War were from their younger selves. When they talk of childhoods spent under the gloom of paraffin lamps, huddled round a smoky peat fire, of daily meals of brose and neeps and saps, and of the trudge to lug a bucket of water from a distant well, or talk of night time forays into the smelly dankness of the toilet hut out in the backyard, of holidays spent, not in Florida or Majorca, but at an auntie's in far off Stonehaven or on an uncle's croft at Lumsden, then they seem to be peering back into an age of primitive practices and narrow privation.

But, they will tell you, that is not how it seemed at the time. Ask them whether they ever judged themselves to be 'deprived' and they will respond with, 'Ach no! we didna ken ony diff'rent'. The compensations are readily listed: the freedoms of the fields and of the village, safe in the assurance that there would be no-one around to harm or to molest them; the shared pleasures of homemade games and the satisfactions of necessary tasks properly done; the security of an enfolding domestic life when families were large and remained unbroken; the warmth of community life where everyone knew everyone else and all were sure of their roles in its enduring structures.

More than that, they will go on to explain that. 'Aabidy wis in the same boat – an we aa pulled tegither'. It is a comment which moves us from simple description onto the level of a moral judgement. If their period was one of hardship and elemental toil, it was also one of difficulties overcome and of characters formed, of values which, as they fray and erode before the easier circumstances of the twenty-first century, are to be cherished still. The common struggle to work with the basic forces of life – the sea, the weather, the frailties of body, of dying and giving birth and, above and below all, the land itself – well, this is the native soil in which the traditional folk virtues of thrift, of prudence, of proud self-sufficiency and mutual respect, of a wisdom that is cannily practical and of ready hospitality and a pious work ethic, may take root and be brought to fruition. And they will lay claim to these qualities, not in any boastful or loud voice, but with that dryly self deprecating good humour and modest courtesy which are themselves evidence of, throughout the North-East, their unexceptional possession.

Consequently, it is not surprising that, running through the treasured evocations, there is an undertow of regret at how deeply the changes of the second half of the century have bitten into the social landscape of their North-East. Though balanced by an acknowledgement of the comforts of the contemporary world, they express a bemused concern at the extent to which these seem to have been hire-purchased through a glib materialism. They fear that the old community values of thrifty self denial and plain hard living have now, apparently, come to be regarded as superfluous and downright quaint.

This is why their reminiscences often dwell upon the old institutions of the local church and the parish school, not necessarily because either was enjoyed at the time, but because they were simply there, unchanging and without compromise or complication. That is why, too, when they revisit their pasts, it is to the nearby features of corner shops and travelling vans, the hours and hours spent freely roaming the surrounding fields, or into gatherings down at the village hall, that they will go. These might have been days when life was restricted to a small clump of endlessly repeated activities which were local and artlessly straightforward, but they were also securely familiar and at the service of the whole community.

There is, of course, something paradoxical about such claims. The elderly witnesses who evoke such past satisfactions, when simple contentment and neighbourly support were at everyone's door, will, in so doing, also be restoring a picture of existences that had to be struggled for on the floors of cold, bare cottages and up crowded tenements, where the lavvy stood across the mud of the open back yard, and in habitations where most families had an experience of a premature death from the kind of common condition which the antibiotics of the post-war NHS would banish as a matter of course. There are tales, too, of harsh, tawse-wielding classrooms, of stiflingly dull Sundays seated on itchy hard pews, of educational careers stunted through simple lack of money, and then of early working days passed in wretched bothies, as 80-hour-a-week maids-of-all-work, or as galley boys, churned about in the North Sea on some nauseous bucket of a trawler. And they will be conjuring up all these good old days in sitting rooms which are bright and carpeted and centrally heated, the wide screen TV in the corner, the colourful photographs of gleamingly healthy grandchildren on the walls.

Yet it would be a disservice to the integrity of the lives from which such memories have been extracted, to read them as data that have now diminished into a record which is merely historical – or, worse still, as a sepia-tinged snapshot whose clear outlines have become blurred by the roseate glow of selective memorisation. These people and their stories have much to teach the 21st century.

Listen to how clear they are about who they are and where they have come from. What is striking about the hundred or so witnesses, who fill the pages of this volume, is how firm is their sense of their North-East as a place that is both distinct and distinctive. This is partly a matter of geography, of their awareness of the old counties of Moray, of Aberdeenshire, Banff and Kincardineshire as being spread within a shoulder of land which shoves its way into the North Sea and is demarked from the rest of Scotland by rivers and Cairngorms, by sea and by Firth.

It is also a question of quality. Asked what they admire about their region and time and again they will turn to the words 'real' and 'balance'. They recognise, and their earlier lives bear witness to it, that theirs can be a hard land, but they know too that within its boundaries lies a rare combination of arable plain, of valleys, hills, water and mountain and small, tightly-drawn settlements in which men and women may lead lives that are quietly poised. These are the strengths that are daily given voice in the richly expressive Doric whose vocabulary and rhythms speak so intimately of the elemental realities of their land.

What is also remarkable among the range of witnesses is the idea of the 'North-East', and not simply of their own village or small town, as a presence which is felt to have nourished their own developing identity. Its terrain, in all its diversity of hill, river, forestation, heath and billowing farmland, its seas of fish and oil and windblown tides, and the peoples who have had the strength of purpose to master them all, gives the framework within which they have been able to make sense of their own 'ordinary' lives and the struggles and the satisfactions that have attended them. Its values of thrift, of hard work and shared endeavour have given them a standard by which to measure the worth of their own lives.

But the 'balance' and the practical realism of which they speak point in another direction too. It is a matter not simply of place but also of period. It was the novelist L.P. Hartley who stated that 'the past is a foreign country; they do things differently there'. The representations of the past contained in this volume bear out both the truth and the misrepresentation of this claim. The specifics will have changed and changed utterly, but the values that impelled them forward into our later age are with us still.

Perplexed though they may be at the consumerist pace and technological whirl in which their grandchildren are living, not one of the speakers in this volume would wish to thrust them back into the circumstances of their own childhoods. Their lives have been devoted to making something of themselves and by that they mean using the traditional North-East qualities of hard effort and neighbourly endeavour, of good sense and mutual respect, to improve not only their own but the lot of those who have come after. Just as their lives grew out of what their own parents and communities gave them, so they, in their turn, have striven to hand on something of value to the later generation. Their memories are more than a simple fireside story; they are our bequest. They show that their tellers are not the survivors of an alien age but our compatriots still.

A phrase which several speakers use, when asked to sum up their lives, is 'We've had the best of it!' The words are a tribute to an era and to the place. They recognise that the children of the last sixty years have lived through an age of soaring living standards, one of comparative peace and of universal social welfare and in a country that has been, on the whole, liberal and well intentioned towards its individual citizens. But they are also expressing gratitude that their span of years has been sufficiently long grown to have been firmly rooted in a land where the hard and decent lives of their own elders were there to give them the character and the example by which to win this later fulfilment. Just as the best of what they have been grew out of their own past, so should their histories guide and nourish us.

They have seen the North-East of the twentieth century as a good place in which to have grown up. For them it has provided a combination of time and place in which its mix of inherited wisdom and continuing effort, of independent spirits and communal support, of social responsibility and a sharply practical intelligence, have given integrity and coherence to the individual life. For the farmers, the teachers, the fisher folk, the mothers, the craftsmen and all those who have worked within its hard-won acres, around its coasts and upon its upland reaches, for all its various sons and all its daughters, the North-East has proved to be a good and fitting place in which to have passed their formative years. Looking back upon the unfolding of their years, they see lives which have made sense, their own and those of all their others. For them the North-East has been a land whose rugged contours contain a very human soul.

# A PROPER UPBRINGING

**The family gathers**
for Dr and Mrs Barclay's
Golden Wedding. Alexina Fleming
is sitting far left with her nephew
Allan on her knee.

**Alexina Fleming**
on her 103rd birthday.

# Daughter to the 'Banffie'

My father, William Barclay, was the editor of the *Banffshire Journal*. All through my childhood, my father was writing, writing for the paper. But we knew very little about his work; he just never talked about it.

At home, we had to be very, very quiet, because he did a lot of his work there and we were all in the one room – the study we called it. It had walls filled with these dark bookcases, which went from the floor to the ceiling; they were full of encyclopaedias and histories and all the classics like Dickens and Sir Walter Scott.

We would be seated at the table, all six of us children, doing our different lessons, and he'd be at the end, scribbling away and if any of us said even the smallest thing then out would come this 'Shoosh!' You'd whisper a question, 'What's the Latin for so-and-so?', and it would be 'Shoooosh…' He was a very remote person, for a father. Busy all the time, always writing, writing.

He was very well respected in the town. When we were out, people would touch their caps and say, 'Good morning Mr Barclay; good afternoon Mr Barclay'. He knew everyone in Banff, but none of them were invited to the house. It was all reading and writing with him. He was always too busy for friends; he was completely devoted to his work.

He had left school at 12 and, really, he was self-taught. He was one of 13 and he was the second son. The eldest boy went to Aberdeen and trained for the ministry but there

**Sixty-five years of unbroken service:** the presentation of a silver salver to mark William Barclay's retirement from *The Banffshire Journal* in 1946. Alexina's sister Betty is standing directly behind him.

wasn't the same money for him. Father went to the *Journal* and worked his way up from message boy and then the boy who would set the type. The editor retired at an early age for his health and Father got the chance to step in.

He wasn't exactly strict – but you just knew where you were with him, that you had to keep to the rules. Our only free time was on a Monday evening because that's when the paper went to print. He would be off at his office and we wouldn't see him again until the next morning, so we had the evening to ourselves. That was the time in the week when we could get our friends in and make as much of a row as we liked.

On a Sunday he would take it in turns to go to a different church each week and he would sit there and take down the sermons in shorthand. He particularly liked going to Alvah to hear the minister there. At the breakfast table he would just announce, 'We're going to Alvah!' And we would have to trot out to Alvah, four miles there, four miles back. We couldn't say, 'Oh, not Alvah again! We don't want to have to walk out all the way out there!' We couldn't object; it was the law!

Both our parents were very keen for us to get on at school. There were lists every term and they were printed in the paper and he would scan them thoroughly. He would look out for our marks in all the subjects: mental arithmetic, dictation, spelling, reading, writing – they were all laid out in different columns for everyone to see. 'Why didn't you do better there? Why only second in that?'

We were expected to excel in everything. There was never any scolding about it; you just knew what was expected of you. I remember at the table once, us all sitting around; by that stage there were only three of us still at home. Those who had left were expected to write their letter home, once a week. I remember at one lunchtime, he picked up one of their letters and read it. Suddenly he said, 'A gross grammatical error! There's a gross grammatical error been committed!' We didn't dare ask what it was or who had committed it; we were just glad it couldn't have been one of us. But afterwards, we used to laugh among ourselves: 'There's been a gross grammatical error committed by someone!' It became a joke among us – but not when Father was present…

Alexina Fleming, born 1905: Banff

# A Calvinist upbringing

My father was the village soutar. He was looked upon as a very strong church-going man. We were brought up that way. My mother used to giggle when she saw us going off to church on a Sunday morning. We were like a line of ducks going to the pond, my father going first and the four of us children behind. Everything about Sunday was strict; we weren't allowed to play, to knit; we could read schoolbooks only. There were no Sunday papers, nothing like that. And you had to do the housework on the Friday evening so as not to leave anything over that might possibly interfere with the Sunday in any way.

On a Sunday he would take it in turns to go to a different church each week and he would sit there and take down the sermons in shorthand.

## Mabel Brocklehurst:

Despite her 'Calvinist upbringing', there was still room for some diversions. Here Mabel is pictured, third from the left, as a five year-old, on stage in a local church production.

My Sunday was made up of going to the big Sunday school for the older ones at nine o'clock and when I came out at 10:30 my father would be standing at the gate, waiting for me and the other three to go to the church service. We would sit there, wondering if Father would ever pass around his pan drops. He always had a few in his pocket. The sermons were all hell-fire and damnation.

After lunch I had to go to the Infant Sunday School and play hymns there on the piano. Then, afterwards, my parents and the rest of the family would go for a walk by the river Spey – we'd go round the two bridges for a walk, rain or shine, and always dressed in our very best.

He was very particular about the shoes that we wore; we had to be well turned out. We had our Sunday clothes and our Sunday shoes. These were different from our school shoes. They had to be polished up the night before. I can see them sitting there yet, all arranged in a row and sitting on newspaper, all shining and looking absolutely tip-top.

Thursday was half-day in the town and he used to spend the afternoon in the garden. I remember going up to him when I got my Highers results and he was digging away and he said, 'Well?' and I said, 'I've got all my Highers! I got all of them!' He kept on digging and said, 'Well, that's what you were kept on at school for'.

Dad was very good at numbers. I'd see him in his shop on a Saturday when I went down to help him tie up the parcels for delivery. I used to get sixpence for that. He'd stand there with all these boots and shoes. I'd take down a flask and sandwiches for our tea. He'd go on till about 10 o'clock and I'd still be there helping him. He'd write out, 'Mr So-and-so, one pair of boots' and he'd write in the cost price and the selling price alongside it. He could remember all the costs in his head. He'd sit with this great long till-sheet and he'd put it over the counter and he'd stand there and count the whole thing up, just like that. He had a wonderful computer memory.

Father was a great reader. Very politically minded. I used to listen to him discuss politics

with my mother and it always ended up with her saying, 'Well, if that's what you say, then that'll be right'. He was also very careful about with whom we made friends. They had to be well brought up. There must be no scandal attached to the family in any way. I remember this girl, and her father had been to prison for embezzlement from the bank where he worked. I was sorry for her but Father used to warn me, 'I'm not sure you should hobnob with that family. Not got a good reputation'. The sins of the father were to be visited on the children.

It wasn't social uppityness. It was more a moral judgement. Our friends had to be from families that were known to work hard, that made an effort to keep their children at school. All he appeared to be interested in was getting our feet on the right road for adulthood. Education was very important. He had the old Scottish belief, especially in the North-East, that you had to do anything, take on any job, to bring in the money to give the children a proper education.

I remember Mother telling me about this family of six girls and the eldest one wanted to become a doctor. The minister loaned her some money to put her through Aberdeen University. The money was paid back as soon as the girl got a post and was used to help the next sister's education – and so on down to the youngest one. You hear Tony Blair talking about, 'Education, education, education'. Well, there's nothing new in that because that's what I heard all my young life.

Young people in my day respected their elders. And they were never bored. People now don't know how to make their own fun. But my family was very good: we all had bicycles, we all had skates, we all had sledges, we all got golf clubs and father bought us an annual ticket for the Golf Club. We had tennis racquets and he got balls from the courts after their tournament.

The Provost taught us to swim in the Spey. He would get hold of all the children who couldn't swim and take them to a sandy beach on the Spey. He'd get somebody to go over the bottom of the pool to check for rocks which might have been brought down during the winter spates. At the end of his lessons, we could all swim across the Spey and back again.

I think that Mammon has taken the place of religion. I was made to learn the Catechism. I often feel that we learned a lot by going through the War: sadness, togetherness, supporting each other, how to make do and mend. Children today are given too much money, money they haven't earned. House tasks – we used to put up a list on the kitchen door: 'So and so do the dishes; so and so take in the milk; so and so keep the coal scuttle filled'. We were taught that in this world nothing is ever handed out to you for nothing.

**Mabel Brocklehurst,** born 1918: Grantown on Spey

**'We all learnt to swim in the Spey':** Children swimming at Grantown-on-Spey in the 1930s.

The Provost took all the children who couldn't swim to a sandy beach on the Spey. At the end of his lessons, we could all swim across the Spey and back again.

**Marigold Nicol:**

Water colour of the Free Church in Newmachar by Marigold's mother, Cecilia, the wife of her father, Reverend David R Kerr.

# A home education

I was born in the manse. My father was the Free Church minister at Newmachar. I had a sister; two years older than me she was. There was a perfectly good primary school in the village, but my father didn't approve of the headmaster. In the village he had a reputation of being an efficient teacher, but my father thought he was a brutal man, one who was prone to dreadful fits of temper; he used to beat the children. There was one case I know of a boy hit over the head and who became deaf.

Father didn't approve of the headmaster at all. So, when my sister came to five years of age, he wouldn't send her to the local school. He determined he would teach her at home. He had a friend in Aberdeen who was a master at Robert Gordon's College and he gave him advice on what we should be learning.

My sister went upstairs at the age of five to the study to be taught the beginnings by my father – reading, writing and so on. I was four and I didn't like being left behind down there so I went up too. I can remember the first day up in the study: I was sat down at a table in the corner and started with the alphabet. It was printed out on a sheet, 'A-B-C', and I had to learn this. I can remember my first reading book – 'Dan is in the van', 'The cat sat on the mat'. Yes, I seemed to learn to read quite easily. He also tried to teach us the beginnings of arithmetic, but he just wasn't fond of that side of teaching at all. Maths of any sort he just did not like; he'd had great difficulty with the subject himself.

So we had our lessons: two hours in the morning, 10 to 12, and then later, Mother taught us French, sewing and drawing in the afternoon for about an hour. We kept to that

**On the doorstep of the manse.**

Marigold's parents the Reverend and Mrs Kerr with grandmother, aunt and Jock the dog.

timetable pretty strictly. On the days when my father had to go into Aberdeen for a Presbytery meeting or when he was writing his sermons, he left us work to do. He would set us a line of writing at the top of the page and we had to copy it all the way down.

Later on, with this advice he was getting from his friend at Robert Gordon's, he thought he should teach us the same as the boys there were having. Well, in those days they started Latin quite early. So my sister started Latin at 10. I was only eight and I did it too. I enjoyed it; I just loved it, in fact.

An inspector used to come out once a year to see what we were doing. He always seemed to be quite satisfied. He must have been a bit surprised to find us doing Latin at such an early age, but he never said anything about it. But we never did any mental arithmetic, which I found a great lack when I went to secondary school in Aberdeen later on. I had to count on my fingers. There was a teacher at the school up at Disblair, a widow she was, and she used to come in and do some mental arithmetic. I'm sure she thought we weren't being taught properly. I don't think she approved of us…

**Marigold Nicol,** born 1919: Newmachar

**In the woods** at Newmachar around 1922. Marigold and sister Cecelia.

# Lessons my granny taught me

I was born at Rowan Cottage, Gather Dams, Tullynessle. It had a thatched roof – what you would call a but-and-ben. There was a little bedroom off the door and a bed in the kitchen that could be shut off with a curtain. No electricity; paraffin lamps just. And no running water either; that had to be fetched from the well down the road. But happy days! I had a happy childhood.

My father was a crofter's son. He was called up for the war; he came back home and lived on for six years only. He died at the age of 26. He took epileptic fits because of the gassing in the war and each fit weakened his heart a bit more. I can tell you this: he started work on a farm before he took the croft and the farmer would pay him £3 a week, but always with one pound taken off to cover all the days that he might miss because of the epileptic fits. That was farmers in those days! They had little regard for their men; they would put them and their families into any kind of little box for a home – rats and everything. The farmers, I'm telling you, they got off with murder!

It was a hard, hard life. My granny would make her own mealie puddings for the winter and store them up among the meal; she made oatcakes and stored them up and all. The women had a hard life – all that washing in tubs. Never-ending, what they had to do.

Now, don't get me wrong – I'm not a snob – but there was a lot of what we called cottar bairns at Tullynessle school. These were the children of the men who worked under the feein system for the farmers: the farm labourers. I used to say, 'Oh, there wis the L-children waukin ahin me a the wye tae skeel. I didna wint tae wauk wi them'. But Granny would get me into trouble for this. She would say, 'Nannie, min' this – they're jist human beins tae'. But they seemed to me to be different, to be differently dressed and differently

**On holiday in Ayrshire, 1935.** Marigold and Cecelia with Mother and Aunt Kitty.

> We were taught to behave in front of our elders. I was brought up to respect the headmaster, the minister, the doctor and the policeman. If the doctor came into your house you didn't dare speak. The children just sat there in silence.

behaved. They were rough, rough and ready. It was just the way their homes were, you see.

We were taught our lessons and we were taught our manners; we were taught to behave in front of our elders. I was brought up to respect the headmaster, the minister, the doctor and the policeman. They were the four big people in the parish. If the doctor came into your house you didn't dare speak. The children just sat there in silence. Same with the minister.

Church was important. I went to the church and to the Sunday school every week. It was always full in those days. And in the afternoon we would all go out as a family for a walk, all dressed in our best Sunday clothes. Down the road, up the glen; we'd gather buttercups and other flowers; then we'd bring them home and press them between the pages of a book.

We went on Sunday school picnics. We'd all congregate at the Meal Mill and we'd be piped there to our picnic. We all got a bag of biscuits and they would come round with milk or tea. You don't need money to be happy. A good community spirit, that's the thing.

It's all changed now. I may be wrong but here's my point of view: we are living in a greedy, selfish world. In the old days, in my day, people did things for each other and they did it without having to be asked or expecting anything in return. I'll give you an instance. My granny and my mother were both lying ill – they were down with some kind of flu. There was this old roadman who came past: 'Oh, Annie, I hanna seen ye aboot fer a whilie. Are ye weel? Na? Weel, fan Ah ging hame Ah'll wash masel and then Ah'll cam roon and hack yer sticks and tak in yer coal and git yer pails o' water. And then, maybe in a day or twa, ye'll feel better'.

That's what people did for each other in those days. But nowadays people are just stuck in their own affairs. I'm maybe old fashioned but there they all are, having to work to pay off their mortgages. And you get young couples who start off with everything and then they've got nothing left to work for. But we all had to work for what we got and we were proud of it.

It's just the way we were brought up. My mother and granny were so clean. It was pride, oh yes, pride! There was always food on the table. We were always properly dressed. My mother worked so hard for us. She just went out and worked in the Forbes Arms. She was waitress there. She made sure we didn't want for anything. All my mother got from the state as a widow was 10 shillings [50p], and that was all she got. And the farmers didn't help. I remember when old C- called; well, his wife was unwell and my mother went to help out. It was to be for payment; that was the arrangement, you understand. Then at the end of it he told her, 'Ye ken, Bessy, I canna pay ye till the end o' the year'. She said, 'Weel, fat div ye think Ah've got tae live on till then?'

I never came home to an empty house. My mother or my granny was always there for us. We were never bored. We all felt safe then. There was never speak of all these sex things: homosexuality, child abuse – we never heard of them. We felt secure going out on the roads, into the fields. Mercy, aye. We knew everybody round about us. We didn't chase after boys the way they do now – the Academy's just up the road and you should see what

I see when they go up the lane to the school. Different altogether! Just a different way of life…

A country quine! A happy childhood. It all fits together: happy home-life, happy school, happy childhood. I've a lot to thank my old granny for. She would tell me, 'Nat a'body gings tae the kirk. An not a'body fa gings tae the kirk listens tae fat the minister tells them. But, Nannie, there's a lot o' goodness in his words – jist you listen'.

She gave me a lot of wisdom like that. Granny taught us a lot of good sense. If you've got good sense and good manners you won't go far wrong in life.

**Nan Esson** born 1920: Tullynessle

## Nobody spoke of such things

My mother died when I was born. There were these neighbours who took me in and looked after me for the first three years of my life. Then the man I thought of as my father married again and so at the age of nearly four I was taken back and lived with him and his new wife. What nobody ever mentioned to me was that they were really my grandfather and my step-grandmother. People in those days just didn't speak of such matters; there was such a lot that went on behind the scenes and which was kept under wraps. Oh, they would have been talking about it

among themselves, but nobody told me the truth about myself, not once. There was a lot of hypocrisy about family matters of that kind then.

When I was 12, I passed the exam to go on to Aberlour High School. We cycled over to enrol me at my new school. We were in the rector's office; he was taking down the particulars and then he looked up and said, 'You'll be the father, of course'. Whereupon the reply came, 'No, I'm the grandfather'. And that was the very first time I'd ever had the slightest indication of the truth. It didn't shock me or traumatise me, no; I'd seen things going on in other families and I'd become almost cynical about such matters.

We left the interview and made our way home in silence. Nothing more was said about my situation; there never were to be any explanations. My mother, Mary Grieve, was never mentioned in the home or by anyone else outside it. All that was left of her was a plain gravestone in the kirkyard.

**Allan Grieve,** born 1921: Maggieknockater

**A plain headstone**
The graveyard at Boharm, Maggieknockater, where Allan Grieve's mother lies buried. Her engraving on the family stone simply says, 'In memory of their grandaughter Mary Grieve … who died 15th December 1921, aged 26'.

**The main entrance to Muchalls Castle**
where Geraldine Simpson lived, 1954–1991.

Below, the Great Hall at Muchalls Castle.

# The heiress

I really had the stupidest and oddest upbringing that ever existed. I had a Victorian upbringing past the Victorian age. I started life as a daughter of the manse. But my father was very shell-shocked from the war. Noise upset him dreadfully, especially the noise of the wind as it moved through the trees. That would send him round the bend. When it was windy he couldn't sleep at night and he'd walk for hours outside. Yet we lived in a house right up on the hillside, which caught all the winds that blew. For some reason or other I would cry a lot then – and he was caught in the act, I understand, of trying to strangle me as I was crying. I was six at the time. After that it was considered not to be a very good idea for me to continue staying there. I've inherited his hatred of the wind; if it's windy at night I go right under the bedclothes.

They decided I'd better go and stay with my grandparents, the Pringles who owned the knitwear firm in the Borders. They lived in this very large house and had all their

domestic staff to do everything. And that was a bit of a drawback for me. I was never allowed to go anywhere near the kitchen, or to know the kitchen even existed. Everything was just done for me. Until my husband died I always lived in a household where you had at least six or seven staff – and now I'm well into my 80s and I live in a house all by myself.

Getting on for 20 years ago I landed ill and had to go into Aberdeen Infirmary. They tried all sorts of tests and everything else they could think of and then they told me there was nothing really wrong with me – except that I was undernourished! So there I was, living up in Muchalls Castle and I was suffering from malnutrition! I'd been feeding off hamburgers and chips and any stuff that came to hand.

That was when I realised how little I knew about the practicalities of life. I was very fond of reading; I knew all about castles and how to handle a horse and I'd been taught how to set a table with glasses and cutlery. I'd been taught how to wait at table and how to sit at table. I knew I must never lean back on the chair and never to yawn in company, no matter how bored one might feel. I was also told never to lose my temper or to go to bed bearing a grudge. I was taught never to wet my finger while turning the pages of a book. And I was never ever to take God's name in vain. That's stayed with me: even something like, 'Oh my God!' jars with me and yet you hear it all the time.

All of this was very fine – but of no use to me when it came to cooking the dinner.

**Geraldine Simpson,** born 1921: Muchalls Castle

**'I knew how to handle a horse and all about castles...'**
Geraldine Simpson pictured going through her paces at a show in the 1950s.

**Where it all started:**
West Lodge, Pitfour; here pictured a few years before Stanley Rothney's birth in 1923, with his father and mother standing at the door.

**...and in 2008,** with the 85-year-old Stanley.

# A step up in the world

If you stand by the roadside outside the cottage where I was born and look up to the brow of the hill, a few hundred yards away to the north, there among the trees you'll see a fine baronial style house, substantial and well set up so as to be seen for miles around. Now that is the farmhouse of North Auchmachar and it marks my very first journey in the world. It was a place where time stood still. It was in the ownership of the Penny family of whom only one member ever married and that was the eldest. The rest of them spent all their days on that farm, right up into their 80s.

I could never work out how many of them there could be but there seemed to be about 10 of them – five women and five men, shall we say. All their days the men were referred to as 'loons' and the women were known as the 'quines', even into their dotage. For their meals they would all go into the farmhouse and be fed round the big kitchen table there. And right to the time they departed the face of this earth that is what these old loons did, always in order of seniority, with the eldest the first to take his place at the table.

Despite their old fashioned ways they were excellent farmers and ran to four pairs of horses. Four of the men had their own pair to manage; the fifth took charge of the cattle. Each of the quines had a specific job to do: one to the baking, another to the butter making, a third did the housework and so on.

As I said, time stood still at North Auchmachar: these were folk who didn't go into the world; the world had to come to them. They offered traditional hospitality and were always ready to receive their neighbours. Just after my birth, my mother decided she and I must walk up to the farmhouse for me to be shown off to the Penny family.

Now, the women of the family took in the *People's Friend* each week. They would pass it from one to the other, in order of seniority, of course, and read it from front to back, always with great attention to its advice and information. They believed what they read in the *People's Friend* absolutely. At the time of my visit they had recently read that if you took a newly-born up as high as you possibly could then that would mark the height of his journey through society in later life. The ideal would be the tower of a castle but, fine though it was, North Auchmachar was not exactly that. However, it did have an attic, so they bundled me up and carried me in their arms, right up into the attic at the very top of the house. Nor were they satisfied with merely putting my face up to its window; they got a chair and stood on that, on tiptoe, and held me up to the light. And that was my first journey up in the world.

**Stanley Rothney,** born 1923: Old Deer

# Well dressed, well fed, well shod

I would say it was a hard life for my parents, but I don't think as children we were very aware of any hardship. I mean, you got a hot bottom now and then if you'd been doing something you shouldn't have been doing. But that was about it.

My mother was a very efficient manager and she ran a good home: she made all our clothes. My father cobbled our shoes. We were always well dressed, well fed, well shod. Porridge in the morning, porridge made over the open fire. Oatmeal was the staple food; there'd be home baking and scones over a coal fire. As a baker she was second to none, our mother. There were always plenty fresh vegetables and tatties. We had good thick soups. The butcher called once a week with his van and Dad would bring home a rabbit now and then. We got the odd chicken. If we got kippers they would be done on a brander over the fire. Oh, it was a good healthy diet.

There would have been poverty in the bigger families, but we were all right. Father was a grieve, but the pay itself was sweeties. About £26 for a half year, but with all the hard work and all the domestic skills, the basics of life were always there. Mum always knitted our jumpers and she made us summer dresses. Our boots were fitted out with tackets to make them last.

My North-East background did stand me in good stead later in life. You'd had a good upbringing whereby you were never going to be in trouble. When the war came, I was called up. Now, in the Army you could be easily led and get into trouble, dead trouble. For some of them, it was a question of flying the coop and with all that new freedom they would be led astray. It was all down to the upbringing, I think. More than once I was stopped by my father in the street when I had some lipstick on and told to go home immediately to 'wash aa' that muck aff yer face'. I might be 18 years of age, but I did as I was told. I didn't paint my nails either – well, not in front of him. I'd go into the toilet, do up my nails and then come out with my hands behind my back.

A very strong upbringing. Discipline, the work ethic: we all had our chores to do in the house. My parents were very strict, but they were caring, utterly caring. If they told you to do anything then you just did it. You didn't stop to question it, or say, 'Wait a minute.' You just did it. Immediately.

**Peggy Walker,** born 1924: Udny Green

> We were not very aware of hardship. You got a hot bottom now and then. But that was about it.

**Peggy Walker:** in 2008, outside Cairnfechel, the cottar house near Udny Green where she spent much of her childhood in the 1930s.

**'She was aye the sort who never stopped working...'**

John's mother at the sheaves at her father's croft Upperton, Oyne, in the 1950s.

**Brought up to work:**

the three-year-old helping his father at Cairnmore, Rhynie

**The first suit:**

at the age of 12.

# Simple respect

I had to walk the three miles to school and back each day even when I was only five and just a little loon. The way back was over this narrow wooden bridge, over the Bogie burn. Now this bridge, the tinks all used to camp there, for the clear running water I suppose. There was this old tink and he once called out to me, 'Ah'll skin ye alive jist as ah dae the moles!'. The tinks would catch rabbits and moles and sell the skins off them and get a few pence for them, you see. He was just tormenting me, but to me they were a desperate looking lot and I got a real scare. I ran off like the blazes, all the way back home.

They would go round the houses and sell you pegs for hanging up your washing, or a besom which they made out of the heather. One day, this old tink came to the door and asked my mother whether she could spare any food for him. My mother was aye a kind-hearted woman and they knew she wouldn't send anyone away empty. But she didn't like to invite the tinks to step over the door; she was aye feared they were unclean and might be carrying lice. So this day – it was a cold kind of day – she told the old man: 'Jist you sit

doon there aside the door an Ah'll gie ye a plate o' soup'.

Now, I aye mind this: there on this cold day when he sat down for his soup, this old tink, he took off his bonnet and laid it to the side and took the soup bareheaded. It was respect you see, respect for my mother and what she was giving him. And nowadays you'll see the young folk going into houses and – I've seen this a lot – they never think to take their caps off. But that old tink, he knew what he should do. It was respect, just, simple respect.

**John Robb,** born 1932: Rhynie

Now, I aye mind this: there on this cold day when he sat down for his soup, this old tink, he took off his bonnet and laid it to the side and took the soup bareheaded. It was respect you see, respect for my mother and what she was giving him.

> In those days babies and how they came into the world, all that was just not spoken of. I'd been given no warning at all; my mother hadn't even told me she was expecting.

# The facts of life

When my young sister came along, that was a complete shock to me. I hadn't been told that such an event was going to happen and when this strange new baby came onto the scene, I resented it. I remember looking down into her cot and thinking to myself, 'I don't know how you got here, but I don't want you'.

You see, in those days babies and how they came into the world, all that was just not spoken of. I'd been given no warning at all; my mother hadn't even told me she was expecting. I remember once asking her what a midwife did exactly and being told to be quiet and ask no questions. The only help my mother ever offered was to hand me a poem which was entitled, *To the child who enquires*. It started off, 'You were born of a beautiful love, dear, a love both Daddy's and mine'. I read it right through, but was none the wiser.

My upbringing was, I suppose, quite a strict one. My mother was the main power in our lives and she demanded quite a lot of us. My father was a gentle sort of man, not the kind who ever wanted to administer punishment. He'd had a hard life. When he was 16 he fell off his bike and broke his leg. The leg was never properly set and the result was that he had to wear a special boot and was left with a limp for the rest of his life. This was rather sad because he was just full of music. He had taught himself to play the violin and the piano, but after the injury he could no longer dance – and if there was one thing he and my mother loved, it was dancing.

He had started off as a painter, but that hadn't worked out. Mother's people were fisher folk from the Black Isle and an uncle came over to show him how to set up in the fish trade. He got a van and started a delivery round, house to house. The business did well enough and Mother was a great household manager and a great saver. She held the purse strings and we had quite a comfortable life, but I did feel sorry for my father: he would go off early in the morning, right over to Tarland sometimes, and he wouldn't get back and have something to eat till after four and then he would still have the van to clean out and get ready for the next day. The supplies came out from Aberdeen by train each day, at five in the evening, and that had to be seen to as well.

I don't think he really enjoyed his job, but he had a family to provide for and just had to keep at it. Sometimes it seemed as if all his day consisted of was the van, coming home, cleaning it, getting ready for the next day and then locking up before going home to a meal and his bed. When he was on the brink of retirement he just dropped down dead. He never did get any rest from it all.

Mother set high standards for us. She had come to Ballater to work as a maid in the big houses here and so she had mingled with the upper classes. She had learned how to cook really well and she could do embroidery and lace-making. We had to mind our manners, always say our 'please' and our 'thank you', eat properly at the table and never ever to use bad language.

She didn't allow us to speak the way the locals did; we were brought up to speak Standard English. To her, from the Black Isle, that was how she spoke anyway, but to us on Deeside, it proved to be a bit awkward. At school the other children would brand us as

snobs because we didn't use the Doric. They would ask me, 'Far are ye gaain?' and I would reply with a 'I'm going home' and they would make fun of me. Maybe that's why my best friend was an evacuee from London – she didn't speak the local way either.

Willma Sim, born 1932: Ballater

## Setting the standards

My mother was a brilliant household manager. A marvellous pair of hands, she had, and could make anything with them. We were always well turned out, most definitely. My brother was a baker and she'd get these old flour bags from him. They were washed and then they were put out on the green and they lay there for weeks, bleaching and getting all the flour out of them. And then they were taken in and boiled till they were pure white. She'd make skirts for us; she'd make pillowcases and table cloths, all from these old flour bags. And all our clothes were knitted; even our stockings were knitted by her.

She was an amazing cook, just amazing. She made chutney, she made sauces, all sorts of things that other folk couldn't. We had a good country diet: a lot of broth and pea soup and fish soup. There were tatties and fried onions; we had chappit neeps, cabbage with cream, kale – I never liked the kale, but I had to eat it. Eat or want, that was the way of it, eat or want! We had saps, using the old dried bits of bread – nothing was wasted. She was a dab hand at the dumplings and bread puddings; we never went hungry.

My mother could turn her hand to anything – even to giving us a good walloping. She was strict, very strict, with us all. Time-keeping had to be adhered to: if she said a

**'We had no time to be bored...'**
Isobel McRae with the 1st Old Deer Guide troop at the annual camp at Arnage, 1946. Isobel is front row, fourth from right.

Eat or want! that was the way of it. We had saps, using the old dried bits of bread – nothing was wasted.

> **The spoons were all Brassoed so you had to put them in soda water to get the black stuff off. Then you had to polish and polish them till they were sparkling, and fit enough to pass her inspection. Oh, I detested that job!**

certain time then you had to be there on the dot, otherwise, a walloping. I got plenty: that's why I've such a broad backside! If you were stuck into the middle of a game outside and the time was up then that was too bad: you just had to run home. The bus would come up the village at 6.45 and you knew that your mother had seen it as it went up the street. We'd be all down at the Square, caught up in our game, but we knew we'd been told to be home at seven sharp and no excuses. Whether you came in no later than 7.05 it made no difference – a walloping was what you'd get.

If you broke a dish – and that happens – you knew you were for it. If you came back with a tear in your clothes, then that was it – wallop! We were kept right about everything. Our manners had to be perfect. If we were by ourselves then you got the same plate and cutlery for the soup, the meat and the pudding – this was to save on the washing up. But if anyone came to the house then everything had to be just so. All our 'pleases' and our 'thank yous' had to be in place; if you wanted a piece of bread you couldn't say, 'Pass the loaf'; it had to be, 'Please may I have a slice of bread?' You couldn't leave the table without asking for permission to do so.

If Mum asked you to do anything, you didn't dare say 'No'. Once she asked me to go to a neighbour about a meeting or something and I was busy playing. I didn't say 'No' but I did let out a 'Well!' and she caught it: 'You say "well" once more young lady and you'll be for it!' So, what did I do but let out another 'Well'. Clatter! She knocked me sideways. With her there was no such thing as taking a careful aim; she just let you have it. She would use her hand or fetch a slipper; sometimes it was even the carpet beater and the blows could land anywhere.

But my mother was no monster, no, no! In some ways she was of her time; there were plenty others like her in those days. She had had such a hard life herself that she couldn't afford to waste time and energy on feelings. Work, work, work was her motto. You must never be caught about the house doing nothing: you must either be reading a proper book, or doing a bit of knitting, or getting on with the sewing. We did play games in the house, but there was no laughter or any mucking about; cards, ludo – they had to be played seriously.

When our two grandchildren came to stay with us, I can mind Daniel sitting down and saying, 'Granny, I'm bored!' 'Bored'– now that was a word that just wasn't allowed when I was young. If you didn't seem to have anything to do, then my mother would hand out some horrible task or other, like knitting or opening some wool for her to make blankets with. The worst one was cleaning the spoons. They were all Brassoed so you had to put them in soda water to get the black stuff off. Then you had to polish and polish them till they were sparkling, and fit enough to pass her inspection. Oh, I detested that job!

Besides, there was always something going on in the village. There were sales of work and there were concerts. In the summer there was the Gala. For the Brownies there was Mintlaw and the Guides were at Old Deer. In the winter we'd go into the Pitfour Estate and watch the curling on the lake there. Four great men from the village would be at it:

Dr Kemp, Dr Dixon, Captain Curran and Fred Martin. You'd see them going hard at it with their heather besoms.

In the war we had evacuees from Glasgow billeted with us. Now they didn't just bring themselves; a whole herd of little visitors came with them – nits and lice! My mother noticed me scratching away one night and, well, six o'clock the next morning, I was yanked out of my bed and marched straight to the bathroom. She bent my head over the basin and then scrape, scrape, scrape with the been-kaim. Every time she got one there was a crack as she did for it and then I got a dunt in my back. Crack, dunt! You'd have thought it was a herd of jungle animals she was battling with. Then my hair was swathed in Dettol – oh that was nippy, I can tell you! – and then she took this black soap and scrubbed away at my scalp. Boy, was it tender!

Lice, you see, that was regarded as a shameful thing. Cleanliness, tidiness, good manners: she was setting us standards, putting us on the right path. She taught me a lot about the skills and the manners necessary to run a household. And don't forget that for five years of wartime she was by herself; all her men folk were away at war: her husband was a POW in Poland and her oldest son had been taken prisoner by the Japanese at Singapore; the youngest was at D-day.

She had to do all the raising of us, making do with very little in the way of cash. Yet every Monday I would go to the school and put £1 into the savings bank – 6/8 each for me and my two sisters. She took in lodgers, she did all kinds of odd jobs. She kept the household going. She was hard; she had an awful temper, but she brought us up to do right. I can't really fault her.

**Isobel McRae,** born 1933: Fetterangus

# Holding hands after Bible class

Banchory was a good place to grow up in then. Everyone looked out for you and saw that there was a limit to the mischief you could get up to. It was a close knit, familiar village, one that shared the same strong values and made sure its young were going to be brought up to follow them. Honesty, thrift, hard work, family life, respect: these were the guiding principles. Education was highly valued; the local school was held in great respect, as were the teachers. The headmaster was one of those pillars of the community who was automatically held in esteem both by virtue of himself and of his office. The same went for the minister and the doctor. My father was a member of the John Watson Guild and this was a body of community-minded men who would distribute coal to pensioners at Christmas time and would donate money to cases of hardship during the rest of the year. It was a happy, safe place to grow up in.

These were happy, carefree times. I have a memory which captures its quality. At the back of the house there was a croft and we could play freely all over it. I remember playing hide-and-seek under a harvest moon, in and out of the stacks in the corn yard. A

Then there were the Glen o' Dee woods and homemade cairties; we had second-hand tennis rackets, we played hoosies and shoppies.

**'Several life-long partnerships had their beginnings in some hand-holding in the dark...'**
A turn of the century 'Come to Banchory' poster.

magical, special memory of a safe and free childhood! Then there were the Glen o' Dee woods and our homemade cairties; we had second-hand tennis rackets, we played hoosies and we played shoppies. Although I was an only child I could always find someone to play with and a place to go to. You'd go out to play and only go home when you were hungry. Someone would shout out, 'It's tea time!' and you'd rush off home; the hours had just slipped away and we were never bored.

There were also organised activities such as the Guides and the Scouts and a tennis club. The height of our sophistication was to go to the Bible Class on a Sunday evening and then to walk to the café at the Bridge of Feugh, through the darkness, as the street lighting only went as far as the Bridge of Dee. Once inside we enjoyed hot chocolate and what we believed to be sophisticated debate on the issues of the day, such as the partition of Cyprus. Several life-long partnerships had their beginnings in some hand-holding in the dark on the mile long walk home – so daring, so very grown up…

Moira Jolly, born, 1934: Banchory

## Home discipline

I come from farming folks. I was the youngest of seven. Times were very hard then. I got hand-downs, never any new clothes, just hand-downs. But we were well enough fed. In fact, they reckon that the diet during the war was the best ever, for health. My mum could make a plate of soup out of nothing. Hares and rabbits used to be an important part of our diet. We'd catch them with the dog. Mother would make soup with the flesh through it – lovely. For our tea, well, have you heard of saps? That was our tea, often enough. Just stale bread with boiling water over it and milk on top of that. It was fine. And brose and sometimes, for supper, milk porridge. They'd turn up their nose at any of that nowadays. But I did get sweeties now and then. My father used to go to the auction mart on a Friday and on his way home, he used to buy some pandrops or some pear-mints. I only ever had one toy of my own: it was a little wooden engine. It was the only toy that was ever bought for me.

At the school you were kept in line with the belt. And if you'd gone home and said, 'the teacher did this, the teacher did that', your parents would have given you some more! George Milne, he was brought up at Montgatehead, the neighbouring farm to us. Well, just as we'd be walking back from the school, George's uncle Willy, he'd be working in the fields and he would turn his head and cry out, 'Weel, loons, did ye get yer licks the day?'.

It was all punishment in those days. Your parents were like that, too. I can remember when I was about seven, my sister and I were up in the loft one Friday; my father was away in Aberdeen at the mart and we were up in the loft picking the sprouts off the tatties. There was a skylight and one of its panes of glass was broken. So, I started to ping the little tatties out through this broken pane. Well, what happened? I hit the other pane and broke that one! Oh, God, it was the end of the world!

I decided I would go and tell my father as soon as I could. So, I went down the road and met him and told him. He just flew off the handle, completely. 'Right, efter that, ye'll git yer bluidy licks!' But you didn't get them right away. He'd make you wait till the rest of the family was there. And then he'd make a great thing of it. 'Right!' He took the razor strap that used to hang outside the door, that would come down, and so would your breeks, right there in front of all your brothers and sisters. And you got it on your backside. The fact that your breeks had come down was a bigger punishment than the belt itself. Humiliation, you see, rank humiliation.

Now, you mustn't think my father was unusually cruel. It was just the done thing then. He used to make you wait; that was the worst bit. But you didn't often need it. It was a deterrent, no question about it. I never forgot it. It wouldn't have been so very hard, the pain; it was the humiliation, the pants coming down like that in front of them all…

**Eric Brown,** born, 1935: Bridge of Muchalls

# Back from the dead

Ahappy home! A crowded home with the six of us sharing the three rooms in our wee croft. But we had the freedom: we'd be forever outside, playing all round the district, in the woods, down by the burn, everywhere. A country life's a good way of life for a bairn, isn't it?

Our parents left us to learn by experience and never fussed over where we'd been or what we'd been doing. In those days everyone knew everyone else and we all looked out for each other. My mother would be at her sink looking out the window and she'd say, 'Oh, that's the doctor's car doon at the Morrisons'. Then she'd wait for it to go and it would be, 'Ah'll jist awa tae see if they're needin a wee bitty help.' And before you knew it she'd be away on her bike, pedalling into Keith to get a prescription for them. There was nothing nosey about any of this; in those days everybody looked out for each other. The Morrisons were an elderly couple and she was just caring for them, being a proper neighbour to them. That was the way of it then, in the country.

But I do mind one instance and it nearly cost me my life. I was out playing by the burn – I couldn't have been more than two years of age – and the burn was in spate and I fell in. If it hadn't been for this man out in the field hyowin I would have been a goner. He came rushing over and put his hyowe out into the water and he told me to grab it and hold on. He managed to pull me to safety.

But that wasn't the end of the danger, not by any means. The water had got into my lungs and I took the pneumonia. At that time there were no antibiotics. I was put to bed and it was feared I would die. But this old doctor, Dr Watt he was, came to call and this I do mind clearly: he hung his coat up and he sounded my chest and then he spoke to my dad. And I heard him saying this, 'I doubt we're going to lose her!' And then – and this I

I started to ping the little tatties out through this broken pane.
Well, what happened?
I hit the other pane and broke that one!
Oh, God, it was the end of the world!

> **I heard the doctor saying this, "I doubt we're going to lose her!" And then — and this I mind clearly — he shook hands with my father.**

mind clearly — he shook hands with my father.

But I made up my mind I wasn't ready for death, not by a long way. That's when I had this 'near death experience'. I can remember flying along this tunnel at a phenomenal speed, just like a plane it was. Then there was this pinpoint of light at the end of the tunnel and I was getting nearer and nearer to it and then I stopped and woke up and found I was in my own bed and back in the world and alive.

I remember trying to tell my dad all about where I'd been and he was telling me that I could have been to no such place. 'Ye've niver bin onywhwere and Ah ken because Ah've bin here aa the time, watchin ower ye!' Then he pointed to the little oil lamp that was burning by my bed and told me that this is what I'd been looking at and that this must have been the light at the end of my tunnel. As for the journey, well that must have been a dream, just. But I couldn't accept any of this; I just felt he hadn't been listening to me properly and taking in how real my experience had been. Then my mum came to the door and she was red-eyed with tears. I heard her say, 'Is that Mabel Ah hear spikin?' and Dad replied, 'Nat only is she spikkkin, she winna stap spikkin!'

It's all crystal clear to my memory. I can mind nothing of being in the water or of near drowning, but the near death experience itself is as vivid to me as the hand in front of my face. And I can mind later hearing my father outside in the bonny spring air at his motorbike and I was greetin because I couldn't get out to play. My father came in and took a spoonful of this malt and said, 'Noo then, lassie, tak a speen o' this each day an ye'll seen be ootside playin agin.' And so I did and that's what happened. I've aye taken the malt and I've aye been healthy ever since.

**Mabel Cowe,** born 1937: Keith

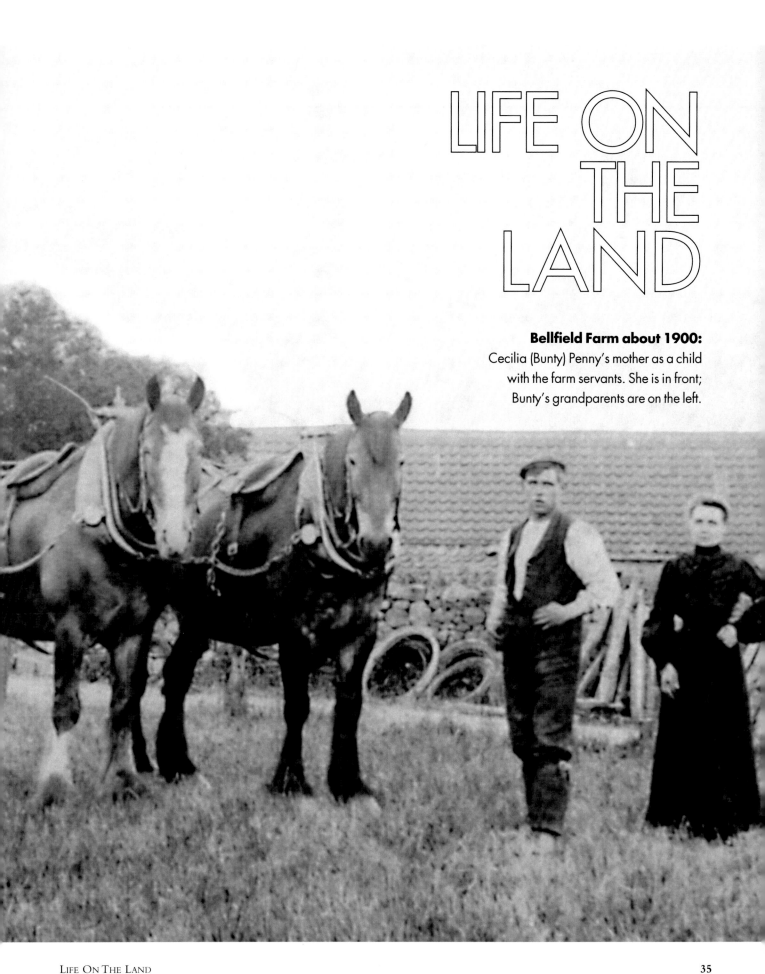

# LIFE ON THE LAND

**Bellfield Farm about 1900:**
Cecilia (Bunty) Penny's mother as a child
with the farm servants. She is in front;
Bunty's grandparents are on the left.

**A long-lived family,**
Christmas 2009:
George aged 93 with
his sister, Margaret
Thom, aged 99.

# Never cross the farmer

My father was the blacksmith in Barras. I went to the local school, about a mile up the road from us. The headmaster was Mr Carson. Here's the ballad we would sing:

*There is a happy land*
*Down at Barras School*
*Where Dominie Carson stands*
*Teaching like a fool.*

*Oh, we would happy be*
*If we got him up a tree*
*We would gie him tattie bree*
*Three times a day.*

Round about the school there was this field; it had bad ground. The farmer used to plant what we called marshly in it – a mixture of oats, beans and peas. Now, the wood pigeons liked to come down and feed off these peas. I was coming out of the school one night and I saw that the farmer had set snares made out of binder twine and that about a dozen birds had got caught up in them, so I let them go.

The next day when I went to the school I found the headmaster standing at the door with the farmer, waiting. They were looking at me – very hard. When I went into the room, Mr Carson came in and said, 'Come out here, Carr. You know what this is for, don't you?' and he produced his big leather strap. I got a right belting.

Farmers were the really important people in Barras; there wasn't much else there then. I had made the mistake of crossing one of them.

**George Carr,** born 1916: Barras

# Escaping the farming community

Knockandhu was our farm and it lay on the Arndilly estate near Craigellachie. Money was scarce and life was hard. The expectation was that I would simply go into the farm. The Thirties were the time of subsistence farming; you'd be at it for long hours, even through the worst of the weather. I could see this way of life looming up ahead of me and I wanted no part of it. Even at an early age I would tell myself, 'There's got to be something better than this,'.

But being an only child I was already being involved in the work. We had cows to milk – the milk was not only for our own use, but we supplied some of the houses round about. My job was to deliver the milk on my way to the school. I'd set off with these flagons of milk, in pints and half pints, and I would have to call in at all these houses en route until I ended up with the order for the school house itself.

We kept a lot of poultry and there was always poultry to rear and poultry to feed. We also kept a couple of pigs. Nothing was to be wasted; the swill and the offal had to be fed to them. There was a lot of cheese to be made; the milk had to be skimmed; butter had to be prepared. There were always byres to be mucked out, and there were indoor chores as well. The work was non-stop.

The grocery van would bring us our other provisions and a kind of barter system was employed; you handed over eggs and butter and you got groceries in return. You never seemed to make any cash profit that way: however many eggs you had they would always be translated into goods and nothing for your pocket. However hard you worked you never seemed to have any cash to spend on yourself. It all seemed to me to be very insecure. And the work, well the work was just unrelenting. While I was at the school the hired man looked after the horses, but when I left he wasn't kept on and I had to take over. I was being caught up in the farming.

My plan was to go into Foreign Service. What that was I wasn't exactly sure, but I had this vision that there must be something out there, some other world that I could escape to. I remember that the ploughman would sing to himself as he worked in the fields this song, *Springtime in the Rockies*, and I thought to myself, 'I'll go to the Rockies'. I wasn't quite sure where they were, or what I would find when I got there, but I knew they had to be an escape from Maggieknockater.

And in those days most people smoked and there would be these cigarette cards lying around. I remember being fascinated by a series on 'Outposts of the Empire'. You'd pick these cards up and you'd be looking a picture of a man in the uniform of the Kenyan Police or astride a horse in Rhodesia; they all looked splendid but some of them, I reckoned, must have started life from a place like mine.

I left school at 14. By the time I'd become 16 I was, I suppose, one of the junior leading lights in the area. I would go to the social club and I was on one or two committees. I was even a contributor to the *Banffshire Journal*. In those days, the *Banffie* would get its stories sent in by unpaid reporters scattered about the various districts. They would send in items such as, 'Twins have been born to Mr and Mrs MacDonald of Bents Cottage', or 'This week, in good conditions, the Mains of Mulben started its harvest'. That's what counted as news. For that kind of thing my payment would be one complimentary copy of the paper each week. But still no money.

In fact, I wasn't getting any real payment from anywhere, not even when I started to work full-time at home. I got my keep and maybe half-a-crown for the dance on a Saturday, but that was it. It was decided that we would keep sheep and so my father bought in a small flock of 10 ewes. These were handed over to me as my responsibility; any profit would be mine – and that was to be my wage, and no more pocket money.

And farming methods in those days were harrowing. It was real hard labour and much of it was self-inflicted. In other words, irrespective of the nature of the soil, the traditional set methods had to be adhered to. For example, some of our land was never going to be productive of oats, but it all had to take its turn for the crop, because the seven-year rotation had to be obeyed. And we milked three times a day – morning, midday and

The work was just unrelenting. While I was at the school the hired man looked after the horses, but when I left he wasn't kept on and I had to take over. I was being caught up in the farming.

The attitude
was that you
could always
get another
servant at
the feein
market.
But a good
broken-in
horse,
that was
something
altogether
more
important.

supper – and you can imagine just how binding that was. You'd no sooner returned the beasts to the field then you would be going out to drive them back in again. We had this cow which refused to suckle her calves unless we stood over her and threatened blue murder, but would we get rid of her? Oh no! 'She's a guid beast really…' So much of the husbandry could have been done better with a little more flexibility and thought, but that would have been 'new' and 'Weel, we've aye dane it this wye'.

I just had to get out of all that…

Allan Grieve, born 1921: Maggieknockater

## The feein system: 'a lot o' shiftin aboot'

I was born in 1924, at a cottage over at Banchory. My father was working on a farm there; he was a farm labourer. The feeing system was on the go in those days and we had to shift about quite a bit. He was at the Home Farm at Ury; he was foreman there for two years but he and the grieve just could not get on, so he had to flit. From there he went to Elfhill, up the Auchenblae Road out of Stonehaven. He went there as horseman and, to start with, the farm was in the laird's own hands on account of the fact that he couldn't get it let, but after six months a new tenant came and he brought his own horseman along with him. My father took over the cattle for six months and then he went over to the Bents of Maryculter. He bade there one year but he didn't like it, so he then left and fetched up at Hillhead of Glasslaw. He was there for five years, but then the farmer gave up the tenancy. From there he went to Upper Cullie, Auchenblae, and he was there for a year and then he took up a position at Lyne of Skene. He was there six years and then he went to West Carmont, Stonehaven.

A lot of shifting about, but that was quite common in those days, more or less, yes. The married men stayed at a farm for one year, the single men for six months. Not always, but very often. It was the feeing system, you see. You would shift about on the lookout for another few pounds in the year; you would always be looking for something a bit better, or you might simply fancy the change. Some farms made the men work outside all weathers, and at some places you might not be fed so well, or the farmer's wife might be difficult to get on with, or the grieve might be a real so-and-so.

They stopped that during the war when I was just 16. I thought, 'What a bloomin' shame, no more feein' market!' But when you look back, it was the best thing that ever happened. That's when folk started to stay at their farms and that's when the farmers began to respect their labour better. When I left the school, the farmers thought more of their horses than they did of their men. To them a horse was really valuable – you had to pay for your horses, you see. The attitude was that you could always get another servant at the feein' market. But a good broken-in horse, that was something altogether more important.

And accommodation could vary a lot. I mind when I was with Troup of White Stone

at Skene and there were four of us to this one bothy. There was the foreman and me – I was second horseman and I was only 16, but no matter. Then there was a cattleman and then the young loon. All in this small black bothy with no running water and without heat. I was there a year and I tried to get away, but it was the war, and there were these 'Stand still orders' and the farmer wouldn't let me away.

I argued that my reason for wanting away was that it wasn't healthy, the four of us in a bothy of that size and in that condition. This was on the Dunecht Estates and after my complaint something was done: the bothy was made a bit bigger, a bath was put in, so was a built-in wardrobe, hot and cold water for the sink and a fine new fireplace. So I stayed for another two years.

**James Edwards,** born 1924: the Mearns

**'The farmers thought more of their horses than they did the men.'**
A typical showpiece picture of the day: a farm servant with a fine pair, Waterside of Thornton Farm, near Laurencekirk, 1930s

## The cottar quine

My father was a fee'd farm servant and we shifted around quite a bit from farm to farm. I was the youngest of five. So I was what was known as 'a cottar bairn'. Although I wasn't so conscious of it then, looking back I realise there was a bit of a stigma associated with it. To be a cottar bairn was to be at the very bottom of the pile, almost to count as nothing. But when I was a child I was one of many cottar bairns

**'Helping' with the hairst:** cottar bairn, aged two.

Our diet was sufficient, if a bit monotonous. Everything was made to fill us up – tatties, kale, skirlie, brose, neeps and 'hairy tatties'– tatties and salted fish. There was also plenty soup: tattie, lentil, broth.

all through the surrounding countryside and I thought of myself as just 'ordinary'.

I can recall the days at 'term' time when we'd be off again to a new farm. The night beforehand, you had to fill the mattresses with fresh caff and sleep on the floors, because all the beds had been dismantled. The next day our goods – not that they were many – were loaded onto a horse-drawn cart, or maybe even an open cattle float, which came over from the farm we would be going to.

The cottar houses were generally very basic – concrete floors, no running water, only water from a pump or a well outside. That meant you had to carry buckets in and be careful not to waste any. I can remember my mother saying, 'I'm jist awa for a fracht o' water'– that was two bucketfuls. The best you ever got on a floor was a piece of linoleum. But we did have a rug to place by the fireside; this was home-made, from strips of rags clicked through a piece of sacking. This was a job for the evenings; a rug would take more or less a whole year to build up – there was always a new one every year.

Heating was by a fire and lighting by paraffin lamps and Tilly lamps, which at least did give off a bit of heat. On Sundays the big tub was brought in and we had our weekly bath; I can smell that carbolic soap yet! Mondays was wash day and for that mother would use a wooden tub along with the scrubbing board. She'd spread the whites out on a bit of grass to bleach them in the sun. For furniture we had the dresser, a horsehair sofa, a wardrobe and a chest of drawers.

There was no running water, so our toilet was an outside lavvy. We used an 'Elsan' pail which contained disinfectant. For toilet paper Mother would cut squares from the *People's Journal.* Going to the toilet was a cold and draughty business and we didn't linger any longer than was strictly necessary. My niece is astonished when I tell her this; she just can't imagine such a primitive way of life. She claims that if she'd been me she just would have refused to use it – but I think she would have had to.

For food there was the meal girnal; a supply of meal was one of the farm worker's perks. Cooking was done on the big black range and this had to be black-leaded every week. It had an oven which was heated by the fire and a flat top where you could make pancakes. Mother would be baking almost every day, it seemed; we had a constant supply of oatcakes, pancakes and scones.

At most places there would be a bit of garden where Father could grow some vegetables and tatties. We also kept hens, so there were always fresh eggs. For us children the hens became pets: I can remember one hen which got into the way of bringing her chicks into the house whenever it rained; she would then sit on the footstool and watch over them. Mother would sell her eggs to the grocer's van which came round each week and this helped to pay for the messages.

So our diet was sufficient, if a bit monotonous. Looking back, I can see that everything was made to fill us up – tatties, kale, skirlie, brose, neeps and 'hairy tatties'– tatties and salted fish. There was also plenty soup: tattie, lentil, broth. On Sundays there might be something a bit more special – some broth and some boiled beef and mealie dumplings. We'd use our soup plates for the second course and maybe even for the pudding – we didn't have so much crockery you could just change it for each course.

Puddings were filling: rice and raisins, bread pudding, jam roly-poly. The great standby was the milk pudding – rice and tapioca with some jam or rhubarb spread on top. Father liked his 'murly tuck'; this was hot oatcakes crumbled into milk. Whatever was left over from dinnertime would be recycled for supper: the dinner tatties would be fried up and so on.

Sweeties and treats of that sort were a rarity. A cake of McCowans 'coo' candy had to be divided out between all of us.. On a Sunday night I might get one square from a cake of Fry's cream chocolate and I would suck and nibble at it so as to make it last.

Christmas day wasn't a holiday on the farm, but we did celebrate it with boiled chicken, broth, mealie dumplings and tatties, followed by a clootie dumpling. Mother would give us some excitement by wrapping a threepenny bit or two in greaseproof paper and hiding them in the dumpling for us to find. And my parents always made sure we could wake up and find a stocking by our beds. There wouldn't be much in it – an apple, orange, a school ruler, pencil, something useful like a home-knitted jumper or cardigan, socks and always a pair of bottle green or navy knickers for school. But it was always a thrill to wake up in the dark and to put your hand out to feel what might be there, waiting for you. I was always hoping for my very own dolly, but I made do with the hot-water pig.

My parents had to be very hard working. I never ever saw mother sitting idle; if she wasn't baking or washing or cleaning she would be sitting in her chair with some sewing or some knitting on her lap. Then she had to help with the farm work and she was required to work in the dairy, washing the cans. But she never complained; after all, what she was doing was what hundreds of others like her were also having to do.

Until we arrived at Uppermill I grew up as a fairly isolated young girl. This meant I was very shy, timid in fact, and not used to dealing with anyone outside the family. And even though I was the youngest, I can't say I was exactly petted at home. I can't remember being hugged or spoken to in a soft and loving way. But that was just the way of it then; my parents weren't being unusually cold or unkind, they were simply far too busy. We did sing together on a Sunday evening. Certainly, they never raised a hand to us. The worst that would happen was if father was reading his newspaper and we were getting a bit rowdy and then he would shuffle his paper about – and that would be enough. Mother was the one who sorted out right from wrong.

Don't forget, they were both of them hard at work from morning till night. They just didn't have the time or the energy to sit down and play with us. We had to make our own amusement and this we did by playing outside: we built little hoosies, we played shoppies, that kind of children's game. We played rounders in the field. In the winter we used to break off the long icicles which hung from the spouts and suck them as if they were ice-lollies till they chapped our lips and made our mouths sore.

'Cottar Bairn', born 1930: Buchan

My parents always made sure we could wake up and find a stocking by our beds. I was always hoping for my very own dolly, but I made do with the hot-water pig.

**'It wasn't a good house, really, just a shack, but my mother kept it so well'.**

The Fraser family at Burnside of Enzie, in 1941.

There were nine of us in the house at Muldearie. Upstairs, it wasn't even filled in. We had to sleep up there and it was just rafters.

# The farm servant's son

In the Hungry Thirties my father was forced to take a job as a farm servant. So, I come from a farm cottar background. My mother never did like the term 'cottar' – 'cottage' if you like, but 'cottar' never. She was of the opinion that if you were a cottar bairn you were a lesser creature on the scale of things. A lot of people would look down on you.

There was a fair bit of shifting around among the fee'd men then, though generally only over a small area. That's only human nature, to try for something that bit different, that bit superior. The normal perquisites were tatties, meal and milk and you could expect that wherever went. But then at this farm, the house might be a wee bit bigger, or a bit better positioned. And then, my goodness, there could be big differences in the food you got. Now on one farm I heard about I know for a fact that all day, every day, all the men got fed with was a bowl of milk with bits of bread floating in it. Saps, it was called, just saps. But then at another one, well, there the woman was a tremendous cook. At the end of the working day, men from other farms would come over for a game of football, or throwing the hammer, or just a bit of chat and they also knew they would be getting a really super tea. A different world altogether.

My father didn't do all that much shifting about compared to some. He went from Cullen to Banff to Fochabers to Keith and finally to Enzie. The farmers would come to know such a worker. They'd advertise in the paper and you'd look at the *People's Journal* and you'd see they needed a horseman here, a foreman there. He landed up at Burnside of Enzie, two miles inland from the Moray Firth, as a foreman; this was reckoned to be one of the best farms in Banffshire and that's where he stuck, for 20 years.

Before that we'd been at Muldearie and the house there was just a shack and there were nine of us altogether. Upstairs, it wasn't even filled in. We had to sleep up there and it was just rafters. Mother would try and make it better by putting in bits of old carpeting on the sarking boards to stop us from catching our heads on the nails. The wind would come whistling through. Downstairs the floor was bare concrete.

There was no running water in the house; just a well for that. I think the first time she got water from a tap would have been at Burnside and that was in 1941. She never had an inside toilet, not till 1949. My whole childhood was spent without these facilities. But what strikes me now, looking back, is what an effort my mother made to turn that house into a home. She would be forever going off to a roup and coming back with an odd bit of linoleum or something like that. People in the cottar houses could be very house-proud. I remember Mrs Hendry on the next farm, the Braes. Her house was right in the middle of the steading, but you would go into it and she would rush to dust the seat before you sat down and then she would rush to dust it when you rose up. My mother liked her house to be just so. When she finally got a council house in Fochabers, well, that was like a palace to her.

I don't really see my childhood as all that tough, not at the time. I often think about it now and compare it to today's childhoods. My grandchildren have been to Florida twice – it's just a different world! But you see, life in the country is different from that in

the town, especially then. You got out of the school and you were immediately into the open air. At the age of 10 onwards, I would be driving the tractor or caa'in the neeps. I set snares; I would go ferreting rabbits.

**Allan Fraser,** born 1930: Enzie

# The crofter's daughter

I was born at Woodside Croft, Crooksmill. That's just two miles from Keith, along the A96. Woodside was what you'd call a 'twa-coo craftie'. My grandfather just dug it oot, in the old fashioned way. You paid a fee to the landowner and then you could put down the foons and build up your own house on the site and that's what he did.

My father scarcely knew him. He died in 1907, my grandfather. You see, my dad's mother had gone to him as a housekeeper when his first wife died and then she married him. He was real old by then; all my father can faintly remember is this old man with a white beard and that was his father. He was only three when he died.

The croft is still there, but greatly altered, with extensions, new fencing and all sorts of renovations; it's even been given a new name. A different place altogether. When I was growing up on it, there were wooden hen houses and a little steading at the back. There were six acres of land – that was about the stretch of it – enough for the two cows, their calves and grazing. We also kept hens; my job was to see to them. I would go out and feed them, muck them out and take the manure to the park in my barrow. Mother reared geese for Christmas and we also had cockerels which we'd bring up for nine months and then

**When it was still possible to park your barrow on what is now the A96:**
Woodside Croft in the time of Mabel Cowe's grandfather, about 1900.

**No running water in the house:**
Mabel and her two brothers by the broken door which covered the spring from which they had to fetch the family's water. The geese are being raised for the Christmas market.

> My granny had a milk house with stone shelves for her butter and cheese, always with a cloth to keep the blue flies off them.

kill and pluck for Christmas. Not interfered with in any way; just lovely for the table, they were.

My father was awful good with his hands and he did a lot to improve the croft. For water, we just had to pump it from the well, but in the old steading out at the back he put in a bath and a toilet, all by his own hands. Our old toilet had been a wooden bench in the shed with a bucket underneath and this had to be emptied, physically emptied, but Dad's new toilet was plumbed underground; you still had to put buckets of water down it but now we could just pull the plug and the waste would run down the brae and just disappear into the ground. Very advanced!

It was a three-roomed house: a living room and two bedrooms and a little wooden kitchen at the back. In the house the furniture was very solid and quite practical. My mum had an old-fashioned washstand at the bottom of the bed and this held a big basin, a jug, a thingy to hold your toothbrush and a little bowl for the soap. There was a large wardrobe, made of solid dark wood. The living room had a nice old sideboard with a mirror in the middle and these stands at each side, with two little mirrors. The bottom had a pair of lovely bevelled doors. We also had a chaise longue.

Looking back, this furniture seems to me to have been good solid pieces made to last and handed down through the family. But we went through a spell – we weren't the only ones either – of thinking all this heavy, dark old stuff was terribly old-fashioned, and so they were taken out into the yard and hacked into sticks for the fire. We replaced them with lighter utility stuff, which didn't last.

In the kitchen there was another old sideboard. This is where Mum sat her milk and made her cheese. I've never ever tasted home-made cheese like it. She'd heat the milk till she got her curds and then she would pack it down in the cheese press, put a wooden lid on top, and, with one more crank of the handle each day, she would squeeze and squeeze till the juice ran out of it. Then, once it was nice and solid, she would store it in the cupboard; this had an air vent to keep it fresh. And guess what: I never thought to ask her for the recipe. If only I'd thought to get hold of her secrets then, I'm sure I could have set up a factory and exported the family cheese, the quality of it was so good.

In those days the farmwomen would run their own little cottage industry for dairy produce. My granny had a milk house with a cool flagstone floor and stone shelves for her butter and cheese, always with a cloth to keep the blue flies off them. I mind once being over to see her and this man came by off the Moss, all sweating, with a terrible thirst on him. He'd been casting peats. So my granny gave him a mug of buttermilk and he drained it all in one go, just like that. I remember standing there watching this man tip the glass back and back without pausing for breath till it was completely drained. It was a wonderment to me to see it. He had whiskers and afterwards you could see the white liquid all over them.

I wouldn't have said anything; in those days when there were adults about, there was a good bit of the seen-and-not-heard. When callers came to the croft we would go outside and play; we knew not to interfere. I remember one Christmas when King George came

on the wireless to make his broadcast and I started chatting. Oh, the looks I got! I remember shrinking back in my chair; you mustn't speak when the King's speaking. There was a great respect for royalty – and that went for the minister and the dominie too.

Growing up on the croft was a round of hard work. My abiding memory of childhood there is the continual cry of 'Hurry up! Hurry up! Let's git the job dane an then ye can ging oot tae play.' We had a lot of fun and games, make no mistake, but we knew there were jobs to be done too and that they always had to come first.

There wasn't much of the huggy-huggy, kissy-kissy either – but we grew up knowing we were loved and cared for. Just knowing you were an essential part of the family's life, that was so important. We grew up happy and loved.

Mabel Cowe, born 1937: Keith

**A communal affair:** tattie picking in the 1940s with Granddad and some neighbours. The young Mabel is next to the dog, on the left.

# The small-holder's son

I was born on a 40-acre holding. It was something rather bigger than a croft, but not as grand as a farm. What, in Buchan parlance, would be termed 'a placie'. It was picturesquely called Thistlehillock. My parents went there in 1925, the year I was born. They went with the high prices – just before the slump came.

The house we lived in had two upstairs rooms; you could scarcely call them bedrooms, just rooms; downstairs was the kitchen, bedroom and then 'the Room'-the one that was kept for visitors. No bathroom. It was a dusty, old, old house. We also had a loft and I would aye imagine that one day I would go up there and come across some ancient harp – with maybe an angel to play it, too. But angels were in rather short supply at Thistlehillock…

The toilet was a little hoosie in the traditional sentry-box shape. We used an old-fashioned wash stand; we used an old piece of hessian that wasn't too rough, if we could find one, for our ablutions. Then there was the fire, which being peat, had to be kept in at all times. The last thing at night was to let it go low and then to take the tongs, get hold of the embers and, with the shovel, make a space for them under the wall, after which they would be covered with ash. This was known as 'resting the fire'.

Now, in those days the rule of thumb for a tenancy was to produce evidence of capital at £10 the acre, so 40 acres postulated £400. It helped if you were reckoned to be 'a real decent chiel', but you had to have that cash to lay out. Dad had three, mum had two hundred, but that left them with no elbowroom at all when things got tight and in the Thirties they did. Came the slump and we had to grow up with the svalue of siller – or the lack of siller – well dinned into us. I remember once asking Dad what 'rates' were and his reply, 'Ah laddie, ye dinna get tae live in this world for nothing.' And there was this grieve up at Blackhills, talking away one fine Sunday morning, and he was saying, 'We'll hae tae pay for aa this guid weather yet,' and me thinking to myself, 'Not another thing – how the blazes can we pay for the weather as well?'

Dad was actually an intelligent man, but the hard times had made him very pessimistic. I remember meeting him one day in the cornyard and taking it into my head to ask him what his favourite colour was. 'Black,' came the immediate answer, 'it's black.'

The work ethic was very important. Education had its place, but if you were to be seen wandering about with your head in a book, well that wouldn't do at all. Education had to have a practical value; it was not something you pursued for pleasure or for its own sake. And you'd go to the library and get out these children's story books and look at the pictures of the farms in them; they all seemed so neat, with the yard swept clean and the children nicely playing in it, and you'd think on the way in which your own yard would be pock-marked with cow pats and mired in hen droppings…

**Charles Birnie,** born 1925: Balearn

## The dairyman's son

My father ran the farm, a dairy farm of 55 acres. When he had taken it on it had been a poorly run place; it had fed no more than half a dozen cows, but he built it up into a good going business with more than 30 head of cattle. He had his own milk round in the district. The milking was done twice a day and the milk was treated and prepared for sale on the site. We had a cool cellar room beside the kitchen to keep it in and the milk we produced was good quality – there was a bit of flavour to it – much tastier than today when everything's become so overtreated and so standardised. In those days the customer was getting milk more or less fresh from the cow.

Before the war we would milk by hand, put it into cans and then deliver it door to door. We did this on a cart, a kind of gig, pulled by a large pony. The cans had a tap at the bottom and the customer would come out with her own jug and buy the milk from us

**How it used to be:**
the dairy team at
Jackston Farm,
Rothienorman, 1935.

**The future dairyman at play:** Monquhuitter Cub pack, 1937. Ally is back row, second left.

out there on the street. The only problems was when it got windy, because that's when the milk would get all frothy and fly all over the place. The Milk Board fixed the price; we got twopence-halfpenny a pint.

The milk cart was pulled by a Shelt. I never did get on with that animal; when I took it to the water trough after the round it would deliberately plant its hoof on my toes, and a real heavy hoof it was too, and refuse to budge. It was a large animal and there was no way I could shift it; I just had to stand there and grin and bear it. That pony also once nipped the wart off my father's finger – and he never suffered from it again.

My father was popular with his customers and part of the job was to stop and have a word or two about the weather or the latest goings on in the village. He was actually a quiet kind of man, never up or down. This meant that he just took all the comments about the milk in his stride: he never got upset when they remarked that the milk hadn't been so good yesterday. It wasn't that the milk really varied from day to day so much as the customers did. If they had had a problem with his milk then he knew that it was probably due to the fact that they hadn't stored it in the right way – a common problem in the days before there was a fridge in every home.

We didn't have any refrigeration either, just this cool room next to the kitchen. But we worked in an hygienic way; it wouldn't have paid us to be careless about that. The great enemy of the dairyman is mastitis and I was aye careful to wash the clusters with disinfectant and keep everything spotless. After all, we weren't the only dairy in the district

> My father and I both milked by hand. Sometimes I would put my arms round one of the cows, feel her warmth and the softness and give her a cuddle.

**'Aye the farmer's daughter':**

As a University student back on the farm with mother, niece and lamb, Kinghorn, about 1950.

and there was plenty of competition. But after the war things changed: there were more and more regulations and milking machines and bottles came in. A lot of the smaller dairies fell by the wayside. Not that all our customers saw this as an improvement: they seemed to enjoy the personal contact of buying straight from the cart and having a word or two – and maybe hoping to squeeze a wee bit more into their jugs than they would be getting from the regulation bottle.

My father and I both milked by hand, of course. It's not such a difficult job to pick up, not really. The important thing is to get a nice easy rhythm going, up and down, hand and hand about. When you come to the end, then give a nice smooth caress down the udder and a gentle squeeze to get the last of it out. Mostly this was straightforward; the cows usually wanted to be milked and quickly got to know you and to trust you.

You developed something of a personal relationship with the cows, very much so. Sometimes I would put my arms round one of them, feel her warmth and the softness and give her a bit of a cuddle. When I took them in from the field for the milking I would be speaking to them, nice and easy. I'd say, 'Come on, darling, come on'. Not so different from dealing with a woman, I suppose! But later when mechanisation came in and herds got bigger, they became a number only. When I finally sold up the herd it near broke my heart to watch the last of them going off to other people; I think of it yet and, 40 years on, a sadness will come over me.

My routine would be to get up at five and then, if it was summer time, to go out to the field to get the cows in for their morning milking. The cows would be already waiting for me at the gate and willing to come and get rid of their milk. Once in the milking shed they'd go straight to their own places, all by themselves. When you milk by hand you'd sit on a small low stool, so as to get at the right height. I must admit that some mornings with your head resting against the warm flank and the rhythm of the milking you'd doze off for a second or two – especially if I'd had a late night out!

**Ally Irvine,** born 1926: Cuminestown

## The farmer's daughter

I was a Rennie and members of our family had three farms in the Newmachar area. There was Louis Rennie, my father, who farmed Kinghorn; Westside was the main family farm and that was Uncle Jim's and then there was Rennieshill, over beyond the railway station, and that was Uncle Alec's farm.

My father had a very basic education, just at Newmachar School, but looking back I can see that he was a naturally clever man. I remember how he used to do all these calculations concerning the farm and I would look at them and think, 'What's all that about?' He had never been taught any approved method for any complicated arithmetic, but he'd found out his own way of doing it.

My mother came from Bellfield Farm at the Bridge of Don and went to Balgownie School. But then she went on to the Demonstration School and there she got things like literature and Shakespeare. She was an interesting woman; she liked to read. She was the one who made sure we were all well educated. My father would have wanted us to go into the farming life and he didn't bother too much about all that education.

My father was very much one of the old type of Scottish farmer; not the kind to hand out praise or to give us cuddles. But I knew he was proud of us and that he wanted us to get on in the world, though more by growing up to do the right thing than succeeding academically. My mother was a bit different: she was a warm and couthy woman, everyone liked her. She read and recited to us a lot and encouraged us to learn. I'm now a storyteller at the Buchan Heritage Society and I reckon that I got that from her.

Kinghorn was a 90-acre farm – small by today's standards, but large enough in those days to support a moderate-sized family like ours. It wasn't an easy life and the whole family had to pull together to make a living. When I was a little girl my father employed a horseman and usually had a young loon to help with general tasks. The chaumer at the farm was still in use then. At times of heavy work like the harvest and again when we had a visit from the travelling mill, helpers from round about would come along to help. My mother must have spent her whole life cooking, cleaning and washing, but there were moments of enjoyment too.

It was mixed farming – sheep, pigs, cattle, oats and barley, tatties, neeps and hay. We also had poultry, including turkeys and geese. We didn't have a dairy herd, although we kept a family cow for our own use. As a girl my jobs included getting in the sticks for kindling, feeding the cats, fetching in the water and seeing to the hens. They were, of course, completely free range and you'd have to go hunting for their eggs in every little nook and cranny, far from the henhouse. I liked doing that, but I never could stand the geese – horrible hissing creatures that would come running after me with their necks stretched out and their little black eyes fixed on where they could peck me next.

We always kept a hard-working collie dog and they would become my especial friends. One of them, Teddy, saved my life. I was just a toddler and I'd gone wandering off. It was some time before any alarm was felt – I was generally given plenty of freedom to play about the place. But eventually my mother realised she hadn't clapped eyes on me for a while; she also remembered the mill was on and that the lade would be full of water. She rushed outside, only to see me coming round the corner of the steading with the dog beside me and my clothes all dripping wet. 'Teddy pulled me out,' I told her. I'd been playing with my bat and ball beside the lade. My ball had fallen into the water and in trying to get it out, I'd fallen in too. Nobody would believe that a collie would have

**'An interesting woman':** Bunty's mother in a gig at Bellfield Farm, Bridge of Don, about 1915.

My father was very much one of the old type of Scottish farmer; not the kind to hand out praise or to give us cuddles. But I knew he was proud of us.

**'Oot fer a flop'.**
Taking a wee break during the hairst; father and one of Kinghorn's life-saving Collies.

**The threshing mill**
comes to the farm. Kinghorn, 1952.

jumped in and pulled me to safety. So the next day my brother went up to the dam and pretended to jump in. Sure enough, Teddy grabbed his clothes and pulled him back away from danger.

I loved those dogs, but there could be no sentimentality on the farm when the end of their life came. My father would take them to a quiet spot, usually the barn, and shoot them. That's what life had to be like then, on the farm: no nonsense, hard work and every penny counted. Our house was big enough, but when I was a little girl our water came from the well until it was later piped into the scullery. The lighting was by Tilly lamps. The toilet was the 'wee hoosie' out at the bottom of the garden. There was a chunty under the bed to get you through the winter nights. I actually grew to accept these arrangements. It was my library and refuge, a peaceful, private place that I could retire to and philosophize about life, out there amidst the peace of nature.

Farming was simple in those days – little of the chemicals and the specialized machinery of today. We were all organic in those days, without knowing it. I drove a Fergie when I was a student. I did it for my board. If I ever protested about the work my father would just fix me with a withering look and tell me, 'Be quiet, quine! Ye're nae payin fer onything while ye're awa at that university o yours'. I grew up among the life of the farm and the fields and loved it all – except the weasels, nasty evil little creatures. They could even scare the collies. But I would always look out for lapwings and skylarks– they were much more numerous then. It was still possible for the tractorman to stop his slow tractor out in the fields and carefully lift a nest clear and put it in a safe spot at the side, returning later to replace it in the original place. Now that doesn't happen and the birds which make their nests on the ground are fast disappearing.

At harvest and at the hay time, all kinds of folk would come in to help out. There'd be male nurses from Kingseat. My father always had a laddie to help him after school in the evenings or at weekends. Then we had prisoners of war; I once wrote a story, 'The United Nations at the Farm' and told how the Germans and the Italians had a fight up at the dam. One of the Germans had insulted my mother's soup and was challenged to a duel by an Italian. So many people came to our farm; I remember the old Italian POW, Alessandro Revassio, who made wooden bats for me to play with. We had a Palestine policeman and Alex, a Polish patient from Kingseat Hospital. The whole world came to Kinghorn.

**Cecilia Penny,** born 1932: Ellon

# Feein day at Alford

Twice a year the feein mart would hit the village. I actually found Alford a scary place to be a boy in on those days. The pubs had permission to stay open all day and, gee whizz, you'd be coming home from school and a lot of folk would be wandering about the streets absolutely plastered. Farm servants would come in, looking to move on after their six months at a farm, they'd strike their bargains and then off to the

Haughton Hotel to get drunk. There was only the odd fight, but folk would be jostling about and crying out to each other in loud voices. In the old days the feein would have taken place on the Market Stance, but when I was a young lad it all seemed to be happening out on the streets and things could get rowdy. The streets leading up to the school, round the hotel and the fountain, that's where they all congregated, and it could be quite intimidating to try to make your way home through them all.

Another exciting time was the sheep sales at the end of the year. As soon as the school was out I'd throw off my bag and rush off to the mart. There was great excitement because that was the time when the sheep would be going off with the train and the streets would be full of them being herded along down to the station. It was our great fun to get in among them and try to jump on their backs and the drovers would be shouting, 'Hey you loons, git oot o there!' In those days the sheep weren't floated in but were just driven along the roads, miles and miles. It was said that at the back end of the season – beginning of September – the sheep would just know to make their own way down from off the hills and then they'd be driven all their way, along the roads, from the Cabrach, home to winter in Alford.

One of the things that kept Alford going as a centre for business and for shopping was the Tuesday cattle marts. That's where the auctioneer's so important. We were lucky in having Melvin Dalgarno at Alford. A top auctioneer's able to sum up what his customers are wanting, how far they are prepared to go, what the mood of the sale is. He's got to be quick with his banter and command the ring. When Melvin Dalgarno took over the difference was immediate: the farming community began to make sure they didn't miss out on what was happening at Alford; it became the mart to go to.

In those days Alford lived by agriculture; the majority of folk either worked on the land or served those who did. You seemed to know everyone you met; you could place them, tell where they were living, know the farm they worked on. Now that's quite impossible: the village is full of newcomers and commuters who have no connection at all with the farming life.

Robbie Gordon, born 1933: Alford

**'A scary place for a young boy':** Market day, Alford, about 1920.

The pubs could stay open all day and, gee whizz, you'd be coming home from school and a lot of folk would be wandering about the streets absolutely plastered.

**'Always well turned out...'**
With her three younger siblings, in front, left to right: William, Alan, Mary. About 1920.

# EARLY CENTURY LIVES: 1
## Isabella Wilson

# Forty years a teacher, forty years retired

**The young teacher**
ready to take on all comers.
udio photograph, early 1920s.

They used to say my mother was a snob. But she wasn't a snob, not really. She maybe didn't take up with the rest of the street; nobody came into the house unless they were asked.

I was born in April 1903. I was a pupil at Fetteresso School, here in Stonehaven before the First World War and I ended up being a teacher there, just when the second one was starting. As a girl I had always wanted to go in for Cookery, but Mother Wilson wasn't going to allow that, oh no, so a teacher I became.

I retired in 1965. For the past 10 years I've lived here in the Abbeyfield homes. This is a fine room. I like it because I look over and see the Carron flowing by and I can see people coming along the path by the river, beneath the cherry trees over there. In the springtime when the blossom comes out it's really lovely.

My father was in the Post Office and mother had worked in a big house as a table-maid. That's where I got my very good training in life: she knew everything. I had a sister and two brothers. I was the eldest and now I'm the only one left.

We didn't seem to want for anything. My people didn't have much money to spend, what with four children, but I can tell you that we were always very nicely dressed. We were very happy. I can't remember any time when there was any trouble or quarrelling in the house. We were never bored; there was always something to do. Father was very good at sitting with the boys and playing with their Meccano. He also saw we all did our lessons; he was very strict about that. Father and Mother were both keen that we all got a good education; they wanted us to get on in life, no doubt about it.

Do you know, they used to say my mother was a snob! But she liked to see us all well turned out and properly fed and all the rest of it...she wasn't a snob, not really. She maybe didn't take up with the rest of the street; nobody came into the house unless they were asked. There was no going backwards and forwards to the neighbours or anything like that. That just wasn't on at all.

Our family all went to church. My father was an elder and Mother did a lot of church work. We all had to go to Sunday School. I can remember Mother and Father stepping out with the four of us on a Sunday. The family pew just held us and no more. My brother Bill could be a bit of a rascal; you had to watch him. So I had to go in first, then Jean, then Alan, then Bill, and he had to sit beside Mother and Father, because you just couldn't tell what he would get up to. He'd start to play trains with the hymnbooks and all sorts of things. He wasn't bad, just a bit of a nikkum and the church could be boring for the young ones. But father was a staunch churchman. Father would sit with his Bible at night. If you ever said a bad word in his presence...oh no!

We all had little gloves; we were all dressed up for the church, and I can remember a

button came off one of my gloves and because it was a Sunday, it couldn't be sewn back on. That had to wait until the Monday. Mother wouldn't do anything on a Sunday, you see. We weren't a holy family… we were just what you would call good living.

I was five in 1908 when I went to Fetteresso School. I do remember my first day, I do remember that. Mother had got one of the other girls to take me to the school and I had to wait for her to take me home for lunch and I just stood there howling. All I wanted was to go home. But that was only the first day: I was all right after that.

I can remember the headmaster there – old Sorrie. He used to go about the corridor and he had a strap, a kind of cat o' nine tails, and he'd put it in his jacket pocket, but he couldn't get it all in so you always saw it dangling out. It was a kind of warning to us all.

We got mental arithmetic till it was pouring out of our heads. First thing, Miss Chalmers used to put a ring on the board, point to the numbers, and off you'd go. Sharpened up your brain, all right. We always got Religious Instruction in the morning and the minister used to come once a year for Bible inspection. I can remember him exactly: a white-haired man. He'd ask us a series of questions on the Bible and we would have to get them absolutely right.

We couldn't use the Doric in the classroom. If you were outside, in the playground you could but, oh no, not in the classroom – they were very strict about that. We didn't speak Doric at home either – you see, Mother liked us to speak properly. You certainly couldn't speak broad Scots to her. I can't remember anyone who spoke like that to her.

We didn't want for anything. There was always plenty of food, good food; we never went out with a hole in our clothes. There was a family we were friendly with, Strachans the baker people and their four children. We'd go out playing with them on a summer's evening and we were always told to be back at a certain time. Mother's instructions were for us to come home as soon as we heard the clock in the Market Square striking eight. Well, this particular night, we simply didn't hear it, and who had to come along and fetch

**'A dead hole of a place?'**
Luthermuir in the 1920s, when Isabella was a young teacher in the village.

**Note the hats!**
Parents and dog in the
back garden of their
Cameron Street,
Stonehaven, home.

At
Luthermuir
there was
nothing to
do at all,
just nothing.
A young
female
teacher like
me could do
nothing in
my spare
time but sit
in my room
and do a bit
of sewing or
read a book.

us but Father! But he just said, 'Come along home now'. There was no punishment involved. There was nothing like being hit – we were just told to go straight up to our beds; the rule was to be washed and fed by 8.30 so as to give Mother some time to herself. We were very well brought up. I've no regrets, none at all.

We all went to Fetteresso School, the four of us. And we all went on to Mackie Academy. The rector was Billy Riddoch. But he had to go off to the war in 1914; he was a captain, you see. But Billy came back. By gum, you wouldn't cheat that man…a very good disciplinarian, no nonsense at all. Hard but very fair, he was. He didn't use the belt a lot either. I never used it myself. I had one, but in all the years I was teaching I never brought a piece of leather against the skin of a child. I didn't need to and I never wanted to. I liked to think that when the children came to school they would respect me, but I don't know if they respect their teachers now. The times are so different.

I was happy at Mackie. I would say I got a sound education there. Then, I went to the Teachers' Training Centre in Aberdeen. We had to be tidy in our appearance. But as a teacher you always had to be properly dressed – almost as if going to the kirk. Always gloves and a hat. Never went without them. In those days men wore hats when they went into the school.

My first post was at Luthermuir; in those days there weren't many jobs around and you had to take what you were given. Oh, I could tell you stories galore about that place! That headmaster there was just a ninny. He wasn't married; he lived in the schoolhouse by himself and his two Alsatian dogs. He wouldn't come and open the school in the morning. Rain or sleet, the two female teachers had to wait outside, before we could get in. Well, I said to the other assistant, Marjorie, 'There's a backdoor key; I'm going to take it because it'll lead to my room'. So, I just took it. Once we got in, you could open the front door and let our own children in. We left his ones playing outside. He never said boo; his kids would be playing till after 10 o'clock, in the snow and everything. Well, we weren't going to allow that for our classes, certainly not.

Eventually he got the sack. He would go out playing football with the kids. They all smoked with him too. This carried on and on. Mr Miller was Director of Education and he came out several times. They eventually got the headmaster dismissed. Then I went to Johnshaven and oh, what a difference! I never regretted going there because Mr Kerr was an excellent headmaster. You had to be on your toes all the time. It was very good for me.

At Luthermuir there had been nothing to do at all, just nothing. It's all different now – lots of new houses – but in the 1920s it was a dead hole of a place. The village was just a straight row of weavers' cottages, all made of clay and painted white. The weaving had really finished by then and the heart had gone out of the community. A young female teacher like me could do nothing in my spare time but sit in my room and do a bit of sewing or read a book.

As for the pupils, there were some very poor ones – I used to feel very sorry for them. A lot of them were farm servants' children. I'd start a class and by the time November came, you didn't know how many would still be there, because of the feeing. Another

thing: there were weeks and weeks of potato gathering and the mothers would come and take them away because the little ones had to be with them out in the fields and their older children had to look after them. But when they came back, what a difference! They were so beautifully dressed. Poor kids: when they were at school before, they were just in rags.

I went to Fetteresso in September 1939. Just about my first duty there was to organise places for all the evacuee children. It was when I left that the great changes were taking place in education. So I said, 'It's maybe just as well I'm going'. I had enjoyed it all. You did a lot for the little ones. You weren't finished at 3:30, oh no. You had to carry on – homework, preparation, putting things on the wall. And the news bulletin – teaching children to speak properly and sometimes getting stories about what their parents had been up to you didn't really want to know. Never mind. The object was to get them to speak in sentences. We'd talk about the weather and any sensible news they wanted to tell me.

I enjoyed my life in teaching. I had lots of laughs. No regrets – oh, no. I thought when I gave up that the first day when the kiddies went past after the holidays I would be a bit sad. But no, I'd had a long career. I felt it was time to go. So that was that.

**Isabella Wilson,** born 1903: Stonehaven

# SIMPLE PLEASURES

**The adults had their fun too...**
Meal and Ale Night, Fetterangus Hall
around 1930. Sheila Wells's
father is seventh from left, with
raised spoon and cuff showing.

**'It was painted brown with gold leaf decoration...'**
Queen Victoria's Jubilee Fountain, Saltoun Road, Fraserburgh, 1920s

# Playing in the street

The road wasn't made up then; it was just compacted sand and gravel. In the summer the water cart would go along to sprinkle water and lay the dust. All the children had great fun running along behind it and playing about in the spray. In the summer we would all go about barefoot, across the Links and down to the beach.

We had plenty of freedom; we played out of doors all day long then. We had seasons for games. There was a skipping season, and then there'd be a season for playing on the pavements: we used to draw a circle with chalk and you had to get your buttons into the centre of it. Then we played beddies – hopscotch. No, we were never ever bored; we didn't know the meaning of the word. Hoosies, we played at shoppies and hoosies: you'd get a cardboard box and you'd fill it with seashells and pebbles from the shore and this would be your sugar and your tea and then you'd sell it to your pal for buttons.

We made our own amusement, you see. We had guessing games: you'd start off by saying, 'I'm thinking of a flower that begins with the letter "m"' and they would have to guess whether it was a marigold or a marguerite or whatever. There was certainly no sitting about in the house. And we had our dog and you'd take him for a walk along the beach; you'd go paddling and at low tide you'd be looking for shells in the pools. Fraserburgh had a nice clean beach then. You'd go off for the day with a flask of tea and a biscuit and that would be you.

Another memory I have is when they were putting up the war memorial, which was at the corner of Strichen Road and Saltoun Place. This was erected where Queen Victoria's Jubilee Fountain was. The Fountain was then moved to its position almost opposite this house. It was painted brown with gold leaf decoration on it and this was put on, using little gold pieces of paper. After the workmen had finished we got the gold pieces that were left lying around and stuck them in our hands. Simple children's fun.

**Violet Johnston,** born 1909: Fraserburgh

# Queen of the May

**Bringing in May Day**
Alford c1920

Every first of May we had the May Queen in the village. We would choose a May Queen and a May King and May Maids. I was never good enough or clever enough to be chosen as Queen, but I did become a Maid once. We would march to the fountain at the top of the village and we'd sing, 'Tramp, tramp, tramp, the boys are marching'. We would sing all the way. And we'd go into gardens and pick the spring

**'Tramp tramp the boys are marching...'**
May Day Alford, c1920

flowers. But, you know, I've seen us having to shake the frost off the daffies on the first of May. Then the shopkeepers would give out sweeties and drink. Then we'd go back to the school and have a real tuck-in. But in those days there might be snow on the road as we marched along in our long white stockings and our white cotton dresses and white canvas shoes. Oh, but we didn't mind the weather: we thought we were really lovely!

**Isabella Cowe,** born 1911: Alford

There was a spot on the Leuchar which was known as the Dooker. In the summer it would run pretty dry and then I could try to guddle for trout. You'd stand in the shallow water and wait for a trout to come along and catch it in your hand.

# The school run

When I was 11, I went to Robert Gordon's. The great thing in those days was that two buses would set off to take us country pupils into the city. They would race each other all the way. If one person was standing waiting at the stop, the first bus would pass by and leave it to the next one to pick him up. And if the engine began to misbehave by any chance, one of us lads would lie along the mudguard and work the throttle; you'd keep an eye on the driver to see how fast we should be going. Then on a Friday when the bus would go round by the Lyne of Skene, the driver might let one of us take the wheel. There wasn't much else on the roads then.

**Ronald Smith,** born 1913: Dunecht

# A shot in Paradise

We moved up to a cottage, at a spot above the village, called Cornyhaugh. It was a primitive place: no running water, no electricity, just a range fire. Alongside were sheds and that's where the dry lavvy was, and next to that the washhouse and then the coal shed. We had to get our water from a pump in the washhouse and in the winter when the pump froze we had to take our bucket along a track at the back of the cottage, down a brae to the well there.

No water, no amenities – but a lovely, lovely place. Once in later life my brother sent me a photo of the old place and on the back he wrote, 'Our beloved Cornyhaugh'.

It was such a free and outdoor life for us boys. You'd go out the back, down a track and you'd come to the Leuchar burn, which comes down from Loch of Skene into the village and then falls into the Dee. A magical place! You could go across a field, then along a path and into what was known as the Den. You'd come to where there was a fallen tree trunk and this made a kind of a bridge. You'd cross over the burn, go up the bank and then you'd arrive at this lovely flat field. We'd go there and take a picnic.

There was another spot on the Leuchar which was known as the Dooker and this was a pool where we could play about in the water. In the summer it would run pretty dry and then I could try to guddle for trout. You'd stand in the shallow water and wait for a trout to come along and catch it in your hand. I was never any good and the trout would just use my hand to vault over, but I had a pal who was so quick at it that he once went home with a catch of 22. Sometimes I'd use a bent pin on the end of a stick as a rod, but again, not much success.

Then, just down from Conyhaugh, there was Newmill farm, with a sawmill on one side of the yard and a barley mill on the other, both driven by a waterwheel off the Leuchar. At the back was a beautiful lush green field which we called the Haffy. The farm servants would come and play in it, practising for the Highland games. There'd be throwing the hammer, tossing the caber, jumping, vaulting – the whole lot. We watched and we'd try to imitate them.

But here I come to a very sad story, one that makes my heart sore yet. We had a dog,

Jack. He was just a mongrel, a tan coloured mongrel, but he had a faithful, loving nature. One thing about a dog: if you're good to it you'll get it all back tenfold. Human love seems to fade after a few years, but a dog's love is yours for life. That's the way it was with Jack; he would go everywhere with us. Well, this day we made our way to the Haffy, but for some reason Jack was following on later. I was there at the far end of the field watching all the sports when suddenly I heard a yelp and a shout. I turned and there was Jack grappling with one of the sheep that was grazing there. He had it by the leg and they were struggling together; then the pair of them tumbled into the burn with a great splash. I just couldn't understand what I was seeing: Jack had gone everywhere with us, among cattle and among sheep, and he'd never made to bother any of them.. Anyway the farmer, a man called Charlie Smith, a hard type of a man, came dashing up shouting, 'Ye'll hae tae pay for this! Ye'll hae tae pay for this!'

My guess is that Jack had been in a hurry to get to us and he'd strayed near one of the sheep and she must have kicked out at him. Then Jack naturally reacted by getting hold of the leg in his teeth. Really it was hardly anything at all; he was just holding onto the wool – at the most the sheep would have got a wee bruise. But we understood the way it had to be in the country; we knew that Jack would have to go. The vet stayed in the middle of the village; we would have to take him there the next day.

That night Jack was out in the shed and I was the one to take his last supper out to him. He wagged his tail and licked my hand in his usual way. I stayed with him while he finished the plate. The next day when I got back from the school, he was gone. He was just a young dog, a lovely young dog. We never had another dog after that, just cats. As you can see I can't tell the story of how Jack met his end without the tears still coming to my eyes – and it's 80 years ago.

**William Booth,** born 1914: Peterculter

# A penny for the Prime Minister

I can visualise the Infants' Room yet and the teacher we had in Primary 1. She always wore this old Fair Isle jumper with a v-neck. Every time the headmaster came into the room we'd watch her and we'd take great delight in seeing her go bright crimson with embarrassment and see how her skin would turn red right down the length of that 'v'. She was scared of him, you see. And that wasn't really surprising, because he was such a very formidable personage. He was Benjamin Skinner and he had a rather grand manner about him. Whenever he spoke to us girls it would be 'Mistress Smith' or 'Mistress McDonald', never the first names.

He was the President of the EIS and little did I think then that one day I would have a daughter who is in that very position [Kirsty Devaney]. He often had to leave the school to go off in order to catch a train so he could attend a meeting in Aberdeen or Edinburgh. We always knew when because then he would appear in a dark suit. The rest

'Can you tell me how the Prime Minister is different from our own minister here in Strichen? There's a penny for you if you can.'
I knew the answer to that one: 'Our minister wears his collar the other way round'.

**'Wearing the woollen dresses knitted by our mother,'**
Tortoston School 1922. Winnie Brown is second row, third from left and her sister is fifth from left.

of the time he would come to school in knickerbockers and stockings. He could put the fear of death into all of us. He ran a very strict regime and Strichen prided itself on the high standards it achieved. You could take Latin and French; quite a number of First Bursars came out of Strichen school.

I once won a penny at the school. I must have been about six when it happened. Mr Skinner came into our classroom. He had this newspaper in his hand and he held it up in front of us. It had a photograph on its front page. 'Can anyone tell me who this gentleman is?', he asked. Well, I hadn't the faintest idea, but I did have very good eyesight and I could already read so I was able to make out the words. 'He's the Prime Minister,' I told him. 'Very good. Now you all go to the church, don't you? But can you tell me how he is different from our own minister here in Strichen? There's a penny for you if you can'. I knew the answer to that one too: 'Our minister wears his collar the other way round.' I did get the penny for that; oh, you could spend ages with your face pressed up against the sweetie shop wondering what to get! You could buy such a lot for a penny in those days.

**Catherine Strachan,** born 1915: Strichen

# Walking to school

The country was a good, good place to grow up in. Things are so different in the evenings and the holidays now: the kids just sit inside and gape at their screens. But we'd be up first thing in the morning and away outside. We had complete freedom and we wandered about wherever, all the day long. Now they are taken in cars everywhere, but then we would have to walk to the school each day. We had miles to go; we enjoyed it. You picked up all your knowledge about the country that way. We knew all the birds and all the flowers; we had collections of birds' eggs. The rule was not to take an egg from a nest unless there were at least five in it. We held that birds 'canna coont mair than fower', and wouldn't miss the fifth one.

We would walk to the school through the fields. If we went by the road then someone was aye sure to see us. When the fields were newly ploughed you'd see the teuchits [lapwings] scraping away at the earth and you'd know that's where their nests were. It used to take hours to get home; in the morning we had to hurry to get to the school, but coming back we could take as long as we liked – and we did.

Childhood for most of us was extremely happy, but then came the real world and then by… I better watch my lingo! There was a lot of poverty around. I've got a photo of the whole of Tortie [Tortoston] school taken in my second year there. You can see Hattie, my sister and me, sitting in the same row. Both of us were wearing woollen, dark red dresses, which our mother had knitted.

I was happy enough at the school. All my pals were there. The playground was quite different, quite separate from the classroom. There, you'd be belted if you did or said anything out of line, but the playground was our world. We could speak how we liked and play our own games.

**Winnie Brown,** born 1916: Inverugie

## Shakespeare beneath the trees

Kemnay was a secondary school in those days and you could go all the way through from age five to your Highers. Dr Minto Robertson was the Headmaster, a great Shakespeare man, very much so.

It all started quite gradually: there had been some sort of a strike and the pupils who went by train were stuck at the school because they had to wait for the train that went at 20 minutes to 7. So Dr Robertson started this little gathering after school and they would do a scene or two from a Shakespeare play. It's something that just grew and grew. And he also seemed to celebrate every possible occasion. At Empire Day there would be some kind of ritual, some kind of ceremony in the school and most of the parents gave their support. Really, he seemed to rope in everybody!

My own first venture was as the fairy Mustard Seed in 'Midsummer Night's Dream'. I was six and stood in awe of it all. At the end of each June there would be this performance of a full length play – 'Much Ado' or 'Winter's Tale'' or

whatever – out at Kemnay House in the open, in front of the great tree there. Very ambitious, but it was all done in the three weeks leading up to the performance, after the exams. It was very busy, those three weeks - you'd go home for your tea, then come back at five for the rehearsals. It was a very happy time.

**Ella Michie,** born 1917: Kemnay

> The rule was not to take an egg from a nest unless there were at least five in it. We held that birds 'canna coont mair than fower', and wouldn't miss the fifth one.

**'Winter's Tale' beneath the trees,** Kemnay School mid 1930s. Ella Michie is seated on the ground, right.

> Old George Wilson, the banker, used to say, 'I wudna marry a McPetrie even if she cam to me wi a goldmine stuffed up her airse!'

# Scouting for boys

For the young males of the village, there was the scouts, the First Torphins Troop. This was under the command of James George Campbell, the soutar. He had been a sergeant major in the First World War and he treated us all as his soldiers, though with little success. His attempts at military standards of discipline were somewhat undermined by an unfortunate speech defect which resulted in each barked out command being punctuated by a distinct farting noise. 'Company, form fours! – fart; company quick march! – fart' – and so on.

In his day job as shoemaker, Campbell had been used to holding court in his workshop, surrounded by any local yokel who cared to drop in and be treated to his dogmatic opinions on how the country should be run. His mouth would be full of tackets and sprigs that were always in danger of showering the listeners; he would thump a flat-headed hammer up and down to give added emphasis to his words. His wife had been a McPetrie and she resembled a witch in appearance, sporting one solitary front tooth. Old George Wilson, the banker, used to say, 'I wudna marry a McPetrie even if she cam to me wi a goldmine stuffed up her airse!'

Despite these shortcomings she bore three children. The eldest was Archie who became an architect – an attainment which his mother would always pronounce with a soft 'sh' – 'Archie is an arshitect, an arshitect!' Archie was married in Ireland and on the boat back across a very rough Irish Sea, his father was violently sick and vomited his upper and lower sets of false teeth into the deep.

His daughter fancied herself as something of a singer and would treat the village to renditions in the hall in a howling soprano voice. At her version of 'Ye banks and braes are bonny', my brother would remark that this was an excellent choice, since she was so expert at braying.

The youngest succeeded to the family trade. He it was who regaled the youth of Torphins with his story of how he had seduced Mary, the Stewarts' maid. 'I took her into the widdie at the North Kirk and took doon her knickers and there she lay wi her fanny winkin up at me, so ah jist gart her fud dirl'. This was the forest, in which we would build our tree houses and gather bundles of kindling wood, and which also served as a meeting place for the sexes and their somewhat scruffy little seduction scenes. Later you'd see Mary riding around the village with a self satisfied smile on her face.

**James Morrison,** born 1917: Torphins

# A fine wee village

**Edna:** We were both born and brought up in Torphins and that's where we still live. **Alan:** This is going back to just after the war – the First World War. It was a fine wee village in those days. We had our own brass band – our father was a member – and then there was the curling pond and lots of home-made entertainment. You used to be able to walk down the street and everyone you bumped into was a kent face, someone

you could stop and have a news with. It's not like that now. And there used to be so much visiting, from one house to another. Folk would drop in and make an evening of it - a game of whist, a tune or two, or just a blether.

A trip into Aberdeen was like going abroad to us.

**Edna:** Yes, father would sometimes suggest it and we would tell him, 'But we're quite happy here in Torphins!'

We had our animals. The croft had a milking cow and there were ponies. We'd put the dogs and cats in the cart and pull them along; we'd try and guess how long they'd stay there till they jumped out. Then we kept rabbits and we'd let them out and get the dogs to round them up just as if they were sheep.

**Alan:** We'd go and look for birds' eggs. We collected them, but you'd never take more than the one from a nest and then you'd blow it and keep it in sawdust. We knew all the birds: blackbirds, chaffinches, sparrows, the tits – we recognised them all, instantly. We'd play in the woods or we'd take the dog up to the golf course and hunt for balls. We'd make fishing rods out of sticks and fish for trout in the burns. We'd take them home and fry them in oatmeal.

**Edna:** And all the wild flowers too. We'd pick daisies and sit on the green and make chains out of them. Our toys were home made. You'd make tops out of cotton reels and then spin them to see who could go the longest. Or you'd get a penny and flick it and send it spinning and guess where it would stop – heads or tails.

**Alan:** We had Shetland ponies and when I was a little wee lad father made a wooden snow plough for me. The ponies would pull it and I'd go round all the houses in the village and clear the paths up to them. Those ponies could go up all the steps, no bother. I'd be given a penny here, a penny there, and think I was rich.

**Edna:** People would come out and see their paths all nice and clear and say to themselves, 'Young Alan Stuart mist hae bin roon wi' his pony!'

**Alan:** A penny was a lot of money then. I used to spend my earnings on lucky tatties. This was a kind of toffee with a cinnamon flavouring and if you were lucky you might find a halfpenny in it.

**Alan and Edna Stuart,** born 1921 and 1917: Torphins

**Torphins Brass Band 1890s.**
Alan and Edna Stuart's father is the young member seated with the drum.

Our toys were home made. You'd make tops out of cotton reels. Or you'd get a penny and flick it and send it spinning to guess where it would stop – heads or tails.

'Hundreds of horses'

– and people too. Aikey Fair in the 1930s

# The great days of Aikey Fair

One of the great highlights of the year was Aikey Fair. This was the great annual horse fair which was held on a hillside the other side of Maud. By some wondrous means of calculation, Aikey Fair and Rathven Market were deemed to take place annually as follows: Aikey – the first Wednesday after the 19th of July; Rathven – the first Friday before the last Monday of July, thus ensuring that both would take place in the same week, always. I thought that whoever had worked this out must have been some kind of genius.

The fairs brought a huge stir to the roads all about us. The main road to the fair went past our front door and you could see the horses, the lorries and the machines for the funfair going past in a great stream of vehicles and of people. There would be swings and shooting galleries and roundabouts pulled by great steam engines, and all sorts of other attractions.

But the main thing was the horses: there were hundreds and hundreds of them. The area was renowned as a great breeding area for fine strong horses: Clydesdales, and of such quality that buyers from all over Britain would come to Aikey Fair. After they were sold they had to be marched down in procession to Maud Junction for despatch to the south; many of the large haulage and carrier companies such as Pickford's would come up to buy in those days when the horse-drawn wagon and cart was still the most common way of moving stuff around.

Living in our cottage on the Brucklay Castle estate just by the side of the road, you felt you were in the thick of events when Aikey Fair was on the go. You'd see the traffic of lorries and steam engines and men and animals all processing along the road in front of your house. Then at night, after the Fair was over and the traffic was moving onto Rathven Fair, you'd see and hear the traffic passing up the road again, but this time in the darkness. I can remember gazing on the fire and the glow of the traction engines with the reflection shining out from their fireboxes, as they roared past the house in the darkness.

A lot of men would appear at the end of the Fair and go up to the buyer with a 'Ah'll mind yer horses for ye, sir! Ah'll tak them doon to the station, sir!' This was a way of earning a few extra bob. The usual thing would be for the man to sit on one of the horses and lead three or four others in a sort of procession. One of my early memories is being taken at the age of about four, down to the station at Maud to witness the 'truckin o the horses' – the packing of the horses up into their trucks to go on the long journey south. Most of them would be quite wild and used to the freedom of the open fields; they hadn't been broken in, so there could be real shenanigans persuading them to take up their position in the truck. And these trucks weren't horse boxes, either – no finery about it, the horses were simply packed like sardines into cattle trucks and you'd see them rearing and bucking and generally protesting about the whole business.

The fair also brought tramps and hawkers to it. You'd see characters the like of which no longer seem to exist. Tramps would knock at the door in search of a crust of bread which they would receive in return for a wee bit o' sang. One of our regular callers became quite celebrated later on in the folksong world. This was Jimmy McBeath whose songs were recorded and collected by the American expert in the field, Pete Seeger. Many of these tramps would sleep under the hedges or seek out one night of shelter in the lodging house at New Pitsligo or Banff. They'd go to the police station to get a chit signed as genuine vagrants and that would entitle them to one shilling's worth of accommodation.

**Stanley Rothney,** born 1923: Brucklay

> One of our regular callers became quite celebrated later on in the folksong world. This was Jimmy McBeath whose songs were collected by Pete Seeger.

# Football daft

I was football daft. At the school, in the playground, we would play with a small ball; it was a major job getting a proper sized one even though you could get one then for only 7/6. We had to hold our own collection, with people chipping in a sixpence here, a threepence there, before we managed it. There were no school funds for that kind of thing then.

Aberdeen FC, oh yes, the Dons! Going to Pittodrie was only a very special treat, but my father usually managed to take us in for an early season game or two before the harvest started. I can still recite the names of the teams back in the 30s though I doubt whether I could get half of the present lot right. They were all home-grown names then, none of these tricky foreign ones that they have now: Eddie Colquhoun, Benny Yorston, Willie Cooper, Johnston, Fraser, Thomson, Smith, McDairmid, McGill…

I loved going along, but I was only a small lad and it could be a real job seeing

**Fan-tastic:**
A cup-tie crowd pressing to get into Pittodrie, 1930s

the actual play – no seating back then! We'd get there early and look for a spot down by the dyke which ran around the pitch, down where there'd be no one in front of you to blot out the play. But I dreaded coming out again; they would open this big gate at the Merkland Road end and the crowd would come surging out and I'd be swept along in the tide and with a feeling of near panic rising up inside me. But the crowd were always good-natured then: there was never any fighting or anything nasty, not back in the 30s and 40s.

When I was a boy you could get into Pittodrie for a shilling, boys sixpence; you'd cycle to the station and the fare from Ellon was sixpence. One-and-six for a whole afternoon's entertainment! Now I hear that to go to somewhere like Chelsea it can be £60 for a ticket. But most times we didn't go and then came the problem of finding out the score. We didn't get the wireless till about 1935. What I did was cycle the two miles to Arnage Station and wait for the 7 o'clock from Aberdeen to pull in. This would bring the *Green Final*; I'd get a copy, look for the result and then cycle back. If they'd lost I didn't exactly cry all the way home, but it certainly put you down.

That was fine during the early season, but when it became too dark to cycle down, you'd often have to wait till the Monday to find out; my father wouldn't dream of taking in a Sunday paper. And now it's all instant news: on the radio, by TV, computer, text-messaging, what have you. Nowadays nobody has to wait for anything.

**Arthur Watson,** born 1921: Tarves

## The Friday night dance

Everything was more in the community then; you'd go to a dance at Alford, or maybe the next week to the hall at Tullynessle and you'd find all the young folk of the area there and they'd be all familiar faces. At that time, all the farms round about employed plenty of young male labour. At the end of a hard week's work, they would come pouring out of their cottar houses and make for the local dance hall. The Friday night dance was just a great thing.

Nobody had a car then; they all went on their bikes. You'd go into the hall and the men would be on the one side and the ladies on the other. If you didn't want to be left out of it, you had to get across the hall quickly! The dance floor was always full; everybody was there to dance. If a lassie refused an invitation she could be put out of the hall. And there was no licensed bar, maybe just a stall selling lemonade splits for tuppence.

It was all dancing: no drinking or just standing around. Everybody mixed together; there was none of this grabbing someone round the neck and spending the whole evening with them. No, no, none of that! You didn't pair off till the very end: after each dance you'd escort the lassie back to her place, thank her, then go back to the men's side and wait for the next one. There would also be a couple of Ladies' Choices and that would give you an idea who you might be asking to take home at the end – but you'd aye be hoping she didn't live too far away!

We danced close enough at the waltzes, but nothing more than that – strictly no smooching. That did change a bit when the war came and there were troops posted here. Things became a bit more direct then. I noticed when I was in the Army down south how the girls there were a bit more open about things. But then in those days Aberdeenshire lads were aye a bit shyish kind and slow at coming forward.

You used to get bands come out from Aberdeen. There was Billy Thain; that was a great band. He played the xylophone and the saxophone and his mother was at the piano. They played a good mixture: waltzes, quicksteps, maybe an eightsome reel or two. You'd get all the hits of the day; they were such great musicians. They got £10 for the night, and that included their transport out to Alford; if things were going well you might sometimes offer them an extra quid and then they'd play an extra hour or two.

On a Saturday the entertainment had to stop before midnight because of the Sunday, so mostly the events took place on a Friday. Sometimes they might run on till two or even three in the morning. They would begin at eight. The bars would close at nine and that's when you'd get a great influx; by ten past the hall would be real full. But there wasn't much drinking beforehand – nobody had the money for it. There was no misbehaviour, no trouble. The band had their tea-break half way through and, sure as anything, that's when the bobby would appear and get his cuppie too. 'Aathin aa right, boys?', he'd ask. If anyone was the bit worse for drink, he'd go up to them and say, 'Ah'd like ye to cam ootside wi' me a minute'.

A lot of our courtship was around local events. In fact we'd go to anything local where you could meet other young folk. The Bible classes were well attended and so was the Band of Hope. Mrs Goodall used to play the organ in the hall and you'd go along and listen to that. We aye got a laugh at that; it had one pedal which squeaked and you'd listen out for the 'squeak, squeak!' In the summer we had mixed bathing in a pot in the Don.

I suppose today's young people would find all this real tame kind of stuff. But we knew how to enjoy ourselves all right.

**James Gordon,** born 1926: Alford

**'The men on one side, girls on the other...'**
A line up of lassies, Alford Hall, 1950s

**'All the hits of the day...'**
Billy Nicol's Band, Alford 1950

**George Swapp**
enjoying a celebratory
swim on its 75th
anniversary
(PHOTO BY ANDY THOMPSON)

# The open air pool

The pool was opened in 1934 and I was present at the event. I nearly wasn't because I'd been up to something naughty in the morning – picking buds off plants along the street or some such crime – so the family story goes. My mother told me, 'That's it – you're to go up to your room and miss the opening of the swimming pool!' But after half-an-hour or so she relented and I went. It was something of a grand event, with all the dignitaries and local professional and business people invited, along with my mother, brother and myself.

You could say that Stonehaven was quite a popular resort in those days and that the pool set the seal on its position. It was certainly a great attraction for all of us when we were young; in the summer I would spend day after day there, and when I became a student I got a summer job as a lifeguard attendant. It wasn't simply the swimming that brought in the crowds: there would be galas and diving competitions and parades. There were polo matches and, twice a week, midnight bathing.

In those days Stonehaven had its own resident dance band for the season and they would sometimes be in attendance at the pool to provide background music as well as concerts. It was a seven-piece outfit and it would play the latest popular hits including Glenn Miller. So the pool was something of a magnet for holiday makers and a lot of them would simply pay to be spectators, quite happy to pass away an afternoon just sitting on the benches enjoying the spectacle of the swimmers and taking in the music.

The pool was capable of being heated, but in the war years it was limited by all the energy shortages. The manager of the gas works, Mr Scobie, would say, 'Look, I've only got enough gas for the homes or the swimming pool, not both!' And in the competition between the housewives cooking the family dinner and the bathers, there could only be one winner. But we went anyway; you quickly got used to the bracing temperatures!

**George Swapp,** born 1931: Stonehaven

# The village was our playground 1

You'd play together and you'd learn how to share and to keep to the rules and about playing fair.

We could go out from morning to night; free to use the village as our playground. Kids just don't get that kind of opportunity nowadays and that's a shame because you learn so much that way. For the bairns to get out and learn to communicate with each other – well, you might be having gripes at home with your parents giving you the works or the teacher at the school doing the same and then you could meet your pal and share all your problems with them. You'd play together and you'd learn how to share and to keep to the rules and about playing fair.

The Ugie was our sea. In the summer we'd be there from morning till tea time. You'd go to the burns and catch bandies or tadpoles and take them home in a jar. We'd pick birdies' peas and we'd eat soorex – you call it sorrel nowadays – and make we were having a picnic.

In the winter all the bairns of the village would come to North Place – ' Up-the-Pole'. It was such a good sledging area: the road was tarred and that gave us a good surface. All the bairns of the village came together for that. We'd organise games like Hoist the Green Flag; we'd have skipping games; we had leapfrog; we'd play 'hanky droppit'. 'I sent a letter to my love and on my way I dropt it/ I-d, I-d, I dropt it/ An old man picked it up and put it in his pocket/p-o-c-k-e-t spells pocket and o-u-t spells out'.

For this you'd all be in a circle and whoever dropped a hanky by you as they passed by, then you had to chase after them and if you managed to tap them on the shoulder then they were out and had to sit with their arms folded.

You also learned how to look after the younger ones. Sometimes that could be a bit of a nuisance, but you knew from your parents that if you didn't take your younger sister or brother with you then you wouldn't get out at all. Then if you did something wrong like coming back late you'd be confined to barracks. I'd tell my friends, 'Cam tae the back door an ask fer me oot!' Worth a try, but it never worked!

**'Up the Pole'**
North Place, Fetterangus where both Isobel McRae and Sheila Wells were brought up

For us there were no social divisions, none at all. If there was a fancy dress party then all the bairns of the village would be there; if there was a concert, same thing. If there was a sale of work the whole village would turn out. In the summer there was the Gala, the Fishie Gala. For the Brownies there was Mintlaw and the Guides were at Old Deer. To get to them you got the bus, or you just walked or biked it. There was plenty going on.

Going to Peterhead was the great trip of my childhood. For that you'd get up early to catch the seven o'clock bus and the night before I could hardly sleep for the excitement of it all. Peterhead meant dressing up in your very best – nice frock and a handbag over your shoulder. For us this was our visit to the big town and the chance to shop in Woolworth's. I'd be given a little money, enough to buy a book, which usually cost sixpence. That was my treat.

**Isobel McRae,** born 1933: Fetterangus

## The village was our playground **2**

I was brought up in a house 'up the Pole'. This was a circle of newish council houses built at the top of North Place. A lot of the houses had been settled by families with young children, so there was never any shortage of playmates. It was a wonderful place for us children. We could play out in the street; we had skipping, hopscotch, ball games. One of our favourites was to use the gates of the houses around the circle as stops for our rounders. One of the houses didn't like the ball to go into the garden; he would come out and confiscate the ball, so you had to do your best to duck down and creep in to get it before he could spot you. But most of the adults took the view that it was the bairns playing and let us be. In the winter we could use the incline of the street as a sledging track – it was ideal for that. But then one day the doctor had to make a call and the very next day the council came round and put sand down and that was the finish of the sledging. The sledges were just home-made affairs: a plank of wood with a metal runner.

Those were the days when you had to make your own amusements and the toys to go with them. One of our tricks was to take a couple of old two-pound syrup cans, punch holes in the tops and then fit them up with long bits of string that you could hold in your hands while you walked along on top of these cans. Stilts, home-made stilts! Sitting here 60 years later all that seems unreal now, but that's what we did – no TV or computers for us then! You remember going along to a birthday party in someone's house and playing putting the tail on the donkey, or getting out the board for a game of snakes and ladders or ludo at home.. Just simple fun, made out of nothing. And we were very happy.

**Sheila Wells,** born 1937: Fetterangus

> In the winter we could use the street as a sledging track. But then one day the doctor had to make a call and the next day the council came round and put sand down.

# Pigeons were big at the Broch

Pigeons were a big thing in Fraserburgh in those days; and there would be racing pigeons set off to fly all the way to France. Father gave us a wee plot of land to keep round the shed at his allotment and he warned us, 'You kip that – that's yer job noo. If ye mak a mess o' it, then the pigeons'll go!'

As lads just, we couldn't afford to buy any racing pigeons for ourselves, but you'd see lots of wild ones flying about, so we decided to try and catch one and train it up. The school had a broken window, high up, and we could see the pigeons going in and out of it. We'd watch them and talk about which one we fancied. There was one which had a kind of broken leg and which could only hop about – we called it Peg Leg.

When it got dark, we climbed up a drainpipe and got into the school through a skylight. We managed to crawl along the rafters in the pitch black; you could hear the rats going past but we didn't care – we were going to get those pigeons! At last we saw the broken window and we knew we'd got to the right place. I caught hold of a pigeon and put it in my jumper and managed to crawl back with it. We had to be absolutely silent because the janitor was in the school with the cleaners. I was dying to get down onto the street so I could have a look at the pigeon I'd got. When I did I took it out of my jumper

**A real character...**
Ricksy, the Rennie dog, very much one of the family

and found it was Peg Leg. I just said, 'Oh no, not you!' and let it go.

An old box, an old Fish box, that was my first pigeon loft. I put two pigeons in it with lots of food. I gave them a bath first in salted water so as to kill all their fleas. But when I went to see them the next day I found they'd broken out and gone. I thought that would be the last of them, but the next day I took another look and found one of them there eating up the food. After a few days the other one turned up; it was his girlfriend and before long there were a couple of eggs. Brilliant!

I used to let them out one at a time. The first one I called Twister because he'd eat up all the food and try and break out. He disappeared for a few days but the hen pigeon continued to stay, sitting on her eggs. Then her mate did come back, not for the eggs but the food — that's what he was interested in — Twister! The first time I let the hen out she flew up onto the roof, so I took a tin with peas in it and shook it. She flew straight back in — and that's what happened: every time I went out with that tin and shook it, the pigeons would come back. I'd turned a pair of guttersnipes into homing pigeons, but I couldn't race them because they didn't have any rings on their legs, with my name and address. That's something you can only do just after it's hatched; after five days it's too late.

We had a dog called Ricksy. A real character, one of the family. When we took him past the tennis courts, if a player hit a ball into the road, he'd grab it and run off back to the house with it in his mouth. The players would ask whose dog it was, but we never let on. We got a lot of balls that way.

Another thing we'd do was catch bees and put them in a jar. We didn't kill them; it was a competition. You'd lick the tips of your fingers, creep up on a bee in the garden and then, whoosh! — you'd snap your fingers over the wings and pop it into the jar. When your fingers are still little and nimble you can do that. You'd go round and ask how many bees ye've gat? If you were good at it you could maybe take 20 or more in an afternoon. You never touched the bodies of the bees, just the wings. I can't remember ever getting stung that way by any of them.

We caught bats when they came out at dusk and flew around the street-lamps. We'd take these nets we used for bandies on the shore and catch them. We didn't harm them; the idea was to get them in your net and then throw them out at the girls and make them scream. Once we took Mother's washing ropes and cycled out to Rosehearty. We lowered the ropes over the edge of the cliff and climbed down to get seagulls' eggs. We cycled home and threw the eggs at the kids in the street. But sometimes in the war we'd fry seagulls' eggs for our supper.

The street was our playground. In the winter we'd seen this ice hockey in the newsreels at the picture house, so we decided to have a match. We flooded the street so that it all froze over; we used a cork as our puck and sticks to hit it with. But the bobby soon put a stop to all that. The horses delivering the milk were sliding all over the place. We had to get muck from the gardens and cover up all our lovely ice rink.

**Alex Rennie,** born 1934: Fraserburgh

**The young pigeon fanciers**
Alex Rennie in the front

**From guttersnipe to homing pigeon**
Alex with Twister

**'An old fish-box picked up on the shore...'**
Alex's first pigeon loft

# The home sides

The Huntly Cricket Club is something I grew up with. I was going there when I was scarcely big enough to hold a bat. My father was a great member and player. The club had high standards both on and off the field. The matches would get a fair-sized crowd, but you had to behave properly. If there was too much of a babble then a member would lean over the veranda and warn you: 'Keep it quiet – there's a match in progress!' Shouting was frowned upon; you were expected to show your appreciation by a ripple of polite applause.

Once it was the done thing to go the Castle Park on a summer's day to watch the local side, but nowadays it's only a small sprinkling of the faithful who turn out. But the club continues to thrive. I'll often be stopped during the week when I'm out on the street with some such remark as, 'I see the team won again,' so there's still quite a bit of local pride in the cricket club. We run three elevens and have some good young players coming through. I've been secretary since 1985 and intend to see out a few more years yet.

Next door is Christie Park where the town's football team plays in the Highland League. I was never a great football follower, but when I was a boy it was regarded almost as a duty to go along and support the local team. For us it was a family event: both my parents would go, along with a collection of uncles and cousins. We stood at the same spot each Saturday, the very one that the Congregational minister could be found; he was rather good at shouting, I remember! Another vociferous supporter was the local coalman, Willy Lorimer. During the week you'd come across him plying his trade in the streets, always with a bell to announce his arrival. On Saturdays he'd take it to the match and ring it loudly at the exciting bits. If we felt the team was beginning to flag we'd turn to him and tell him, 'Time to ring your bell, Willy!'.

After the match we'd all troop back to my great-grandmother's house and talk over what we had just seen, offering deep analysis of the team's failings and giving out advice as to the changes that needed to be made for the next Saturday. In those days the team was very much a local side, made up of men you could see about the streets during the rest of the week. There was Abbie Rough who was the caretaker at the Stewarts' Hall and Matthew Stewart who worked at the sawmill. I recall one match which was played out on a bitter winter's day. It was absolutely freezing and the players rapidly became miserable and wet. Periodically one or two from each side would go off for a few minutes to get a bit of a warm-up, so at any one time there would only be 18 or 20 on the field. The referee just seemed to allow this on account of the exceptional conditions. Matthew later took pneumonia as a result.

Back then both the football and the cricket teams would gather a lot of support; the two parks would be ringed with spectators and the events of the Saturday would act as the common talking point for the rest of the week. Our great needle matches, of course, were against Keith – Huntly Tinks versus Keith Ceards! In one match the Huntly supporters got it into their heads that the referee was favouring Keith and that he had awarded an entirely unjust penalty to them. After the match a sizeable crowd gathered at the back of the stand to boo him on his way; the whole of the Huntly police force – all three of them – had to muster in order to give him the necessary protection.

Local patriotism ran very high back then. Once the Aberdeenshire Cricket Association printed some posters and caused them to be displayed about the town, warning that spectators must be on 'good behaviour'. I've dug into the old reports and I've come across one match that ended in a mini riot. There's a description of how the opposition – Keith, of course – was forced to make their escape from the town under a hail of stones! It's not like that now; in fact some of the Keith parents come over with their sons to take advantage of our coaching facilities. They can even be seen indulging in friendly conversation with us. Changed days…

**Patrick Scott,** born 1937: Huntly

# A stick of Yarmouth rock

The fishing began in the spring up in Shetland and then followed down the east coast. The shoals would begin to appear in the early spring off Shetland, then down to Buchan for the early summer; North Shields and North England by late summer, then finish at Yarmouth in the autumn. That's what my father did. It was a pattern that repeated itself year after year.

The trip away was a big annual event. The husband would be away for three months, right from August to late November, even early December. That had to be prepared for in

> After the match a sizeable crowd gathered at the back of the stand to boo him on his way; the whole of the Huntly police force – all three of them – had to muster in order to give him the necessary protection.

## They'd bring presents. I always got a stick of Yarmouth rock

the family. Clothes, blankets – it was a ceremony to gather together the quilts and the blankets and then sew them into a kind of bedroll. It was in these that the fishermen would sleep in their bunks, so it all had to be nice and cosy and, at the same time, easily kept together. I always remember that as a great ritual each year.

And then they'd return in the early winter, and they'd bring presents with them. I always got a stick of Yarmouth rock – I used to think that this Yarmouth must be a marvellous place with all this rock!

**Jim Wilson,** born 1938: Sandend

**A Birdslint wedding in the farm steading**

Morag McIntosh's mother to her first husband James Winton 1928. He was to die young, and Caroline was to remarry [see Wartime Wedding]

**Into service**

Caroline Smith, as she then was, when she went to work for a doctor's home in Huntly, c1920.

# Birdslint memories

My mother's upbringing was on a farm – Birdslint – in the Glen of Newmill, four miles from Keith. My grandfather had the farm there. Most of the family worked on the farm at one time or another. They would stay on after their schooling to do that. It's mixed farming – arable and beasts. They had horses to do the work, of course. Donald the horse was a great favourite.

My mother spoke a lot about her early days. I think she felt they were happy ones. My grandmother would make cheese and butter and she'd take it into Keith each Friday to sell. She was also quite involved in the raising of funds to put up a hall in Newmill for

## The whole glen was there.

The Glen School picnic 1910. Morag Mcintosh's grandmother is front row extreme right.

They all had to walk the two or three miles to the local Glen School across the fields and along the tracks.

social functions. The Rural and various dances were held there. She raised over £100 personally, a quite fantastic sum then. My mother would speak about how their father was quite strict and wouldn't approve of the two sons going off to the dances. He was a senior elder at the kirk in Keith. Anyway, they would sneak out to these dances without him knowing. My grandmother knew but her husband didn't. They would then come back in the night and knock at the lower bedroom window where my mother and her sister would quietly let them in.

The whole family were married at Birdslint, in the farmhouse; the old farmhouse was used for the receptions. This would have been in the 1920s, mostly. They all had to work hard. My mother and her sister would have to lift the tatties and would be bent over in the fields, weeding out the carrot field they had. They would also have to see to the hens and milk the cows – the standard female tasks. The two brothers and the father would be out in the fields with the horses at the ploughing and so on. It was hard, but they all managed. She never spoke of any poverty; there always seemed to be enough to eat – hot soups and puddings and eggs with meat on a Sunday.

My mother's schooling was at the local Glen School. They all had to walk the two or three miles to it across the fields and along the tracks. She would speak about them having to do this in the rain and the snow. Then they would go into the room and sit around the fire, with their clothes all steaming away. But their father would always insist they go: the school was important. She was at the one school all the way through till she left at 14. She had the same one teacher too – Miss Jeannie Newlands. When they later got married she would present them each with an embroidered tray cloth that she had done herself.

All her own brothers and sisters went to that school and seem to have had Miss Newlands. My mother told me how, when she left at 14, Miss Newlands gave her a letter to take home with her. It told her father that in her opinion Caroline should be allowed to go on with her education as she had the ability for that. But my grandfather simply said, 'There'll be nane o that nonsense! A girl's place is back here in the hoose'. She was the second youngest and the older ones had flown the nest by now; my grandfather seemed to feel he had to have a pair of daughters about the place. My grandfather did

**Birdslint family**
The Smith parents with their 10 children. Morag McIntosh's mother is seated front to our left of her father. All of the girls' dresses were home-made.

allow her to try the nursing and she started off at the hospital at Keith. But she only stuck it for three days: the bedpan situation was quite enough for her. So he told her, 'Ye'll just have to cam hame and bide here'.

My mother was obviously a good pupil. I've got her prize books at home from that time. She was always good with figures and right up to her 90s was very accurate and quick with her counting. She felt she had been given a sound schooling; she enjoyed it. I think that what they got would have been pretty basic stuff, with no fancy methods, but she did get her needlework and some art, as well as history and geography, in addition to the three Rs. You've also got to remember that they would have learned a lot from the farm itself: she knew all the birds and the plants.

For myself, I consider this rural background to be an important part of what I am. Although I've lived almost all my life in Aberdeen I've never thought of myself as a city person. When I was a child I would hear my mother speaking longingly about her Birdslint days and that made a great impression on me.

I found something magical about it all. Mother would talk about the sister who went off to Edinburgh to go to cookery classes and then come home with clothes that she'd acquired there. She gave Mother a pair of smart boots; she would remember with horror those high lace-up button boots. They were very smart but they didn't quite fit, but granny said, 'Oh they are beautiful'. She was sent round the neighbouring farms to collect for charity and came hobbling back with her feet bleeding. She was let off wearing them after that. There were all these great family stories of that kind that told you so much about what life was like on a farm in Banffshire at that time.

So although I was an only child I never felt lonely. All our country relatives would still come into visit us whenever they came to town and then the talk and the stories would begin again. They'd come in and stay for the whole weekend – to go shopping or to visit the hospital. To me they were an object of fascination: they spoke differently; they had their own views on things, but they were very much part of the one family. All the other children at the school seemed to have their relatives in the town whereas I had none – the Keith contingent were my family. That made me feel a bit different.

**Morag McIntosh,** born in 1942: Newmill

The high lace-up button boots were very smart but they didn't quite fit. Granny said, 'Oh, they are beautiful'. She was sent round the neighbouring farms to collect for charity and came hobbling back with her feet bleeding.

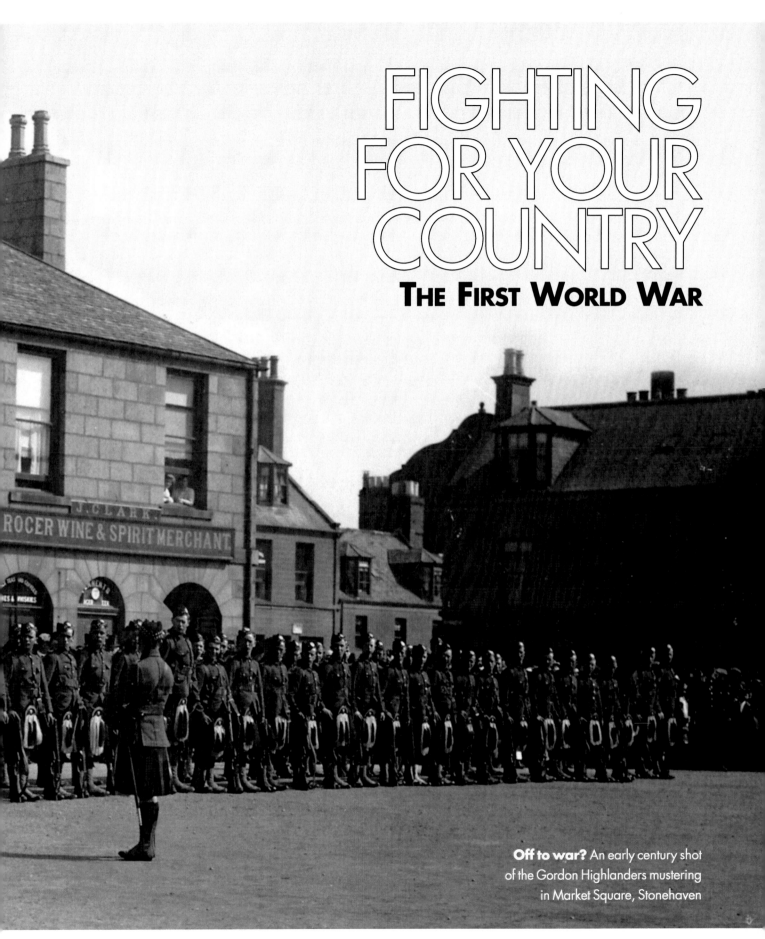

# FIGHTING FOR YOUR COUNTRY

## THE FIRST WORLD WAR

**Off to war?** An early century shot of the Gordon Highlanders mustering in Market Square, Stonehaven

> I remember the day in September 1914 when the Gordon Highlanders left. They marched over the Slug road to Banchory. The man in charge was the Rector of Mackie Academy. A good few of the masters went away. But not a lot came back…

# Through the eyes of a seven-year nipper

My grandfather lived in this very house – it's been the family house for over 150 years. When I was a young boy, he got in the London *Times* a day late. There was a reading room in the town and he paid twopence a week for their old copies and I used to go and collect them each day. His eyesight was poor and he used to sit there and I had to sit just where I am now – I was a young nipper and I used to read all the leading articles out to him. Parliamentary proceedings, international events – he was very interested in all of that. And, of course, I would be reading all the latest news from the Front.

I had to read all these long accounts of battles and manoeuvres and he would be telling me to speak up, speak up. All that was a bit of a bind, really, but it did give me a knowledge of what was going on all through the First World War.

I remember the very start of the Great War and the day when the Gordon Highlanders left. The street from here up to the next corner was filled with people. Where the pub is now was then Alexander's Café and Mary Alexander gave the boys their breakfast before they went off. It was dark on that morning – it must have been September by then, September 1914, that would have been it – and they all got their breakfast and they all lined up and marched over to Banchory, 16 miles over the Slug road. Banchory was where they had their headquarters. The man in charge was Major Riddoch, the Rector of Mackie Academy. A good few of the masters went away. But not a lot came back, not a lot…

**Jimmy Mitchell,** born 1907: Stonehaven

# For King, for country and for God

Mother was the daughter of the minister at Premnay. She had four brothers; three of them lost their lives due to the First World War. An awful, awful slaughter. Two of them were at Edinburgh University when the war broke out; they went to the Principal and asked him, 'We're both well into our Medicine course. What should we do? Stay on and complete it or go off and fight?' 'Oh, you must go off and fight.' they were told. 'It's for your King, your country and for God'. One of them was blown up in a ship off Ireland, the other was killed at the Front. The eldest son was at Gallipoli. He got a CMG, DSO, MC and Bar. The fourth son became an engineer in the Merchant Navy. He got through the war, but then he was on a ship where the captain went down with this dreadful Spanish flu that killed so many. He had to take over the command, but then he went down with the illness too and died. The captain survived.

All this was a terrible ordeal for my grandmother. All they got then was the telegram at the door. They would go into deep mourning with black weeds and hats for months on end. You know, I don't think these deaths would have occurred in a later generation. War and disease, that's what sent my grandmother into all that mourning. Now we've had sixty years without a world war and about the same length of time with antibiotics.

**Margaret Carmichael,** born 1915: Oyne

# Ah'm nae comin back!

At the start of the First World War recruiting sessions were held in the Learney Hall. The local farm labourers would come and take the King's Shilling and sign on for the Gordon Highlanders. Well, most of them did: at the conclusion to one such occasion, the dapper recruiting sergeant was standing at the door, bidding them all goodnight with the words, 'Well, my men, no doubt we'll be seeing you all next week' – to which came the voice floating up through the darkness, 'Awa an kiss ma airse – Ah'm nae comin back'.

When you gaze upon the list of names that are set out on the war memorial, which was just opposite our house, this was a pretty wise decision. Every Remembrance Sunday there would be a service at the North Parish Church and a wreath would be laid. George Gauld, the blacksmith, would play a lament on the pipes, and pretty lamentable it proved too, enough to send our Scottie dog, Tommy, into a fit of anguished howling.

**James Morrison,** born 1917: Torphins

# Prisoner of war on his own doorstep

In the First World War our uncle Jim was out in the fishing boat off Catterline when they were all captured by a German U-boat and taken prisoner. He was sixteen and he was a prisoner of war. There were five of a crew and Germans took them on board, then sailed by Gourdon. They allowed our men to go on deck for a last look before they were taken away to Germany. So that was Uncle Jim's war – captured on his very own doorstep. They were well enough treated; they often went hungry and had to work, but seemingly there was no flogging or anything like that. The village assumed the men must have been all lost at sea; it was over a year before folk got a postcard to say they were all right.

**Margaret Duncan,** born 1928: Gourdon

**But many did...** volunteers to the Gordon Highlanders marching through Fraserburgh, September 1914. Alex Rennie's grandfather (see 'Pigeons were big at the Broch') is in the thick of it, face turned to camera.

Our uncle Jim was out fishing off Catterline when they were all captured by a German U-boat

**Summer 1914**
Ian Stevenson's father (at rear) helping load oatmeal onto train at Auchindachy Station.

**Summer 1916**
Ian Stevenson's father as Gordon Highlander serving at the front against the German army.

# Just getting on with it

My father would just take a look at me and that was enough. He would have raised his hand to you if he thought it deserved, but that was seldom. The look was enough. He was a Gordon Highlander, too. He was in the Sixth Gordons and was called up to the trenches in First World War. Then he was just a ploughman, working out in the fields when he saw the telegram boy coming across to him with a piece of paper in his hand. It was his call up papers; a few weeks later he was in France, deep in the mud and the hell of it. It was funny: the year before the war began he was loading oatmeal onto the horse and cart to take it to the station over by Drummuir and on to Germany; and here he was having to put on the kilt and go off and fight against them. He had nothing personal against them but he had to go. If you didn't, then the police would come round and you'd end up shot. He would always tell us that, 'Ah've git royal blood flowin through ma veins – I must hae: I focht for King an Country!'

He brought back his medal; it says, 'The Great War for Civilisation'. Do your job, just get on with it!

**Ian Stevenson,** born 1931: Keith

# Two uncles lost

I lost two uncles in the First World War; one on each side. My father's brother, Private George Simpson of the Gordon Highlanders was killed in action at the age of just 17 years and one week. He'd actually joined the Terriers when he was only 15. He went along with some other lads to the Aberlour Drill Hall and when they asked his age he told them, 'Fifteen'. But he was a big strapping boy, so the recruiting sergeant just looked him up and down and said, 'Well, just you go out of that door and come back in again – and when you come back in you'll be eighteen – understand?'.

So that's how he came to be shot on a battlefield in northern France in February 1915. When the war had begun and my grandfather realised George was in line to be embarked he did try to get him out of it. He told the military the truth about his age but all he got back as his reply was, 'He's able-bodied and he goes'.

He lost his life in an orchard at a small country place called Seuilly-sur-le-Lys. He'd been lying low in a sniper's trench and the order had actually come to cease fire, but he was determined to take 'just one more shot', raised his head to deliver it and got a bullet right between his eyes.

He was buried in a military cemetery out there. In 1982 we went out to see it. We found a pile of dung just behind the grave with some hens scratching around on it. It reminded me of home; I thought to myself how Granny would have liked the idea of her George having the hens nearby; it would have given her some comfort.

My mother came from a really remote area in upper Cabrach where she was brought up a small house with an earth floor. Her older brother was Willie, Willie Taylor, and he left to train as a wireless operator at the Marconi College in Aberdeen. All this must have represented a huge effort for the family and real determination on his part. He started his education at the tiny local school and then went onto to Mortlach, Dufftown. There's a plaque there yet with his name on it: 'William Taylor, Cabrach, Wireless Operator'. He then had to go into Aberdeen to the college there. At first the family were reluctant to lay out the necessary money, but he was set on going. He came home one day and told them that he knew someone who would help with the finance. They thought he must mean a teacher and they couldn't have that, so they somehow scraped together the cash to allow him to get his wireless qualifications.

When the war came he was in the Merchant Navy; in 1917, on just his second trip, as First Class Wireless Operator and on his way home from New York, his ship, the *HMS Salmo*, was torpedoed and he had to spend 48 hours in an open boat before they were picked up. He said they all sang, *Nearer my God to Thee,* and that the loudest voice was that of the young cabin boy. He caught a train up from London, then out to Dufftown where he simply walked the last 12 miles back to the Cabrach.

But he was a very sick man and had to take to his bed. He lay there for six months

**A strapping 16-year old**
Private George Simpson of the Gordon Highlanders

**Last years of peace**
A young Willie Taylor carrying water from the well to the family home, upper Cabrach.

**Wireless Operator William Taylor,** back row, second left.

> My mother, who was only nine, had to keep the house going. She went to school each day, absolutely exhausted and with her hands all chapped.

before he finally died – of the dropsy My granny took it very hard and, basically, just retired to her bed. She had had another baby just a few months before all this happened and my mother – who was only nine at the time – had to keep the house going. She had to wash the nappies and then hold them up for inspection to show they were really clean; she had to sleep in the same room as my dying uncle and give him his medicine. He was a very religious man, the kind who would go to church each Sunday and then come home and write out the sermon for himself – and so she also had to sit and read the Bible to him. She went to school each day, this little nine-year-old girl, absolutely exhausted and with her hands all chapped.

My uncle died on the 11th of November 1917, one year to the day before the Armistice. That was the day the teacher suggested that the school children should dance and sing their way home, but when Granny saw what was happening she soon put a stop to it.

**Iris Wilson,** born 1942: Aberlour and Cabrach

# THE SECOND WORLD WAR

**Willie Sime,** Fraser's father, recalling the days when the village bobby's house doubled up as the Findhorn air raid warning centre.

**A little respite**
Back home at Torphins on leave with friend Edwin Garden (standing)

**The calm before the storm**
'Pretty horrible, quite soul destroying,' Jimmy Morrison at Capetown before going east and into the fray, 1942.

# My real education

I saw a lot of danger, many deaths. I can't understand all the fuss that's made nowadays, in Iraq and Afghanistan, over battle trauma and the like. Certainly we had cases of shell shock, but that's war: we accepted the daily dangers and just got on with it. But it was pretty horrible, quite soul destroying. The gunnery had a terrible time of it; I was very grateful that I wasn't in the infantry in the desert. Even so you could never be certain that you would be seeing the next day, but we were all in that together; it was the common experience and we just got on with it.

Our living conditions were basic, though the food could be quite amazing. Stuff was piled up for us and rations were quite plentiful, though lacking somewhat in variety. Our 'chef' was a little Glaswegian, Peter, and he would announce to us, 'Tonight, gentlemen, Crepe Suzette will be served'. But, by God, it tasted like no Crepe Suzette you had ever had before or since. Most times he stuck to bully beef and stews – that was more his line.

A wonderful experience and a real education for me. I had just come from the University and was supposed to be well educated, but really all I had been taught was how to keep my head down and to pass the exams. It was the war and the Army which gave me my real learning about life and about people. I found myself sharing experiences with all sorts; they came in all different sizes and spoke in a whole range of accents. We all mixed in together.

Once at breakfast in the desert at Benghazi, a jeep came by and its officer occupant stopped and talked to us. It was Monty – but actually, he was just another gentleman, another officer. It was the ordinary men around me who were my inspiration.

**Jimmy Morrison,** born 1917: Torphins

# From tractor to tank

**Jimmy:** I joined the Territorials in May 1939. War was looming and there was a big push to boost up numbers. It was over at Keith that I joined up for the war, into the Sixth Gordons. I remember sleeping on the floor with just a blanket to cover me. We got four bob a week – and that was before any barrack room damages were deducted. I was with a bunch of local lads, boys that I'd known from around Huntly. These were people I'd always called by their names, but now it had to be not, 'Aye, Jimmy'; Yes, Sandy', but 'Yes, Sergeant; at once, Sergeant'.

I was put on a troop ship and sailed down to Durban, then up to Bombay, then into a train and across to what's now Pakistan. I was a total of eight weeks on that troop ship. In India I got my training in tank and jungle warfare. We had been re-formed into the 116th Gordons Royal Armoured Corps. After training I was shifted east, across to Calcutta, over the Irrawady River and into Burma. That's where the fighting began for me. Our job was to clear the Japs through Kohima, Tongoo and Yamathan and onto Rangoon, all the way out of Burma.

We were anxious to get the job done before the monsoon season came on. At night we just slept out by our tanks. We put the machines into a circle, like a kind of stockade, with men with machine guns to keep watch. The worst thing was the scorpions crawling all over the place. Sometimes you'd hear the enemy moving about at night and shouting to us. Some of them could speak quite good English and it was only the accent that warned you off.

We all mucked in. It was gey rough, I can tell you. The food had to be dropped in by air and it was usually soup and bully beef; bully beef and tomato soup. I was a tank driver. It's not all that different to driving those old Fordy tractors; you work it through your hands. It got really hot inside the tank, real stuffy too, and the noise and the din was

**From tractor to tank**

The young Army piper at Sailcot, Pakistan, in 1942.

I was with a bunch of local lads, people I'd always called by their names, but now it had to be not, 'Aye, Jimmy'; 'Yes, Sandy', but 'Yes, Sergeant; at once, Sergeant.'

**Before the Burma storm**

Jimmy (centre) in front of the Prince of Wales Museum, Bombay, 1943

**Secunderabad, 1942**

With the Headquarters Company, Jimmy is extreme right, third row

terrific. When you stopped and climbed out onto the hatch cover, you'd near get your bloody backside burnt off. Those Japs were helluva boys for digging themselves in real deep, so our job was to blow them out of their positions. Then the Ghurkhas would creep in with their knives and finish them off. They were some boys, those Ghurkhas; it's a good job they were on our side!

**Dolly:** I've heard all these stories from beginning to end, over and over. Whenever Jimmy is with one of his old pals they tell each other all the old stuff about the time out in Burma. Well, I've heard it that often that I just get up and go into the kitchen to get on with something more useful.

**Jimmy:** The Forgotten Army they call us – and when you hear that it's no wonder.

**Dolly:** Of course, I did miss Jimmy and did think about his safety, but you just had to get on with it. Nothing else for it; just get on with it. I spent the war working on farms. I was still living with my folks. I helped about the farm and then every so often there would be a knock at the door and someone would be needing your labour at a farm nearby, so I'd go to help out there. I was always at it, working, working.

**Jimmy:** And there we were out in the jungle with the Japs enjoying ourselves!

**Dolly:** There were plenty of soldiers stationed around here and you'd see them at the dances in the different halls. We'd all go off together, maybe a dozen of us, up the road and then we'd come home afterwards like that. You'd go along till you came to the turning off place and then you'd break off to go down your own track and the rest would carry on. It was sociable just, no trouble, no nonsense. 'Bye bye – see ye aa next wik,' and then back to your own bed.

**Jimmy and Dolly Horne,** born 1919 and 1921: Huntly

# The POW

Our brother, Jock, was in the Army at the very start of the war. But he got taken prisoner by the Germans at St Valery and was kept captive by them right to the end. This was in February 1940 and the nine months after that we heard nothing except for this telegram saying, 'Missing, presumed dead'.

They were taken to near Hanover and made to work at a sugar beet factory. The food was poor; they received these Red Cross parcels – Canadian Red Cross parcels – and he did say that if he never saw another prune or had red cabbage ever again it would be too soon. The parcels always had prunes in them and the Germans dished them up red cabbage day after day. Conditions weren't particularly brutal; the camp wasn't run by the Nazis, just ordinary German soldiers.

They got into the good books of the guards because one of them had slipped them some extra bread and when they were questioned over it none of the British prisoners would give the name away. Jock said they were very impressed by that, because no German would have dreamed of withholding information from the authorities. Then there was this commandant who was nice to them and he was transferred for being too soft. At the end they were marched south for hundreds of miles and were getting desperate with hunger. But then they met up with this old commandant and he told them that he would go ahead to the next village and order the baker there to prepare some food for them – and that saved them.

They were kept marching south, down the Rhine. They would lower bottles into the river to get water and they'd eat berries from the roadside. They looked out for the farmers putting out food for the hens and take that – anything for food.

Jock said it was the bigger lads who really suffered, because they couldn't get enough food to keep up their strength. He was small and wiry and so it was easier for him.

But he found it difficult to adjust when he finally came home. He said that all the bustle and noise of ordinary life was hard for him. He realised that from the moment he came off the train at Waverley and climbed up the steps to Princes Street. He suddenly found himself bang in the middle of trams and cars and that nearly knocked him off his feet.

Back home he was nervy and jumpy; he'd spend hours just sitting by the fire and staring into space. You'd say something to him and he wouldn't hear you; he was lost in his own world. You'd shout, 'Dinner's ready, Jock,' and he wouldn't stir. He told us that he'd developed the knack in the prison camp of being able to shut himself off at will, that he had had to withdraw from all the things going on round him just to keep his sanity. Once an old prison pal came up on a visit for a fortnight and the pair of them would disappear into the hills all day long. That's all he wanted – to escape into peace and into solitude.

**Edna Stuart,** born 1919: Torphins

Our brother got taken prisoner at St Valery and was kept captive right to the end. This was in February 1940 and the nine months after that we heard nothing except for this telegram saying, 'Missing, presumed dead'.

**A bouquet of camellias and boots polished up Army style**

The new Mrs Brand and husband, February 1944

My husband was away all through the war. We'd been only youngsters, going out to the dances together, when it began and were separated practically all that time.

# Wartime wedding

The Moss was a real hotspot for enemy action. There were radar pylons nearby and then there was the Red Moss wireless station over at Nigg, so we got a fair bit of bombing. Then you could climb up the brae above Benty Howe and look down and you'd get a clear view of the coast; my father had a ship's spyglass and you could look through it and see all the splashes in the water as the German bombers came over. Whenever Aberdeen was getting bombed, you could hear the sirens going and then you'd see all the flares and catch the booming of the bombs. You'd go up to your bed and see the places all around alight with incendiaries and you'd lie there and feel the vibrations all through the night. You'd hear the bombs whistling and when the blast went off, you'd be sent going this way and that way, right there in your own bed.

Now you won't believe this next bit, but it's what happened to us, right enough: you'll have heard of the night the Jerries blitzed Clydebank? Well, we heard the sirens go. The Germans came in up the coast beyond Aberdeen so as to dodge the heavily protected areas and then made their way inland down to the Clyde. But what we also heard was the boom of the land mines falling. We heard every single one of them going off. They say that people could hear that boom every few miles all along the geological fault line, the one that starts down there and runs out at Cowie House just this side of Stonehaven; 150 miles away and we heard it all. I went through to my brother's bed and sat with him all through the night and we could both hear it all quite distinctly.

In the morning my sister went to the post office to phone our aunt in Aberdeen to see if she was all right. We thought that the bombing must have been in Aberdeen; when we switched on the wireless and heard that it been in Clydebank, we couldn't believe it. We'd been sure it must have been Aberdeen, it was all so clear, the noise and the boom of it.

My husband Bob was away all through the war. We'd been only youngsters, going out to the dances together, when it began and we were separated practically all that time. He was actually called up in July 1939 before the war began; they were told it was for six months training, but those six months became six years and more. He was at Dunkirk and later at El Alamein and then the Second Front in Normandy.

Then at the beginning of 1944 I got a letter from him from a field post office somewhere in Africa which said, 'I hope to be seeing a bit of granite soon'. He couldn't say any more than that because the letters were all censored, but it was enough – I knew he'd be coming back on leave soon. He said we should get married; afterwards he would be going off to the Middle East for goodness knows how long.

For our wedding cake Eddie Milton, the baker's son, over at Newtonhill, he told us that because of the wartime restrictions he couldn't actually both bake and then ice the cake. During wartime it was often the case that the cake would appear at a wedding with only a cardboard cut-out on top to represent the icing. But he said if we could get it baked he would get all the stuff for us and then do the icing. He got onto a trawler and then appeared at our house in the middle of the night, singing *McGinty's Meal* at the top of his voice; he'd managed to get all the currants and the raisins and everything necessary from them. Now Miss Findlater in the Schoolhouse had this friend who taught cookery at

the Do [Domestic Science] School in Aberdeen and she offered to do the baking for us: 'I can use it as a lesson for my classes', she said. Eddie did the icing right enough and we got a lovely three-tier cake. I kept the third tier back for Bob's homecoming – two-and-a-half years later.

We were married in Cookney Kirk and the reception was held at the Bridge Hotel, Aberdeen. It cost us £30 – that was all you were allowed. My wedding dress was ready-made from Isaac Benzies and for my bouquet I had camellias – they were bought from a florist and my aunt had to get off the bus and then carry them a mile up the road. I can remember going into the hotel and there were all these GIs on the stairs throwing confetti over us. I was all in white and Bob was wearing his Army uniform; he'd polished up his boots till they were gleaming – real Army style. The date was the 5th of February 1944 and there was snow on the ground. The men wore carnations and they were all tinged with the frost.

We did get a honeymoon and that was in Edinburgh. We went down by train. Do you know, I still get a shudder of horror when I go to the station and see a train pulling away; I can't forget the sight of all those trains going off in the war carrying soldiers back to the Front and us women and families just standing there, waving and not knowing when we'd be seeing our menfolk again – if ever.

**Hilda Brand,** born 1921: Cookney

**Wartime wedding, Army style**
Morag McIntosh's parents, Mr and Mrs McDonald *(see 'Birdslint Memories')* in 1941, Aberdeen Registry Office

Looking back on it all, it's not so much the unpleasant job itself that sticks in the mind, but the good times and the people.

# The Bevin Boy from Laurencekirk

When the war came in 1939 I got called up all right, but I didn't go to the Army, not at all. I was sent to the pits instead. There was this scheme to avoid any shortage of coal, whereby two out of every ten conscripts would be allocated to the mines. There was a kind of ballot based on the last numbers in your National Insurance and I was one of them.

So I was a miner for four years, first in County Durham, then up at Newtongrange, near Edinburgh. In Durham I was at the Brandon Colliery. I wasn't very happy about this at the start. There had been a certain amount of excitement at the prospect of the Army, it was what you had been expecting, but here I was, sent down into a hole in the ground, hundreds of miles away from Laurencekirk. But, looking back on it all, it's not so much the unpleasant job itself that sticks in the mind, but the good times and the people. Up till then, I had always worked alongside my father, back in Laurencekirk, and we'd never had a cross word between us. But, you know, I got to enjoy going down there and meeting other people.

I lodged with a widow, Mrs Colne, and her son Charlie. It was a two-room house and she slept downstairs and Charlie and I had the room upstairs. There was the kitchen at the back and this had an enormous fireplace, with a boiler at one side and the oven at the other. The one thing they weren't short of was coal. They did all their cooking there; the boiler had a tap from which you could draw hot water. I was treated as one of the family. I couldn't have left home and landed in a happier situation. Charlie and his girlfriend would take me out with them whenever they were going out to the different places round about.

There were no pithead baths for us and you used to have to haul out a big zinc bath and put it in front of the fire. I was on the fourth shift, from 1:30 in the morning, and would get in again about 11 or so. I'd go into the kitchen, where Mrs Colne would be chatting to her neighbours, and fill up the bath from the boiler there. Then I'd strip to the waist, kneel over the bath and get myself cleaned up. The ladies would just carry on with their chat; to them it was an everyday occurrence. The house had no toilet facilities, just an outside dry toilet. Inside there was no sink, only a tap with a pail beneath it. For the dishes, there would be a basin on the table. It was all much more primitive than I'd been used to in Laurencekirk. There we'd had a sewage system since 1895 and flush lavatories.

**Arthur Bruce,** born 1921: Laurencekirk

# A proud Chindit

In March 1944 we were flown by Dakotas and gliders into a jungle clearing across the Assam frontier in North-East India. Wingate was a great man, trusted by his men. He frequently visited us and addressed us, never disguising from us the dangers we all faced. Despite the fact that we were all in jungle green he would insist on wearing an old Boer War topee. He was rather an eccentric, but a great strategist. I remember the day he lined us all up and informed us that one day we would be proud to call ourselves a 'Chindit'. My response, muttered under my breath, was along the lines of 'Will we f–!'. But he was right: now I can truthfully say, 'Yes, I am proud that I was a Chindit – one of Wingate's men'.

We were really a motley crew of men, from all over. Wingate's idea had been to avoid anything elitist: he wanted ordinary men who could be moulded into a force where everyone would work for each other and where common sense would be the basis of our fighting skills. So there were scaffies and bus drivers from Liverpool and Newcastle, Ghurkhas from the mountains of Nepal, men from Nigeria who carried their kit on their heads – and the odd loon from Buchan, like me. We were a real mixture and we got on fantastically. It was the humour and the comradeship that pulled you through.

Look, I'm a proud Scot, but I hold a British passport and I'm happy about that. All this stuff about anti-English hostility, I just don't know where that comes from. In the war we were all together; we made fun of each other. I might be a 'bloody Jock', but they might be Geordies – 'Scots without the brains' – or 'Cockneys', or 'Taffs', or whatever. Look, if I saw a soldier of the Durham Light Infantry come at my door I would welcome him in as a brother, as one of my own. It wasn't the Scottish or the English Army that won the war: it was the British Army and we were all in it together.

It was humour that kept us alive. We were surrounded by dangers, but you just had to laugh your way through it. There were some great characters and we loved to swap stories about them. We lived with danger in a completely hostile environment. At any moment we might walk into a gathering of Japanese soldiers and we knew what would happen to us then. We were short of food, we had to sleep under the stars, and sickness and disease were never far away. What kept us going was each other, that and our sense of humour. I mean how could you not laugh when you might find yourself out in the jungle, the tropical rain pouring down on you and the Japs never far away, waiting with baited breath for what was going to happen and then hear a voice piping up with a 'What a bloody place to have to die in!'.

My job was to act as the saddler for the mules who carried our loads. I kept the harnesses in good repair. I had been picked for this role on account of the one week's experience with the shoemaker at home – typical Army! But I did manage to carry out the job reasonably satisfactorily.

Conditions were tough. We lived on USA rations which had been put together by American dieticians so as to enable a man to survive for six days comfortably. We had to exist for six months on it. We lost stones and stones of weight. We looked like Belsen inmates. We were driven to search out extra food wherever we could find it. One day we resorted to boiling up one of our old mules, which had been badly injured. He was Albert, a very popular and friendly old beast, but we reckoned that needs must. But he proved to be a tough old boy. I sat there masticating old Albert, thinking to myself how he must now be in his equine heaven looking down on us all and laughing at our efforts to digest him.

**The young Cameronian**
Stanley Rothney in India, 1944

**'Like a Belsen inmate'**
Rifleman Rothney, Singapore, 1946

**Fifty years on**

An 72-year-old Stanley Rothney to the fore in the Burma Star's 50th anniversary march past down The Mall, 1995

It was all very hard going. We had to carry wireless equipment, three-inch mortars and Vickers machine guns. We had engineers and RAF men attached to us. Our goal was to get into the soft underbelly of the enemy, to cut his lines of communication and then cut and run before he could lay a glove on us. Then we would regroup and hit him somewhere else. We used road blocks. It was all a matter of hide and run. It proved to be very effective; we always had the initiative; we decided where to strike; we were the ones setting the scene.

At the end, when a medical examination was carried out, it was found that of 900 men we were now down to no more than 90 fit ones left. I was one of them – why I couldn't tell you. When we eventually got out of Burma, the mules were handed over to those who stayed. I can only imagine that as soon as we got round the bend they were taken out into the forest and shot. A pity, because they had given us good service; they were faithful, hard-working creatures – but that's war for you.

When I returned to Maud my mother was now clerk at the station there. So when I got home to Maud Junction I was greeted on the platform by my mother who had resumed the clerk duties she had first taken up in the First World War. It was she who took my ticket when I stepped off the train.

She had taken the post when she became widowed in 1944. My father suddenly died at the age of 50. It was completely unexpected; in fact, when I got back from Burma I found a pile of letters waiting for me and started to go through them. I came across one that was in my sister's hand. When I opened it the first words that caught my eye were: 'Today was Daddy's funeral'. I hadn't even known he was ill; I then got some more letters that had been put in the wrong sack and that's where I found the one she'd written earlier to warn me that Dad was ill with pleurisy – the kind of illness that would be cured easily enough nowadays.

When my father had accompanied me to the station back in 1940, I'm sure there had been tears in his eyes. He was recalling his own grim time in the First World War and was convinced that this would be the last time he would see me. He was right about that, though not in the way he thought.

**Stanley Rothney,** born 1923: Maud

# Bombs over Gourdon

The war was a memorable time in Gourdon. We got some real sights. One night the lifeboat went out to some oil tankers which had been hit. We were all standing on the top of the brae and you could see right out to sea, all the oil and the fire and everything. It was just awful. The lifeboat had no guns and there were German planes shooting and bombing overhead. The word went out they were needing blankets to wrap the men in when they were got ashore. Within minutes people had gone to their homes and come back with armfuls of blankets – just like that. Everyone pulled together like that in Gourdon.

In the Second War when the men came home on leave there'd be some serious drinking down at the pub on a Saturday night. Black Cherlie would get drunk and put on a comical show down at the memorial. All the kids would gather around for it; he would march up and down and shout, 'Blasted Germans!'. Then he would go down on his knees and make to get out a machine gun. 'Rat-rat-rat-tat! I'll kill them aa, they blasted Germans! Rat-rat-rat-tat!' Then he would get up and sing us all a song. We kids loved it.

Another day I was walking along Queen Street and across the bridge over the railway, when the siren sounded off. I was running a message to the butcher's and I was clutching a half-crown coin in my hand. That was a lot of money back then. I just kept on running, but there was an old man who was a warden and he was patrolling the bridge and as I went up to go over he gave me a push and shouted, 'Run lassie, run! The Germans are comin tae git yer bluid'. I ran for it all right, all the way back home. When I got there I found the half-crown had disappeared, so it was an expensive escape.

You'd see the German aircraft coming along the coast, looking to carry out a raid on some fishing or cargo ships, or to do some damage along the harbours on the East Coast. There were usually four or five in a pack and you'd see them coming over. All we had in the house as our shelter was the kitchen table. We would get under it and Mum would try to follow – but there was only room for her head, so she'd be there on the floor with her head underneath and her backside still sticking out for the Germans to aim at. But we never did get a direct hit – despite that.

In Gourdon everyone mucked in together into the war effort. Most of the younger men had been in the Naval Reserve, so they were called up immediately the war started. My mother ran a Comfort Fund and the women would all come to the house and sit together and knit socks and helmets. She ran concerts, too, and held sales of work to raise money. By the time the men came home from the war there was enough funds to present them each with some money.

We used to listen into Lord Haw Haw, just for the laugh. We'd ridicule the claims he was making about the state of Britain and how we were bound to lose the war. One night Mum was in the kitchen making the tea and Haw Haw was going on about how all of us were starving to death. She got so angry that she went straight up to the wireless with her frying pan and all the bacon sizzling away inside it and held it in front of his voice. 'Smell that ye bugger, jist you smell that now an see if we're starvin or no!'

**Margaret Duncan,** born 1928: Gourdon

> I was going across the bridge over the railway when the siren sounded off. An old man who was a warden gave me a push and shouted, 'Run lassie, run! The Germans are comin tae git yer bluid'.

**October 1939**
Gordon Highlanders
marching to the station
at Huntly to go to war.

## School or drome?

There were distractions all around. This was wartime and Buckie had an aerodrome, over at Dallochy. By 1944 planes were going off and coming back all the time to attack the Germans up in Norway. You could see it all, the planes coming back with only one wheel operating and sliding along the runway. School was very dull in comparison to that. I had this friend, an evacuee from King's Lynn, and we would be cycling to the school in the morning. We'd look at each other: 'School or drome?' Usually we ended up watching the planes.

**Allan Fraser,** born 1930: Buckie

The pilot jumped out and asked, 'You wouldn't have a couple of dozen eggs, by any chance?'

## A Spitfire came to call

I grew up on the farm during the war. I've got one wee story from those days. There I was working at the hen houses at Cairnieburn when I heard this great roar from across the way. I looked up and saw a Spitfire taking off from the fields. 'What the hell's he doing there?', I thought. Later that day my pal from the neighbouring farm called round. 'Well, we fair had some excitement the day!' he said. He explained how he'd been working away at the farm when suddenly this Spitfire came and landed in the field beside the cottar houses there. The pilot jumped out and asked, 'You wouldn't have a couple of dozen eggs, by any chance?' Well, they could only let him have one-and-a-half dozen. 'That'll do,' he told them. 'The canteen's run out of eggs and the boys are hungry for their supper!' And with that he just took off again and disappeared back to one of the bases in the area.

**Bob Soutar,** born 1932: Netherley

## The home front: **Alford**

My mother started up a boarding house in Alford. It was the old bank house and she ran it as a guesthouse. Alford was considered to be a safe area, so people would come out to stay with us from the city. We had these two children, the Streets, aged eight and nine, who had come up from an estate in London. Their father was a baker, but they had an aunt who lived in Aberdeen and she had recommended my mother's place to them. They came from a very religious background. They were with us for a couple of years.

A rather odd, though sad, thing happened to them. The children got a letter to say that their mother and father would be coming up to visit. In those days, Alford was on a rail line and had a station that was easy to get to by train from Aberdeen. One of my jobs was to go down to the station with Heather the pony to meet guests off the train and transport their luggage back to the house. Well, on the day of the expected arrival, the two children rushed down to the station; they could scarcely wait for their parents to arrive. They returned to the house in floods of tears. 'What's wrong? Didn't your mummy and daddy come off the train?', my mother asked. 'Oh, Daddy was there, all right, but the lady he was with wasn't Mummy!'

**Geraldine Simpson,** born 1921: Alford

## The home front: **Bridge of Muchalls**

The war did come to Muchalls. The biggest claim to fame was the day a German plane machine gunned the postie in the smiddy close. It was a Junkers 88 and it had been chasing a train along the railway line all the way up from Montrose. It dropped its first bomb at Blackhills, but he missed the line and it got itself buried in the soft ground at the embankment without doing too much harm.

Those planes carried just the two bombs, so when he came over the top of the smiddy he now had only one left and wasn't going to waste it on us. But he did open up with his machine gun and the postie had to dive off his bike and take cover under a binder. You could see the pilot quite clearly. Dad always claimed that he was a very lucky man because if he'd had his rifle handy then he would have got him.

Then the plane went back to the railway line and dropped its final bomb onto the viaduct as the train was passing over on it. But he was too low for the bomb to explode and it just bounced up again and nearly hit him on his tail. When it came down again there was a small explosion, but all it did was to blast out the windows of the final carriage.

We just stood and watched it all. Mum shouted at us, 'Get inside, get inside!' but we were held by it all; we just stood there amazed.

The other wartime excitement was the meetings of the Muchalls Home Guard. They used the smiddy as a base. It was quite a serious business, really. Well, serious to them; fun to us kids who'd watch them all at the manoeuvres. But we were on the one direct road

A German plane machine gunned the postie in the smiddy close.
It was a Junkers 88 and it had been chasing a train along the railway line all the way up from Montrose.

that ran up the East Coast from the south and there was concern that any invading force would come our way. The Home Guard was led by men who'd been in the First World War so there was a certain air of professionalism about it all. Dad volunteered to do night shift for the Coastguard lookout. They were issued with rifles, but to begin with no bullets. Later on they did get some – a grand total of three to each man.

There were dugouts and barriers and trenches constructed all over the country around us. Bunkers were made to guard the main road. If you were within a certain distance from a main road and on the coast like us, then you had to have a plan in place as to where you would go in the event of enemy action and that applied to the animals too. Our cow was to go up to Blackbutts and the children would be evacuated to Drumblade.

I can't say I was frightened, but we were very aware of the war and its progress. We listened in to the wireless and when we went into Aberdeen, Dad would insist on us going into the cinema to catch up with the latest newsreels. I remember how after Alamein the mood seemed to change and things seemed to swing our way. Of course we were going to win! As a nine-year-old when the war broke out, I firmly believed that Hitler would be defeated. Probably our parents did have some concerns, but if so they hid them from us.

Nina Smith, born 1930: Bridge of Muchalls

## The home front: **Stonehaven**

One of the excitements of the war was the arrival of the evacuees. At the start they were welcomed with open arms; that was the patriotic thing to do, but very quickly they fell under suspicion as a source of disease and unwelcome behaviour. I've read a report in the *Mearns Leader* where the local MP is proposing what would have amounted to a sort of quarantine camp to which the incoming children would be sent for delousing. The headline, 'Criticism of verminous evacuees rampant' appeared and, we are informed, the proposal met with 'widespread support'. I know my mother was very wary of me mixing with them, because she feared they would be bringing scabies and nits with them. The fuss died down quite quickly, chiefly because the majority of the evacuees soon disappeared back down to Dundee or Glasgow once the initial fear of mass bombing faded.

Stonehaven received no direct enemy action, but the signs of the war were all around us. A large Army contingent was close to the town and some of the bigger properties were commandeered. You'd see soldiers on the streets; a popular ploy among us boys was to go up to them and ask for a cap badge. They were quite friendly towards us; they'd reply with, 'Have you got a big sister at home I could meet?'.

Towards the end of the war Polish troops were housed in Nissen huts at Ury. I can recall the atmosphere there at the end of the war. For the rest of the town VE Day meant euphoria and public rejoicing, but the mood in the camp was quite sombre. The Poles realised that their country was being taken over by the Russians and all that victory meant for them was that they were exchanging one brutal dictatorship for another. We felt sorry for them; they had become very much part of the life of the town later in the war.

There was quite a bit of action off the coast. A minefield was laid all down the coast to protect our ships and you could watch convoys sailing south within its six miles zone. The English Channel was too dangerous a lot of the time, so they tended to sail right round the top and then come down to Newcastle, Hull, or wherever, right along the East coast. Sometimes they would attract German air attacks and then you might see the tracer bullets lighting up the sky. The ship *Taurus* was bombed and although it stayed afloat, its plates were buckled and it went down off Catterline several hours later. Of course, none of this was publicised at the time, but word spread around all right. Up in Bath Street you could look out over the North Sea and catch the action. It became quite common for your phone to ring and when you picked it up you'd hear a neighbour saying, 'Have you looked out of your window recently?'.

**George Swapp,** born 1931: Stonehaven

# The home front: **Findhorn**

It's a very sad sight to go into the graveyard at Kinloss and read the ages of the RAF men killed in action from the base – 18, 19, 20 – appallingly young. You could count the planes setting off on a raid and then count them all back in again – there could be as few as 25 percent making the return journey. They reckoned that if you were a rear gunner then half-a-dozen sorties would represent your time up. The local undertaker was kept so busy making coffins that my father – the local bobby – would go in to lend him a hand from time to time.

One of the reasons Findhorn was so much in the war was that the layout and the conditions of the beaches resembled those of northern France, so they used them to practise the Normandy landings. It could be quite dangerous. You'd go along of a morning to the shore and you'd come across two or three upturned boats. It was my father's task each daybreak to walk along the shore towards Burghead and meet the policeman from there about half way along. Their job was to look out for any bodies that had been washed ashore. There were lots and lots of losses like that, incurred during those practice exercises, but the public never got to hear about them.

My father also had to patrol the beaches at night, in the pitch black – no lights allowed, of course, in the war – knowing that around any corner there might be a soldier with a gun who would shoot him first, questions after. He was in constant fear that he would be mistaken for the enemy. All he had was a small torch to shine on any bodies that he might discover.

My mother also had a vital role to play in the Findhorn war effort. She was a trained nurse and was forever bandaging and seeing to cuts and bruises; some folk would call in two or three times a week for treatment. Occasionally she'd get a wee present for her

You could count the planes setting off on a raid and then count them all back in again – there could be as few as 25 percent making the return journey.

Later he was asked, 'Surely you managed at least to take off the new tyres and swap them for old ones?' But he hadn't even done that.

pains, like a few eggs or some vegetables, and she never complained of all this extra work. But the most useful gift was if anyone had access to the RAF base and could get hold of some bandages for her – she was expected to supply her own.

She also had her air raid duties. In the early days of the war the siren for Findhorn was at the police house. She'd get a phone call with the first warnings and then she was required to step out into the garden and go to a large brass trumpet spirit pump she'd been supplied with and pump it up and down: 'Parp-parp-parp'. Then she'd get a 'blue' air raid warning and this indicated that the bulk of the enemy action was now over and that she was to wait for the 'white' warning. When that came it was the 'all clear' and then it was out to the pump again. You can just imagine this young mother having to rush outside to this primitive warning system and then pump it up and down while the German bombers were approaching.

**Fraser Sime,** born 1937: Findhorn

## Jist spare me this ane!

The area round about us all was farming, farming and yet more farming. When the war came my father was the wrong age for being called up. He had just invested in a brand new cattle float, but he lost it completely to the Government. They commandeered it and away it went. I'm not sure he ever got any compensation for it; he just had to hand it over for war purposes and that was that. Later he would be asked, 'Well, surely you managed at least to take off the new tyres and swap them for old ones?'. But he hadn't even done that.

He lost it all. But he refused to be done down. He got hold of an old bus, cut its body off and used his joinery skills to construct a new body onto it and made a cattle float out of that, and then he simply carried on his business. I believe that in the First World War the Government would come to the farms and go off with the horses. What they used to do then was to hide the best horse and offer an inferior one up. They would be quite cunning about it: they would make a show of being reluctant to give the less good horse up: 'Oh no, this ane's ma best animal; please spare me this ane,' and so the Government would grab at it, and leave the better horse safely behind.

**Bill Sinclair,** born 1937: Quilquox

**From bus to cattle float**
Bill Sinclair's father with his home-made wartime haulage lorry

# We had nothing to celebrate

Fetterangus was the whole of my early life: it's where I was born, where I lived the first 45 years of it and where I worked. My parents were Fetterangus folk too. When the war came, Dad was working in the quarries at Kininmonth; a lot of what they were working on was materials for the roads. He volunteered to go into the 706 Construction Company, because they would be sent to do road and aerodrome repair and construction tasks.

Dad died when I was five. I can just about mind him in his Army uniform going off to the war. That was the last any of us saw of him. He was on a boat that was torpedoed by a German U-boat; although he got out of the water he died later in a hospital in Musselburgh. The news came through on Christmas Eve, just after my fifth birthday. I can remember a policeman coming to the door to break the news and then hearing the voices. But Mum didn't tell me that night. She asked Kathleen, my older sister, to explain to me what had happened, the next day. She just couldn't bring herself to tell me.

The body came back and was buried in the cemetery at the top end of the village. But I never saw any of it; on the day of the funeral I was put to a neighbour's, out of the way.

This was really hard. Mother now only had the war widow's pension to live off and bring us two up on. That came to £2.7.6, so she had to go out and pick up any odd jobs she could to keep the home going. When VE Day came the village held a celebration; the children all dressed up in Union Jacks and waved flags. But we didn't join in; we went away from the village for the day. 'We've nothing to celebrate,' my mother said.

**Sheila Wells,** born 1937: Fetterangus

**Workers at Kininmonth Quarry** Some volunteered for war and entered the Construction Company. Sheila Wells's father is in the light cap, behind the leftmost drum.

**'Nothing to celebrate' – but some did**

Three Fetterangus children decked out for VE Day. Margaret Simpson *(see 'The village was our playground')* is centre, flanked by Lilias Greig, left, and Mabel Junor.

# A North-East homecoming

Dad came home from the war. That was, of course, a great day, but one which we played in a distinctly low key, North-East fashion. My mother told me to go down the road to Methlick. On my way down to the village I saw this soldier striding up the road, his kitbag hoisted up on his back. You will have seen reconstructions of other such family homecomings in which the returned warrior is treated like a conquering hero and where his small children are shown rushing towards him, arms outstretched, eyes shining, as if it's Cathy running towards Heathcliff. For us it wasn't quite like that: my father simply smiled and then held out his hand. We linked fingers and walked together up to the farm in almost complete silence. It was all very quiet and without any sense of show or drama – our father was back home, safe and well, and that was enough.

**Charlie Allan,** born 1940: Methlick

A full and vivid account of the speaker's early life is to be found in his *The Truth Tells Twice* [Birlinn, 2008]

# EARLY
# CENTURY
# LIVES: 2
# Eliza Watt

**Stonehaven's grand old lady**
December 2008: Eliza Watt
on her 104th birthday

You'd get
your bitty
homework
to do,
although we
often did it
on the way
to school.
We'd all help
each other,
but the boys
would grab
your pencil
and do all
the copying.
We'd never
clype.

# Oldest wifie in town

I'm just an old wifie, a real old wifie! I'm 104, you see, 104. I was born at a place called Ardallie. Do ye ken far that is? Near Ellon. December 1904, that's when I came into the world. I had five brothers and one sister. My father worked on a farm and we all lived in a cottage. Later on we moved to a farm at Keith Hall.

The house got a bit crowded but we were happy enough together. We all had our own jobbies and we kept on the move, but life wasn't too hard. You'd go out in the field and pull the neeps; you had to get in wood and coal for the fire and you had to see to the hens. The water had to be drawn from a pump outside and we had to take our turns. I once jammed my hand in that pump – I've got the mark on me yet, near on 100 years later. I hyowed the neeps alongside my brothers, but they would laugh at my efforts. You just pottered about on the farm and saw that everything got done.

Our parents weren't too hard on us. You got on with your tasks and you learned to keep your mouth shut – and you might get a copper or two to yourself. I can see it yet, the coppers laid out on the kitchen table and then the visit to the shoppie to spend them on a sweetie for yourself. My favourite was toffee; you could get quite a lot for a penny back then.

We had to walk to the school, over at Fintry; four miles across the fields. The headmaster was a nice man: Mr Fraser. But he always spoke with a stutter: 'tee-tee-tee', he'd go, and some of the boys would make fun of this, but never to his face. At the school you learned the three Rs, the Bible, how to behave yourself and when to shut up. I never once got the strap although my brother John did; he didn't know when to shut up!

You'd get your bitty homework to do, although we often did it on the way to school in the mornings. We'd all help each other, but the boys would grab your pencil and do all the copying and us girls were aye stupid enough to help them out. We'd never do anything wrong by each other; we'd never clype.

In the winter, you got soup at the school for your dinner. We took a piece with us too – a bit of a loaf with some syrup or jam on it. But walking to school would make you hungry and, like as not, by the time we arrived the boys would have eaten all theirs. Sometimes we'd get a neep from the field and bash it on the dyke and share it out. When you got back home, you'd sit down and take a hot drink, then outside to play, with a ball or something like that – we all played football together. Then inside again for your tea, and that would usually be some porridge or brose. Your father would come in from the fields and he would talk over the events of the day and we'd sit and listen. Then once the table was cleared we had to do our lessons and then it would be time for our bed.

So that was our evenings: behaving yourself, listening to what your elders were saying, keeping quiet. We'd never dream of answering back; we just fitted in with what our parents expected. Our parents never smacked us; a look would be enough. On Sundays it was the church; we never missed a communion Sunday, never. The minister would come to visit; we knew to behave then, all right. It's the way we were brought up.

When I was 16 I went into service as a table maid in one of the big houses at 32 Hamilton Place, Aberdeen. I went with my friend, Jessie, and we lived in, did our work, found out how to do things properly, behaved ourselves; we kept our mouths shut. We were called 'maids', but really we were just a pair of skiffies. You had to get up real early; we'd lay the fire, make the breakfast and then get on with all the polishing and the cleaning. We were treated quite well, although the boss would stand in front of the fire, with his back to it, and that used to annoy me. Really, he was so bossy; we were just like his sheep. I'd look at him, standing there, in the road, all important and warm, and I'd think to myself, 'Ane o these days I'm goin to ging up and just kick you oot o the wye'. But I never did.

When I was 17 the whole family moved to a farm near Auchenblae. I became a housemaid in Woodlands, Arduthie Road in Stonehaven. The man there was blind, poor man, and his wife used to boss him about: 'You're in the way. Get out of there, for goodness sake!' He was such a nice man; he'd tell me, 'I know I'm just in everyone's way. I'm just a damn nuisance,' and I'd say, 'No you're not, not at all'. His wife would laugh at that.

I got married in 1926, to Alfie. He was cattleman at New Mains of Ury and we met at a dance in Stonehaven Town Hall. He worked on several farms in the area, but then in 1936 we moved into Stonehaven and Alfie became mashman at Glenury Distillery. That's where he worked till he retired in 1966.

He was never a boozer, my husband. He got drunk just the once. We were staying in the house on the High Street and he went off with his pal, Geordie, and they both came back bleezin. I can mind the way they clattered their bikes against the door and then came in full of themselves, even yet. I was shocked. I stood there looking at them and thinking to myself, 'Noo, fat am I gaen to dae wi these twa stupid feels?'. They came in and yapped on; they sat there, with their bikes lying on the ground anyhow, as if to say, 'We're baith drunk and we're gaen tae bide drunk, so there'. Well, I waited till the next day and then I let him have it. 'Ye've bin drunk this ance an that's it! Ye'll niver, iver be like that again!' And, he wasn't.

My husband died in 1985; we had one daughter, Jean, and she died suddenly in 1999. I've been living here, in Edenholme, for two years now. But I'm lucky; Andrew my grandson and his wife live just up the road and they come in and see me. On a Saturday morning we still manage to get down to the water front in the wheelchair, with our coffee and our rugs. I still get my breath of fresh air.

It's funny to think I've lived as long as I have. I don't know why, but I'll tell you this: I've never smoked and I've never drunk. Nothing stronger than lemonade has ever passed my lips, I can tell you. Drink – it's the biggest curse in town! A hundred and four – I must be the oldest person left in Stonehaven, the oldest old wifie in town.

**Eliza Watt,** born 1904: Keith Hall and Stonehaven

I waited till the next day and then I let him have it. 'Ye've bin drunk this ance an that's it! Ye'll niver, iver be like that again!' And, he wasn't.

# GOING TO THE SCHOOL

**Still smiling** Iris Wilson with her P5/6 classmates,
and Mrs McDonald, Aberlour 1951.
Iris is second row, fourth from left.

**The twin
Geddes sisters**
with their dominie
father and mother,
on the steps at Cairnhill
around 1915.

**The last of her line**
Mary Geddes on her
101st birthday

# The dominie's daughter

I was born in the Cairnhill Schoolhouse in 1904. I come from three generations of teachers. My grandfather and grandmother, my father and mother, the three of us – my brother, my twin sister Betty and me. Plenty of teachers!

I grew up in the schoolhouse, right next to the school itself. My father was headmaster there. That's where I went for the primary school, along with the rest of the local children. It made no difference. When I was in the school you wouldn't know he was our father; it made no difference whatsoever. The only thing was we were disappointed we hadn't any journey to make to get to the school: from our house it was just two steps and we didn't like that. So Betty and I used to go up the road to meet the other children coming in from all the farms and then walk back to the school with them.

There was an awful easy atmosphere, even though there were 120 on the roll. Father never had fewer than 45 himself – he wasn't happy unless he had plenty. Most of the pupils came from Newtonhill village. My mother made soup, in the kitchen, and on Fridays we got stove potatoes and milk. We had to take it in a bottle like the rest at nine o'clock in the morning; we weren't allowed to go through to the house for it.

I can't remember what we called father in the school. He wasn't fussy about these silly things. We were just treated the same as anyone else, same as the rest. The other children just accepted us; we were just one of them, we just played with them.

We played skipping. It depended on the time of the year; there were periods for everything. We played drawing games; we threw a ball up, twirled round and then tried to catch it. Ball games! There was no TV or radio then – we never missed such things. I think people were better off without them. They got on with their work better.

We had tables to learn. We were also taught these 'addition tables'. '2+3=5'; '1+4=5'; '9+6=15' and so on. We had to learn all these tables and to sing them out. If you got hold of them, you always had something to fall back on. But that's out now. The 'times tables' are out. But how are you ever going to multiply if you don't learn them? You can't always use the calculator. I don't need it – just listen: '6+9+8=23'; '7+8+8=23'. Give me any combination you like, I can still do it very quickly. It's just practice. My father used to give us speed tests.

We also got grammar; we had to analyse sentences: 'Objective clause, Parenthetical clause….' I could do anything like that when I was 12. I was quite clever – but we all learned. My father just seemed to be able to get people to do things. He was good at explaining things. We just took it all for granted.

The other teachers varied. One left, another came. Some of them travelled from Aberdeen by train to the station at Newtonhill. They walked the mile up. You walked everywhere. No buses. If you wanted to go to the doctor's at Portlethen, you might get a train there, but you had to walk back. It's about four miles; quite a trail. We didn't go very often!. We had to stay healthy, though we took all the diseases that children took then – no injections, you see. Measles, mumps, chicken pox, whooping cough…we took the lot. If somebody came to school with it, we all got it. That was thought to be a good thing – get them over with.

We had Geography. I knew the whole world. The only town I didn't know was Los Angeles – it wasn't there then! I knew all the capitals; I knew all the rivers, all their tributaries. The Witham, Welland, Nene and Great Ouse – that's the rivers that flow into the Wash. See, I can still get them off, 90 years later! I learned them and I never forgot them.

If you've got the basics, you've always got something to build on. Some kids can't count; they can't do anything. They haven't been taught properly – because very few can't be taken to a certain standard if you teach them properly. My father used to take those with more ability for an extra hour early every morning, before the school began. He even went without his breakfast to do it.

It was a happy school. Easy discipline. Father could never find the belt; it was always buried under a pile of stuff on his desk, he used it so seldom. He didn't need to. We were all very well behaved; we never thought of being anything else. We were normal children, we did silly things – but we didn't throw stones, break windows; there was no vandalism. There would have been an awful row if we'd done anything like that – blue murder! I mean, we weren't angels, but never destruction, nothing malicious, ever. Now there's no discipline in the home, in a lot of homes. We knew better than to misbehave. Good discipline comes from the home. We would never have dreamt of causing damage. Oh no, we never did anything like that.

**Mary Geddes,** born 1904: Newtonhill

**First year at school**
The Cairnhill School line up around 1908. The Geddes sisters are second row, centre. James Geddes, their father and dominie, is third row right.

**Last of its kind**

The Fraserburgh
– St Combs train, which
took Violet Johnston to
her teaching post daily,
complete with
cowcatcher.

# The ten-to-eight train

I used to travel into St Combs each morning on the ten-to-eight train. It was just a small branch line which ran six miles and through unfenced land. Because of that it had a cow-catcher on its front, the last one of its kind, I think. In fact there was a cow killed by it when I was on the train. Sometimes I would be the only passenger on it and the driver would invite me up into the cab. I would get to pull the whistle when we approached Inverallochy. The driver would aye ask me, 'Weel, fat news frae the school the day?' 'Well, we're doing a new poem today; it begins, *Hark the tiny cowslip bell.*' I also told him I knew only one place in the district where you would find cowslips and that was Mains Brae, before the train reaches Inverallochy. When the train reached Mains Brae he stopped the engine, got out and went into the field there and came back with a bouquet of cowslips especially for me. It was the best field of cowslips in the whole district.

**Violet Johnston,** born 1909: St Combs

# I got belted for being left-handed

We had a teacher who was…well…I was five years old and left-handed and do you know, that woman, she would give me the strap till I could write with my right hand. That happened nearly every day. This was Miss Dalgarno. I was supposed to do all my writing with my right hand and to begin with I wasn't very good at it. Then I'd get the strap for my bad writing. At one time I refused to go to school and my mother went up about it. Miss Dalgarno said she would leave me alone after that – but I swear my mother hadn't even had the time to turn the corner when out came the strap – I got it for telling on her.

I had this terrible stammer. I know now that it would have been all that business over the right hand that caused it. I got into the fourth year and had Miss Low. She was the one who cured me of it. When I started to read out loud and found I couldn't do it, she said, 'You can sing it out if you like' .And that did it. For the first three years I'd stammered at school, but never at home, and Miss Low got me singing out and that got me round the problem.

There were the ones who came from the cottar houses. Very, very poor. I've known some of them come to school with no socks. One family didn't even have shoes on their feet. And there was this family which I'm sure never fed properly – if there were any odd scraps left over Miss Low would make sure they got them. We'd take a piece for our dinner and eat it at the school. But Miss Dalgarno was very strict about leaving any food. Once a syrupy piece got thrown into the bin and she blamed this laddie and I knew it hadn't been him – but she made him eat it all up, out of the bin, till he was sick with it.

To begin with I walked to school, two-and-a-half miles, the whole blinkin' road. But then I got a bike. But I didn't get to leave it at the school in case it got damaged – you'd get your tyres flattened, you see. My grandpa bade at the Square so I had to leave my bike with him.

**Too young
for school**

Dorothy Stuart with
mother and brother,
1918

It was jealousy – not everyone could afford a bike. In fact, there were quite a lot of differences made between those who had money and those who didn't. The headmaster at Laurencekirk, if you were the minister's son or the doctor's son, then he'd privilege you. But the working man's loon, he just ignored. My friend Betty Murray and I, we both won a County bursary and that would have helped us with buying our books, but weren't allowed to take it because it was felt that ordinary folk would never afford to keep it up.

I can't say they all did that kind of thing, but this headmaster, he certainly did. You got on better with him if you came from a higher-class background, very much so. But when I got my first reference from him, I must say it was a beauty.

For writing we got a slate and you got a box. You had to buy your own slate pencil – five sticks a penny, they were. Once a month you got handed the slate home to get the sides of it scrubbed. Then you had to bring a box, a little tin box with a wet cloth in it, and another one to dry it with. You'd see the loons spitting on the slate, but not when the teacher was looking!

You started with the sounds – I learned them by the A–B–C, not by the actual sounds the letters made. We had to learn the A–B–C right to the end of the alphabet. As you got older you had to be able to go through it all backwards and ken every one of the letters in their order, either way. We learned to spell out 'cat' as 'C–A–T', not as 'ca-aa-tu'. And we had to learn up all the tables and say them out, every blinkin' one of them, every single day. But all that has served a purpose – you never forgot them afterwards.

You had to learn everything bit by bit. Everything from the letters to whole sentences. It seemed to come to you, no bother. Then you'd graduate to writing little stories. Another thing we had to learn a lot of and that was poetry. Verses and verses of it. One of them I can never forget: 'He was a rat and she was a rat and down in one hole they did

**Another firm but, this time, fair teacher**
Miss Geddes with her class at Laurencekirk 1919. Dorothy Stuart is front row left.

You'd make soup and then have to eat it; if you didn't like it you weren't allowed to pour it down the sink. The teacher would damn well stand over you till you had supped it all up.

dwell…'. And there was *Young Lochinvar came out of the west*. In our first year at Laurencekirk we had to learn up *Grays's Elegy*. We also had to learn up Wordsworth, Tennyson and all the classics like them. They kept you going. And another thing, which I don't think they do now, we had to learn up 'subject-predicate' and describe all the words in a sentence.

Another thing we had was geometry and algebra and to be honest, nobody ever explained what they were. You had to learn these theorems. There were 33 in my class and in the exam I got 11 marks, and I was third. So you can imagine what the rest of the class was like. Nobody ever told you the reason you were doing all this. You just had to learn it.

English, that never cost me anything, but I was hopeless at maths. However, I could do sums and we got a lot of them in the primary school. There we got bills and counting up in pounds, shillings and pence and halfpennies and farthings. I could do that, but geometry and algebra meant nothing to me. I never could understand what they were about.

I liked art - we called it drawing. I loved making things: I remember sewing a petticoat; I had to embroider flowers in white all around it. We got a lot of cooking. My great pal was Edith Booth; we were the same types. We both cooked at home, but at school we'd get the simple things like scones and overdo it and get a row for it. As a punishment you'd be sent to black the grates and you'd go home covered in the stuff; black as soot you were. You'd make soup and then have to eat it; if you didn't like it you weren't allowed to pour it down the sink. The teacher would damn well stand over you till you had supped it all up. We had to take an old-fashioned scrubbing brush and clean the utensils till they were shining bright. You never got off with anything.

Once a week we'd get singing. We had 'do-ray-me' written up on the board; we'd learn up the song and sing it out. Some of the loons were real ill-tricket. There was this devil of a loon and we'd be singing 'Do ye ken John Peel?' and he'd change the words to, '…with his nose all meal'. But I believe in later life he did well enough; he became an auctioneer.

I left school at 14. My mother fell very ill – she was only 39 – and as nobody was bothered I just left. During that last year she was poorly I played the devil. Some days I just didn't go in at all. My mother died and there were the five of us left. I went home and milked the cow. Then two years later my stepfather died and we were completely alone. We all branched out. I went in for nursing.

**Dorothy Stuart,** born 1915: Laurencekirk

## Terror and romance

In those days Torphins School was a primitive place with primitive teaching methods. It was possessed by these howling female teachers and by pupils rattling around in their tackety beets. The female staff seemed to me to be a bunch of leather-wielding dervishes who treated the task of hammering the three Rs into us as a sacred duty,

punishable by almost any means short of death. Every small error was greeted by another wallop and a howl of rage.

I lived in terror, day after day. Miss Taylor put the fear of death in me. She'd taught my older brothers and they had liked her. But in those days she'd been a bright young teacher straight from the TC, full of idealism and hope. Seven years on and she had developed into a tyrant. She tried to hammer the stuff into you, but all that did was to generate fright and an inability to perform. I practically had a nervous breakdown over my continuing inability to spell the word 'beautiful'. The more she shouted the worse it became. All her efforts did was to give me a mental block.

The head was W.G.A. Morgan. My older brothers spoke well of what he did for the school, but by the time I arrived he was very much preoccupied by his great romance with a Belgian lady he'd met on a Brussels tramcar. When he should have been teaching us, he would be sitting at his desk mooning over the latest letter he'd received from Brussels. He'd been married before, but his wife was now dead. He had engraved on her tombstone in Torphins Cemetery the message, 'She's not dead; she's just away'. As one of the sharp-tongued bodies about the village would always remark, 'Weel, he'd hae an awfu shock if she iver dis cam back an knock at his door ae night!'.

Anyway, these letters would arrive daily; his routine was to send a pupil down at nine o'clock for the post and then to sit at his desk working his way through the latest intelligence from Brussels, with a French dictionary at his side. Then one day he appeared at the school wearing this lovely sapphire ring on his finger; this was him showing the world that he was now engaged to be married. Then came the Sunday in church when the minister announced, 'A purpose of marriage between Mr W.G.A. Morgan MA of this parish and Mlle Renée Juliette van der Roust of Brussels, Belgium'. I'd been at the kirk, singing in the choir that Sunday and when I got home my mother immediately enquired, 'What was happening at the kirk today?'. Our house was just opposite and she'd seen the congregation come out after the service, 'just like a swarm o' bees, all bizzin awa'.

He went over to Brussels and came back bearing his new bride on his arm and duly married her. He was now an elderly man, approaching 60 and she was only 28 and quite pretty with it. But then came the big and terrible problem: she was a Roman Catholic and he was a respected elder at the South Kirk. The pair began to attend the Roman Catholic Church in Banchory and then eventually WGA 'turned' and forsook the Kirk and became a Catholic. Well, that caused a terrific to-do in Torphins; some folk never did forgive him the heresy. But the marriage itself appeared to do well enough, although it was without child. The pair stayed together and after WGA's retirement they settled in Brussels.

WGA was actually a nice man and, until the Catholicism, had been well respected in the community. However, he did have the custom of turning up at the school on the last day of the term, sporting a pair of plus fours. This would give rise to the comment, 'Here cams the dom, wi his shite catchers on'.

**James Morrison,** born 1917: Torphins

# A whole list of schools

I was speaking to my sister last night – I'd forgotten all the schools I was at. It's a whole list. We moved wherever the work was, you see. Either that, or the dole, and none of us would have done that. Wherever the job was, there you went. And aye trying to get a better job – that was it.

The first school I was at was Stuartfield. I think I was a year there. I had quite a lot of experiences there. I fell into the dam and lost my new shoes. I didn't get smacked, but, oh, ho….! Then I had to wear old ones, with darnings and things. Then I was coming home, up the brae – no cars or anything at that time – but a chap run over me with his push bike and broke my arm. My fault. But Jean was telling me last night, and I'd forgotten, she said, 'See the mark on your arm, that was the chap that ran you over'. I was going to my bed last night – it's still there! Of course, I wasn't very big.

Now, where did I ging frae Stuartfield? Bulwark School. There was only us and another two at that school. Five, that's all. I was there six months – a wee school just beside the road. But they closed it. I went to Maud School. No bikes, no buses –we just walked. About two miles along the road – there were roads. On your boots and walked.

Now, from there…let me think….I went to Blackhills School. That's on the road to Fraserburgh from Peterhead. Of course, half the schools I went to are all closed. Bulwark's closed. In fact, one of my brothers came home from Canada and he was going to video all the places that we'd been – and there's just a tree and a few stones lying. Oh, they'll be very impressed in Canada when they see that.

So I went to Blackhills School. I was there one year. No, I've got it wrong! I went to Strichen before I went to Blackhills. Strichen! I would have been … four schools by then. Oh yes, I'm very well travelled. And we went to this little house; it would have been a farm cottage, a cottar's hoose. But we were nothing to do with the farm; we just rented the house. There was a house getting built for us, rebuilt over on the other side of the hill. But in the meantime, that house was never very waterproof or anything. So I went to Blackhill till the other house was built.

Now how many's that? Four? Five? I was at Blackhills, it must have been a year – it must have taken that time to build that house. And then we went back to Pluckshill. That was the name of the farm right at the bottom of the Mormond Hill. I went to Strichen School again then. That's where I finished. I was 14, 1935.

The only thing I remember about Stuartfield School is the singing. The teacher gave me a note home to my mam: Would I sing in this concert? I must have been five. That's all I can mind about Stuartfield. Whether I'd been scared there or what, I don't know.

Bulwark School I can mind. We were asked to take a peat to the school, to heat the little school. I canna mind if it was every day or not, but I can mind on one thing and that's going down the road and taking the peats. And we just stayed at the back of that school. But they closed it.

At Strichen the girls got the strap, as well as the boys. But I was the favourite of the science teacher – he'd give me a penny for going out and posting his letters. I did it during lessons. When I was coming out of the school for playtime some of the boys got on to me, 'Teacher's pet, teacher's pet!'. So the penny wasn't such a good thing. I was scared of the teacher and I was scared of my classmates.

But there was only one teacher I was so frightened of that I wouldn't put up my hand to answer a question in case I got it wrong. It was Miss Smith; it was in Primary 5. I'll tell you why. The time had changed – I can't mind if it was forwards or backwards. A few of us girls – we'd got no watches or anything, not in those days – and we'd forgotten and there we were out playing. Then all at once, we remembered and we were about four minutes late in coming back into the classroom, and we all got the strap. I mind that yet. It wasn't so much it was sore; it was the indignity of it.

My mum said, 'D'ye wint me to gae doon?', and I said, 'No'. My husband, now, he would have tellt you that if they'd gone home and told that they'd got the strap, they would have been asked, 'An fat wis ye deein? It must hae bin samthin afore they did that to ye.' And then you'd get another dose of it!

Any one of the teachers would use the strap if you was needing it. No question about it. But I'll tell you, you would never have answered a teacher back or anything like that. You showed respect for them. There was discipline, outside as well as inside the school. There was never any vandalism. You would never even have thought about it. There was nothing in the village, never a broken window or anything. There was aye something to be doing with your time. We all had our little jobs to do when we went home at night.

We respected adults. There was never even – not that we were goody-goody or anything – but there was never a question that if any grown up had spoken to you and told you, 'I don't think you should be doing that', well, we'd have never dreamed of speaking back.

**Bulwark School**
As it was 100 years ago before it became 'a heap o stanes'.

Any one of the teachers would use the strap if you was needing it. No question about it. But I'll tell you, you would never have answered a teacher back or anything like that.

The teachers were only friendly to you to a certain extent. We were aye in awe. They might come in about and speak to you, but you'd never go up to the teacher and start chatting. Some teachers did show an interest in you. I mind at the school at Boyndlie, the little school there. There was a few crofts round there and they had children, boarded out bairns, foster children from Glasgow – there was a lot of that around Mormond Hill. I can remember Miss Grey and this little girl from Boyndlie and she was sitting greetin in the class beside me. We'd have been the same age, about seven or eight, and so she took her to the front and spoke to her, and the next I knew we had put on our coats and she'd written out a note. There were two shoe shops in the village then, and we was put up with this note, and she paid for this girl to get new boots, new laced-up boots. She'd had chilblains on her feet – oh, her feet were just…! And she'd been greetin because of them. Miss Grey told me, 'You don't mention this at home or anything.' She'd bought her the new boots.

**Violet Cassie,** born 1920: Strichen area

# I only got the tawse once

I had to walk three-and-a-half miles to the school each way. But the roads weren't tarmac as they are today: they were sand with wee stonies mixed in. Some of the cottar bairns had to walk it in their bare feet. But we were always well shod: white socks and sandals in the summer, wellington boots for the winter.

Winters were worse in those days. Snow hardly gets leave to lie nowadays, but then you just had to walk on top of it. It was expected of us that we would get to the school every day, no matter the weather. Now the schools do close – there's so many regulations in education nowadays – am I right? But we had to go every day, no matter what, and line up outside waiting to be called in at the school door. Then you'd go to your room, you'd answer the register and you'd say a prayer. Then there would be a hymn: *The King of love my shepherd is; All things bright and beautiful; Be Thou my vision.* I'll never forget those hymns.

You would start off the day with Miss McPherson playing the piano – prayer first, then the hymn. Then would come our reading, then playtime. Then we would play at skipping and the boys might get their marbles going. In the winter, when it was cold, we would huddle in the cloakroom. Then there was lots of mental arithmetic. We had to learn up the tables by heart and chant them out – a thing of the past now, or is it coming back? I hope so.

Do you know, I wouldn't be a teacher for anything nowadays. Kids, they just don't know the meaning of the word discipline now. But we were all well disciplined. And if you met Mr Masson out of school you would give him a salute and if it was one of the lady teachers you would make a bow.

The tawse was in evidence, oh yes! It began to be used when we got to seven. I got it just the once. We were playing 'Hoist the green flag' and I was the captain. The croft

**Kids just don't know the meaning of the word discipline now. If you met Mr Masson out of school you would give him a salute and if it was one of the lady teachers you would make a bow.**

behind the school belonged to my uncle, Jimmy, and we found ourselves there. He warned us, 'Ye ken, quines, the skeel's in – ye'll get the strap!'. 'We winna – the school's nae in!' I always had an answer. But he was right: by God, the school was in right enough. Well, Nannie had to be the first up to get it as I always told the truth and I admitted where we had been. I got the tawse; we all got it, all six of us.

Nan Esson, born 1920: Tullynessle

## Teachers: the kind and the other kind

My first teacher was Miss Robb and she was really a beautiful lady, beautiful in nature. She was there for generations and everyone always spoke of her in the same way. Gentle, but able to keep good order. I can't ever remember her using the strap – and the strap was used a lot in those days. She was just one of those teachers who could keep command just through her own personality. Everyone loved Miss Robb. But the class next door was taken by Miss Dalgarno and she was very much the opposite; she was an aggressive lady and she used the strap freely.

I've got a story about Miss Dalgarno. There was this Jimmy Adam who took over the Gardenstone Hotel; he was a quiet sort of man, but his wife was a very aggressive lady, very domineering she was. Well, their daughter was in Miss Dalgarno's class and she got the strap for some reason or other. Mrs Adam came marching up to the school, knocked on Miss Dalgarno's door and demanded a word. She was in a tremendous rage. All the pupils were sitting there rigid with terror wondering what was going to happen. These are the very words that, according to my wife's friend – she was in the class that day – fell from Mrs Adam's lips: 'If ye dae that agin, Ah'll knock ye doon an tramp yer guts oot!'.

That wasn't usual: mostly the parents just accepted the teacher's punishment. If you

**'A beautiful lady'.** Miss Robb, who gave her kindly teaching to generations of Laurencekirk children, here with the class of 1950, 25 years after Arthur Bruce found refuge in her classroom. Picture supplied by Sheila Sutherland who is middle row, left.

> She was incandescent with rage and hit him with everything – the strap, her hands, her fists. She had him by the hair up against the door.

went home and complained about getting the strap, then more likely than not you would be told that you must have deserved it and be given some more. Another thing sticks in my mind. In our last year before I was due to go up to the Higher Grade classes, we had Miss Shaw. I didn't like her; I was afraid of her; she would become very aggressive and she used the strap a lot. We used to get 20 spellings each day to copy down and learn up. On the Friday there would be a test and she'd select 20 out of the week's 80 for you to write down correctly. If you made more than two errors then you automatically got the strap. That happened to me a lot because I wasn't a naturally good speller. No allowance was made for any individual difficulty, however – you just got the strap the same as everyone else.

Now, she had this nickname among the pupils: Tatty Shaw. There was this boy in the class above mine and one evening – it was winter and it was dark – he was knocking about in the close between his house and the Co-op, when Miss Shaw came walking by. He saw her coming and he quickly hid himself in the close. After she'd passed, he shouted after her, 'Tatty Shaw! Tatty Shaw!' But she knew well enough who it was, so the next day she left us in our room and went to the one next door. She asked to see this boy – Clark was his name, 'Sookit' Clark, we called him. She dragged him back into her own classroom, got him up against the door and simply hammered him. She was incandescent with rage and hit him with everything – the strap, her hands, her fists. She had him by the hair up against the door. We all sat there terrified; she'd completely lost control of herself. But there were no repercussions; I think the attitude was that the boy had deserved it. Nowadays she'd land up in court for what she did.

**Arthur Bruce,** born 1921: Laurencekirk

# The school photograph

There's one thing I would like to share with you: here's my school photo, of the whole school at Maggieknockater, 1926. That's me sitting front row, centre, the youngest one. To my side are two brothers whose father was a tenant farmer. They came from a big family which had to endure all sorts of hardships, but each year another child would come along.

Now, in those days a small tenant farmer, no matter how good he was, would struggle to feed six mouths or so. So he got into debt. The sheriff's officer came along and poinded the family's milk cow. They were to be deprived even of something as basic as that. They got milk from us. We weren't being charitable; we just recognised that that's the way it had to be. One of the boys became a grieve, but the other was a bit of a crook. He was a cattle-dealer and one of our friends had the unbelievable stupidity of handing over to him an open cheque.

Now this big lad, due to leave school at 14 and having spent all his schooldays at the one small school like most of them in this photo, he was the tail-end of a large family.

Our own land went right up the hillside opposite Ben Aigan. But there was farmland even higher up than us and this was known as the Shians. It was marginal, unproductive land, but they worked it. They kept a billy goat and it stank to high heaven. In warm weather you could sniff that beast even down at our farm. Walter would come to the school stinking of the family's billy goat all the time. His clothes were impregnated by the smell.

Now, this girl – she's one of two sisters whose father broke stones on the roads. They always had an income, but it was a tiny one. Yet although not well dressed, as you can see, their clothes were decent enough for the school. They both went on to become domestic servants in farmhouses. They both got married and were competent housewives.

Now look at the twins here, the boy and the girl. Social crimes are nothing new. Their father was a blacksmith, a real pillar of the community and an elder of the kirk. I remember one day going to their back door to wait for them after their midday dinner, which they took at home. I was standing there; the door was open and I could see through to the living room. There sat the mother, sobbing her heart out. When the girls came out I asked them, 'What's to do with your mother?' 'Oh', said one of them, as matter of fact as could be, 'Father his bin takin the belt tae her'.

So here was a case of domestic abuse, and by a respectable member of the community. Nowadays that kind of thing is constantly being highlighted; it wasn't then but, I can assure you, it happened all right, behind those closed doors. You can imagine what those two small children – and they were the oldest of five – had to contend with. The boy never did work; it was claimed he was mentally retarded, but it was nothing of the sort. He was traumatised, drawn in on himself. The girl suffered the most terrible eczema.

This girl was brought up by grandparents, over at Ben Aigan side. She had a very hard upbringing; she was always having to run to the school because of all the household

**Maggieknockater School, 1926**
Allan Grieve was the youngest pupil, front row centre.

chores she had to do. I'm told that after school she went into domestic service and managed to carve out a little niche for herself in that way.

This one is the son of the gardener at Kininvie estate. That should have been a secure job, but there were ways of giving people the shove in those days – no employment law to protect them then – and that's what happened to him, with all the hardship that meant for the family.

This girl was the daughter of the underkeeper on the Andilly estate. He worked there well enough for two years, but then he fell foul of the head keeper and so he got the bird. That meant no income and, being in a tied house, nowhere to go. Because he'd been fired he wasn't eligible for the dole. Fortunately, there was an unused cottage on one of the farms and they were able to move in there. I can remember going over with the horse and cart and helping to load their goods on it for the flitting. Everyone sympathised; that head keeper was known to be a pig of a man. Later, the family was able to move on; the father got a position as water baillie at Rothes.

This lad had what would be known now as learning difficulties. He had problems hearing and speaking. He was the son of the cook at Kininvie, who spent half the year in London with the laird and half up here, at Kininvie. When he came to school for the summer term he just sat there in his own world. Nowadays a lot would done for someone like him, but then he was just written off.

Now this one was the school bully – as thick as two short planks. As the wee-est boy in the school I was a victim. He would organise gangs and gang warfare. When he left he got an apprenticeship at a joiner's, over at Newmills. But later his wife slung him out and he ended up alone. His sister, however, was quite bright and actually went on to Aberlour High School. But the father was only a railway worker and money was tight, so she had to leave school early. She went into the WAAF and got married.

Now this lad is the teacher's son and the only one of us who was able to go on to university. He went to Aberlour and finished the academic course there. He was never part of the playground gang; he was very much a loner who went home for his dinner and only reappeared at the bell.

So you can see how my first school photograph contained within it a fair cross-section of rural society in the North-East of the 1920s.

Allan Grieve, born 1921: Maggieknockater

# Cairncoullie College for knowledge

I started school at Cairncoullie in 1927. We all had to walk to the school. For me that was three miles there and back and for some of the cottar families it could be even further. Some of those children were very poor. Their fathers might only get £16 to £20 for the six months. That's what they would be fee'd for. And some of them would be large families with maybe six bairns to keep. And they didn't get their money till 28

November or 28 May. Often they had to sub their wages long before that date. They did get their meal, their milk and their tatties, too, but it was still a struggle.

Some of the children would come to the school very poorly dressed. They might be shod, but their boots would have pieces of twine for laces. I mind some of the older boys in my school had dungers to the school and I aye fancied being like them. So I got my mother to make me up a pair, but when I got to the school that day all the other boys, they weren't wearing theirs. I mind the teacher said, 'Go home and take off those workman's trousers'.

You did learn the basics at Cairncoullie; you got your lessons all right. The learning was different from what it is now. They sit in groups now round tables. Then we just sat at desks, though the teacher might go round to look over your shoulder to see whether you were getting it right. No talking allowed; once you were inside the school then you could only speak if you were spoken to by the teacher. It was all very strict. If you did speak out of turn then it was straight out onto the floor and the strap. She used the strap a lot.

Strapping was just part of school life; you just accepted it. If you went home and told your parents you'd got it then you could expect to get into more trouble from them. You'd get the strap for not doing your lessons right, not just for misbehaviour. I think that's wrong: if you can't do it, it should be explained properly, not get you into trouble with the strap. Some of the slower ones would get the strap time and time again. I remember one boy out there on the floor trying to get his sums right, with his fingers behind his back, trying to count it out right and still getting it wrong and then getting thrashed for it. He just couldn't do it.

Each day at Cairncoullie you'd go through your subjects. At the start of the day you'd see the teacher go into the school, then she'd come out and ring the bell. That's when you had to line up, in ones, and march through the porch and into the school. You'd say your 'Good morning', then there would be the Lord's Prayer, then, maybe arithmetic and then some reading and writing work. You had an interval at 11 o'clock for a quarter of an hour and dinner at 12.30. In the wintertime you'd take cocoa to school; the cups would be placed around the fire to keep them hot. There were no school dinners at that time.

**Still getting his sums**
Robbie Gauld seated with slate at a desk in the reconstructed school room at Alford Heritage Centre, 75 years on.

For your essay you got to write with ink. You could make a real mess with pen and ink. The rest of the work was done on slates.

You'd take a piece – maybe a slice of bread with some syrup on it. You might have a biscuit too.

Then in the afternoon you'd get your history, your geography, or maybe some music, or have to do a composition. For that you got to write with ink, for your essay. You could make a real mess with the pen and the ink. The rest of the work was done on slates; you'd rub it clear with a duster or maybe just use your sleeve. You kept the duster in your bag and sometimes you'd use a little bowl of water.

When I was 12 I passed the exam to go on to Towie – most of the others just completed their education at Cairncoullie. There was this saying:

*If you want knowledge, go to Cairncoullie College
If you want to be a fool, go to Towie School.*

I never minded going to the school – you can't do without your schooling – but I must admit towards the end I was much more interested in the farm. Whenever I got home I'd be asking my mother what my father had been doing that day. I was always interested in the horses, in working the land.

**Robbie Gauld,** born 1922: Cairncoullie

## The school in the glen

They said that the distance from the lodge to our school was three-quarters of a mile, but it was a very long three-quarters. We just walked. Two of the pupils came from Tolduquhill and that was a three-and-a-half mile walk each way. They just did it, through all weathers, though the winters were much more severe then and the school would be closed when there was a blizzard. The attendance would go down then and the school had to open a certain number of days in the year. Some years it might have to open up on a Saturday morning to make up for the missing days. Only one pupil might come, but that would count as an opening.

Balloch was the only school I ever went to, for nine years till I left at 14. During all that time it didn't change one iota. It was just 'the school', and that's how it remained. It was a basic building: a little porch on the end for our coats; two toilets at the back, one for each sex. And a coal and stick shed at the end. All very basic. School meals were unheard of in our time. You just took your piece. The teacher would boil up the kettle and make cocoa – but kids being kids, we would often mix it up and just eat it, as chocolate. The doctor came once a year, as did the dentist. The district nurse also. But we were a healthy lot. There wasn't even any lice on us. I wouldn't say there was any deep poverty in the Glen, though life was certainly hard. We could live off the land, you see.

We sat at old-fashioned two-by-two desks with lids and fold-up seats, all of us in the one small room. In the winter it could get pretty cold. For heat there was only the one coal fire at the end of the room. The walls had three or four maps on them – the world,

**Balloch School in 2004,** 60 years after it was closed down.

with the British Empire clearly marked in pink, Scotland, England & Wales, Ireland. There was a blackboard, set up on an easel.

The teacher would give each group something to get on with while she saw to one age-group at a time. We would start off the day with a hymn and a bit of prayer. Then down to the allotted tasks. We used slates and those horrible squeaky pencils. You were meant to keep it clean with a sponge, but often we just spat on them. We were quite well supplied with books and with jotters.

I loved the reading. I'm an avid reader to this day – I don't talk much, you see. I reckon that learning to read books was the best thing that ever happened to me. But I wasn't just so fond of the arithmetic. I could do it but I didn't enjoy it. We'd get one session a day of mental arithmetic, and we'd have to chant out our tables. I can do that yet. I don't know why they ever did away with that, even if it did just turn us all into parrots.

History and geography and the reading often went together. I was good at both of them, especially geography, which I enjoyed. I expect that the geography we learnt was the same as anywhere else for the time. We knew every country and every capital of every country. We also knew the name and the whereabouts of every hill, of every burn, of every wood in the area, but that was nothing to do with the school. What we got was strictly world geography. It was the same with the history – it was 1066 and all that.

I do remember some of the literature we got, especially from Miss Thomson. She had us reciting Shakespeare: 'Hath not a Jew eyes/Hath not a Jew hands…'. There you are, *The Merchant of Venice*. I remember it yet. So you see, for a little place, we did quite well. Mark you, quite a lot of what I learned there was not much use to me in later life. But I will say that we got the basics, that we could all read and write and count. And we did get things

**Balloch School, Glenbuchat, 1904**
when Miss Nellie Singer was the teacher.

We used slates and those horrible squeaky pencils. You were meant to keep it clean with a sponge, but we just spat on them.

like drawing – we had drawing books supplied by the authority. We also did painting, and had singing. The teacher had to be an all-rounder.

I feel my education fitted me out well enough. Later in the army, I mixed with all sorts: people from Shetland to British Columbia, from Glasgow and from London. I got on well with almost all of them. I reckon that the education I'd got at the Balloch – up to the age of 14 anyway – was as good as any that was available anywhere in Britain.

**Billy Duncan,** born 1923: Balloch, Glenbuchat

## Academic sense and common sense

I started school at Tewel. One year there. I left when my father went to Bents of Maryculter and I went to Maryculter West School. I was put up a class and it took me a long time to catch up. I got stuff there I'd never heard of before and Miss Herd, my God, she used to strap me something terrible! The adding sums I had to do there – so much millions, so many hundreds of thousands – I'd never had of any of that before. And when you got a sum wrong, you just got the strap; and if you got more wrong you'd get a double dose. Just ridiculous! I was six at the time and there I was getting the strap every day and it wasn't my fault.

But when I was 13 and went to Auchenblae, I'd come second in the class. So I wasn't stupid. It wasn't that I couldn't do it, but my mind was aye elsewhere, on working on the farm mainly. The three Rs were useful, of course. Apart from that, not much. There was some woodwork and that was useful. As for the other subjects, well, I hated geography. History yes, but geography never. And I was never any good at analysing sentences: nouns, adjectives, predicate and all that. I couldn't see the point of it; as far as I could make out, it wasn't ever going to be of any use to me.

Now, if our English lessons had used material to do with cattle, horses or something like that… but then, the school never really attempted to bring the outside world into the classroom. The geography we got wasn't local – it was simply world geography, general stuff. I just wasn't interested – it wasn't my world. I'd see me learning my lessons at home, when all of a sudden, I'd be off thinking about the farm; or my father would be there in his chair, reading his paper and he'd look up and mention that he'd noticed some rabbits out in the fields, or how the barley was getting on – and then my mind would just run right away from my lessons!

My eldest sister, she was different: she was academic. She did six years secondary education, but the war came on and money was tight so she didn't go on. She took a job at the Income Tax; she was there a pucklie years and got married and that was that. Her education, as far as I'm concerned, did her no good whatsoever. She'd got no common sense, you see. Now here's another example: this chap who occupied a high position at the academy – ye ken fine fa I mean. A clever man, but common sense he had none. He couldn't even make a cup of tea. Just a big brain and that's all.

> This chap who occupied a high position at the academy – ye ken fine fa I mean. A clever man, but common sense he had none. He couldn't even make a cup of tea. Just a big brain and that's all.

Now, I'll tell you a different kind of example, a boy who left school at 14, went into the bank, nothing special, but, by God, he had common sense. After he left the army, he got into hotels. He got back and took a hotel at Dunkeld and after a pucklie years he had five of them. If a business was going down, he'd get hold of it and bring it up again. All this was not something he'd learned at the school. It's just what he had. Common sense, you see.

**James Edwards,** born 1924: Mearns

# The cocoa was always warm

It was a country school. We could all do the three Rs, all of us. I don't think in all my years at the school I can recall anyone not able to read or write or do basic arithmetic. You were drilled thoroughly, by rote, and every child could do it. That's why this illiteracy thing nowadays just defeats me: I simply can't understand it.

And I remember the walking to get to the school. And the snow! I remember walking along the roads which had been cleared of snow, but with the snow all piled up at each side in these huge drifts. Although we were told to keep to the road we would walk along those drifts, all in our buttoned boots. You don't get winters like that now. I can remember Dad opening the kitchen door at Strichen where the snow had piled up solid against it, and it would just be packed there, a great solid wall on the other side of your door. But we had to walk to the school in all weathers; I don't ever recall it being closed on account of the conditions.

There used to be a coal fire in the classroom. You went in in the morning and put your little blue enamel flask by it for the cocoa. All through the morning there would be this row of little blue flasks warming up by the fire, for the cocoa. When it came to lunch you would have your sandwiches – probably bread and jam just. But the cocoa was always there.

**Peggy Walker,** born 1924: Udny Green

# Champion of the underdog

Annie Smith was the champion of the underdog. Times were hard and she was there for us. You were liable to get your pandies from her. I would get it, for carelessness in arithmetic. She was a local girl and was well regarded. She had her secure place in the community, not least because she would give it some of its annual highlights. One was the school concert, which would be followed by a dance for the adults. I don't know what her record of work looked like for the six weeks beforehand, because we spent the whole time in rehearsal. That concert would realise £20 or so and that would be sufficient to hire three buses from Burnett's of Mintlaw in the summer and

I can remember Dad opening the kitchen door at Strichen where the snow had piled solid against it. But we had to walk to the school in all weathers; I don't ever recall it being closed on account of the conditions.

'This letter is addressed to the Director of Education. This is what it says: "I am sending you a rather unusual present. Please find enclosed the mud-bespattered petticoat..."'

for them to take the whole district off for a day's outing at Lossiemouth or Montrose. For us these places were another world; for many of the local wives they represented just about the only time in the year when they would be able to get over their own doors.

She would begin the day with the Lord's Prayer and last thing at night we would chant:

*Tender shepherd, Jesus, hear me.*
*Bless thy little lamb tonight.*
*Through the darkness be Thou near me*
*While I sleep till morning light.*

*Let my sins be all forgiven.*
*Bless the friends who are not so well.*
*Take me when I die to heaven*
*Happy there with Thee to dwell.*

Then would come some Bible. I don't think we ever got to the lengths of Saul, though we certainly gave Goliath a good clobbering. We went through Abraham, Isaac, and then the New Testament. We had to recite hymns and carols – many of them I can repeat to this day.

Arithmetic was important. We had to repeat our times tables; once we had mastered the twin beasts of the seven and the nine times tables we were given a penny each, once we could say it all off pat. In English we used to be given cards which carried little pictures of scenes which we then had to describe. One such featured a pail of milk which had been accidentally knocked over and I had written, 'The pail had been upset'. Annie praised me as the only person in the whole class who had noticed it and written accurately about it.

But the others would have seen it all right – the point was, I was the only one of them who knew the word 'upset'. Grammar was very important, very much so. 'A noun is a naming word; a verb is a doing word...' I had an outline of grammar in my head by the age of nine, and well before I went to Peterhead Academy to do Latin. I knew all about subjects and objects before I ever had occasion to hear talk of the accusative and the nominative cases.

Annie created a family atmosphere in the school. She was a maternal figure, cosy and warm. She also taught us of the outside world. We learned our history and our geography from the Oliver and Boyd textbooks. This was pretty factual, though she did give it some imaginative touches – the marriage of the Thistle and the Rose elicited from her the information that on that day 'the very fountains were flowing with wine'. We didn't have any exact idea of what that could be: we thought this wine stuff must be like lemonade, only even better.

In the winter time we would make slides in the playground and send the sparks flying. That playground lent itself to the making of slides – it was a muddy, sticky place of glaur and wet. Annie Smith had campaigned long and vigorously to have it tarmacced. One day a girl stumbled and fell her length. Her petticoat got completely covered with mud. At dinnertime, Annie rang the bell; we lined up and then sat down. She thumped the table, it was clear that something momentous was to be announced. Then she addressed us: 'Now boys and girls, I'm going to read you a letter. It's addressed to Mr Morrison, Director of Education, Union Terrace, Aberdeen. This is what it says: "Dear Mr Morrison, I am sending you a rather unusual present. Please find enclosed the mud-bespattered petticoat…".  She got her tarmac!

It wasn't fashionable to say that we were fond of our teacher, but we were. We got a lot more of the world and of the imagination than most would have seen at that period. And yet the three Rs were thoroughly dealt with too. We all learned to read and to write and to count. She commanded the classroom. Indeed, she had a highly-developed sense of justice, even to the point of making a drama out of disciplinary affairs. If something went wrong then we all knew about it, and in high style too. The whole school had to stop until the matter was sorted out.

**Charles Birnie,** born 1925: Balearn

# None of us could step out of line

When I went to the academy, Dr Lawson was the rector and he was a real martinet. He was so proud of Inverurie Academy, you'd never dare step out of line. In the mornings the janitor – real sergeant-major type – he'd ring his bell and line you all up to march into the school in proper order.

One lunchtime I was walking through the Square when I came across one of the Latin teachers. He was in conversation with some other gentleman and didn't seem to see me at all, so I just walked past.

Back in the school in the afternoon, I was in the maths lesson when the door flung open and he stuck his head round it. 'I want to see Hendry.' I was given two of the belt, for failing to salute a teacher from the school when I was out in public. That, I reckoned, wasn't very fair, but in those days you never dreamt of complaining. If I had told my parents, then I would have got a row and been made to bide in; the attitude was that the teacher must be right.

But I'm grateful for the education I got. We had such excellent hard-working, dedicated teachers, teachers who didn't stand any nonsense and who were masters of their classrooms. I have a daughter and a son-in-law who are both teachers and their conception of teaching is completely different to what we got back in the 30s and 40s. Then you sat at desks with inkwells and you got on with your lessons. Now it's all very informal, but then there was no messing about, none at all. Everything was very strict and in its place. You had to show respect at all times.

**Jack Hendry,** born 1925: Inverurie

I was in the maths lesson when the door flung open and he stuck his head round it. 'I want to see Hendry.' I was given two of the belt, for failing to salute a teacher from the school when I was out in public.

**Drumwhindle in its heyday, 1905** when 100 pupils attended and the rector was Lewis Gavin (back row, extreme left). He remained at his post for more than 30 years.

# The focal point of the whole community

Those small rural schools did much more than simply give the local children a sound education; they acted as focal points for the whole community. In those days before the widespread availability of the TV, the telephone or even the wireless, and when people had to get everywhere on foot or by bike, a school like Drumwhindle made a huge contribution to people's social life. In the evenings people would go there for concerts or talks; the WRI would hold its meetings there, usually once a month at the full moon so that people could walk or bike to it more easily.

Drumwhindle, Braeside, Esslemont, Arnage…these places meant a lot to the people living within a three-mile radius of them. At Drumwhindle, the headmaster, Lewis Gavin, ran evening classes; there was also the local Mutual Improvement Association, run by a committee, which would draw up a programme of talks and dances and concerts. I recall seeing my first slide show, on Whipsnade Zoo it was. There was no electricity, so the power was supplied by a carbine gas jet. This was in 1930; I can remember to this day sitting there in the dark, listening to the hiss of the jet and looking in the glow at all these pictures of lions and elephants. Quite magical.

And now all those little schools are being closed down and lost to their communities. Drumwhindle went in 1976. They go with very little ceremony and in the case of somewhere like Drumwhindle with no written record of the important part they have

played in North-East life. Now many of them have been sold off as private houses, converted and modernised so that people can drive by them and never get a glimpse of what they once were and once meant.

It's true that not many of their pupils were able to go on to get a university education – the economics of the countryside of that time were against that. But they did produce some notable people. When I started at Drumwhindle one of the big loons at the school was Donald C. Stewart. He left school at 14 with no qualifications, but 10 years later he had developed a house-building business based at the Bridge of Don and it was one of the biggest the North-East. He had been brought up just beside Arnage Station; his people had only a small place there, the Neuk.

There's a story about this. Just across a wee burn you were into the Arnage Estate. Donald was an enterprising lad and he would scramble over that burn and go into the woods for a spot of poaching – a rabbit or two for the family pot. The gamekeeper was always after him; more than once he was thrown off and threatened never to come near the place again. Well, Donald left school at 14. Ten years roll on and the estate came on the market. In that time Donald had become a very rich man and was driving a Rolls Royce – AV999 it was. So who should drive up to the castle to have a look at the property, but Donald! And who should be there to greet him but the very same gamekeeper, the one who'd warned him never to set foot in the place again.

It was an amazing rise. His father had run a small joinery business and that gave

Donald left school at 14 with no qualifications, but 10 years later he had a house-building business that was one of the biggest the North-East.

**The year he won the class medal**
Drumwhindle School 1928 with Arthur Watson front row, second right

Donald the basics. But I think what his career shows is how lads from this part of the world could get on. What seems to be the essential here is getting the basics at the local school and also acquiring a strong work ethic. And something else too – the ability to spot the main chance and to go for it. Donald saw in the 1930s and in the post-war years that there would be a boom in private housing and he went for it.

Another local lad who made good in that way was Charlie Alexander, the lorry king. He lived in a small croft just beside Braeside School, a few miles from Drumwhindle and like it, it closed down some years ago. Charlie Alexander started off with the one lorry, doing general haulage locally and built up a fleet on the back of it. Later there were great fleets of Alexander lorries going all over the UK, carrying fish from the market in Aberdeen and all sorts of other goods.

I think looking back, that the small school and the rural background has played a great role in North-East life, both socially and in preparing individuals for a career of enterprise. The great pity now is that all that history is being lost as the schools close down and the memories fade away. I've been trying to interest those who have access to the old log books and records to compile some sort of history before it's too late, but so far without much success…

**Arthur Watson,** born 1921: Drumwhindle

> Normally when they came to the lying water they would go up by the side and keep dry, but this time they decided to plough straight through the wet, with the dominie following.

# The dominie gets his comeuppance

We'd walk each day, along tracks and, when the snow filled the roads, on the top of dykes. The headmaster was a strapper. He would strap and strap. If he couldn't get at your hands; he'd strap you round the back of the legs.

I remember hearing the story of my brother's last day at the school. He'd decided he wasn't going to do any lessons that day. So the dominie would give him the strap. My brother decided he wouldn't take it and he just upped and went home. My father was busy with the plough in the fields. Jim came home and told him what had happened. Back at the school, the dominie announced, 'I'm going to go up to the house and see about this'. Then he told my sisters, 'I'll follow you up; you can show me the way'.

Well, the weather had been real wet; normally when they came to the lying water they would go up by the side and keep dry, but this time they decided to plough straight through the wet, with the Head following. And he had on his plus-fours and his shoes. Then they led him through the fields and onto the marsh. Well, Father saw them coming and although he was coming down with the plough, he simply turned the horse round and went up again. The dominie went into the field to try and catch him and had to walk all through the newly ploughed field and mud. This was my father putting him in his place.

**Findlay Chapman,** born 1927: Millbrex, Fyvie

# Is this what you meant, Miss Horne?

There were eight of us in the family altogether; all of us grew up into adults and made careers for ourselves. My mother was desperate that none of us ended up as farm servants. We all had to serve our time and get a definite trade. I was a plasterer, my brother became a motor mechanic; the youngest one actually became a doctor.

She was very keen on our education; to her it was the way out. One Saturday she took me into Buckie to take the Control exam. For my sins I passed it and so I had to go off to Buckie High School. But at the time, the big attraction for me was life outside the school. I couldn't wait for Friday night, when I was at that school. I would cycle home up the hill, or, before I got a bike, I would rush to catch the bus and get off outside Keith and then run up the hill – I was home and it was Friday night!

But my bag would be full of homework. I would have to get out my books and learn up some poetry, so many French verbs, so many Latin ones; I would have to get up a theorem and I didn't even know what a theorem could be, or what it could be for. And there were screeds of poetry: Walter Scott – 'Breathes there a man with a soul so dead' – I was just submerged by it all.

After two years I decided I'd had enough and switched over to the technical course. At 14 when a job came along I jumped at it. Somebody was needing an apprentice plasterer. I didn't really know what it was all about, but I did know it meant the end of school so I went for it and got it. So for the next 20 years that was me: a plasterer. Then I decided that was enough of that and that it was time for something different. So I went back to my studies and became a teacher. I ended up back at Buckie High School.

At Buckie I remember my French teacher was Miss Horne and once, after I hadn't shone in the exam, she told me, 'You'll come to a bad end, Allan Fraser, a bad end!'. Well, after I had become a teacher at the school and she had retired, I met her out on the street while I was with a group of pupils. I couldn't resist going up to her to ask, 'Is this what you meant, Miss Horne?'

**Allan Fraser,** born 1930: Buckie

My French teacher was Miss Horne and once, after I hadn't shone in the exam, she told me, 'You'll come to a bad end, Allan Fraser, a bad end!'

# Crabb by name, crabbit by nature?

Our teacher was Mrs Crabb. She was Crabb by name and crabbit by nature. She was a widow. But she was a real character; she did so much for Fetterangus. She was a very methodical, powerful teacher. Every day was set out exactly so.

There was a great community spirit about the school. This was helped by the fact that all the teachers lived in the village and if anything was going on they were sure to be involved. Mrs Crabb was part of Fetterangus life. In the war she acted as the air raid warden; she had one of the three phones in the village and she'd get the news of any alert. Then she would march up and down the village, clanging away with her bell, warning us all to get indoors. When the all-clear sounded she would repeat this act of going up and down the streets, but this time with a rattle. She was a tiny stocky figure. We used to say that any German aircraft looking down on Fetterangus would think there was a crow flapping about the street, she was that little.

She taught everything: drill, handcraft, music. There were no visiting specialists in those days. She had to lead us all in our keep-fit sessions – if you'd seen her! She was so small and dumpy. She wore these big bloomers and one of our games was to try and catch a sight of them as she moved around the classroom. This wasn't difficult because she was so small and was constantly having to stretch over to do things. She'd turn her back to write on the blackboard; she'd stretch up to write something at the top and there it was – a flash of bloomers! We'd all snicker and she would hear us. Without looking round she would send the duster whizzing through the air and whoever it struck, hard luck, they would have to take it out to her while we all got a rollicking.

She played the piano; she was a true all-rounder. We got sewing at the school from her, too. You'd learn how to make a lapbag and a pair of knickers, or a cookery apron. Mrs Crabb was at the centre of everything in the village. We all respected her. If you met her in the street then you'd give her a curtsey. She was strict but you knew she would always act in your interests and only cared that you got on in life. When I went on to Old Deer for my secondary she became more of a pal than an ex-teacher; I still had dealings with her because of all the events she organised. You'd go to her door and find that you couldn't get much further than the doorstep of her room, because it was packed with all the costumes and the fancy dresses she was keeping for her next production.

Isobel McRae, born 1933: Fetterangus

# Belt! Belt! Belt!

I started school at a small place called Tarracroys. The school had two teachers: an old one who was a wicked belter and a young one. I got her. I say 'young' but to me then she just seemed like an old wifie and crabby old wifie at that. In fact she was newly qualified and she began to wield the belt as well. Maybe she thought she had to keep up with her older colleague. Anyway, three sums wrong or three misspellings you'd be called out and – Belt! Belt! Belt! I was a clever wee clogs and I could do the work well enough, but my brother was different and he would get it just about every day and I had to watch him getting it. I became very upset, much more than he did. His attitude was, 'Ah'm fer the belt the day an Ah'm past carin aboot it,' while I sat there dreading it all.

It got so bad I was staying awake at night, lying in my bed with the walls falling in upon me. The doctor had to give me sleeping tablets. My life was being ruled by fear. In the end my parents decided to put a stop to the situation. My mother made an appointment with the Director of Education and requested for me to be transferred to Keith Primary School. It was much the same distance – two miles – and I could take the service bus in each day from just outside our house.

So that's what happened: I moved over to the town school and immediately felt much better. I had a lovely teacher; I couldn't believe a teacher could be so human and so nice. Ironically, the young Tarracroys teacher got a transfer to my new school and took her belting ways with her. But just about the first day that happened, on the next there was a queue of parents out of the door, coming up to complain. So she stopped using the belt and settled down to become a perfectly acceptable teacher.

But it's interesting that all the time she'd been at Tarracroys no parent had ever made a fuss; even my mother when she went up to the Director of Education had never explained the real reason why she'd been asking for a transfer. She wouldn't have liked to be seen causing any fuss. Country parents are like that, whereas the town ones just wouldn't stand for it. Just accept the situation and get on with it; that seemed to be the attitude. Teachers out in small country schools before the war could get way with all sorts of things that wouldn't have been tolerated in the town.

**Mabel Cowe,** born 1937: Keith

> It got so bad I was staying awake at night, lying in my bed with the walls falling in upon me. The doctor had to give me sleeping tablets. My life was being ruled by fear.

# Just desperate to start the school

I was just desperate to get to the school. I looked forward to the great day; I just couldn't believe it when it got nearer and nearer. My mother would tell me, 'You'll go there after the holidays' and I would ask her when Christmas came, 'That's the holidays – do I go now?' and she would say, 'Wait for the big holidays'. The same at Easter, so that when the summer came I could hardly believe it. When I got there on the first day I just wanted to go back after tea. It wasn't just the other kids; I wanted to learn.

There weren't many books at home, but there was this one of Burns and I used to write on the back cover. I knew you mustn't just scribble and that you had to set it out in lines and that is what I practised doing. I was just desperate to read and to write for myself. I'd seen my brother reading and I was desperate to enter that wonderland.

I loved Primary 1. I remember so much of it; it was such a huge event for me. Our days would begin with an assembly. We'd go over to the hall for that and join the whole school. Miss Goodall would play the piano and we'd sing a hymn. I liked that; it got the day off to a real start. Then we'd say the Lord's Prayer. For years I thought it went, 'Lead

**Aberlour, 1949**
Iris Wilson, P3,
front row, centre

The gym teacher seemed huge. When I was 12 I found out that this large woman that I'd been so scared of was actually a tiny woman.

us snot into temptation'. That was the way Willy Wood, the rector, barked it out, 'Lead us not into temptation'.

I can remember the Primary 1 room, the abacus and the Smarties Miss Goodall kept in a salad cream jar. She would call out, 'Come away all the Exes'. At home I would play at schools, 'Come away all the Exes. Come away, Iris!'. I can remember the letters for reading: 'D for dromedary; A for apple; N for needle' with the pictures of the camel and the needle with the thread trailing from it. Then we had a poem about the numbers: '1 is the one who stood alone; 2 is the duck that sails in the water; 3 ate all the porridge and so had a big fat tum; 4 is a bunch of flowers; 5 is a fish caught on a hook; 6 is the horse's tail; 7 a walking stick; 8 – oh, I forget 8; 9 is the one who stood on one leg; 10 is the greedy one'.

The first hymn we had was *'When He cometh to fetch His precious jewels'*. I loved the sound of the words. In fact, I loved everything like that about the school – the numbers, the words, the poems and the songs. I can remember the slates and how they were stacked up on the windowsill. Then there were the prickers: we had these felt pieces; there would be the outline of an elephant drawn out on the felt and you'd take this pricker and pick out little holes around the shape so that you could then push it out – and there you had it, a felt elephant.

I remember going to the hall for gym. We had to go along this long dark corridor and the gym teacher seemed huge, with a huge voice: 'O-o-one!' Then she left to have a baby and I didn't see her again till I was 12: I found out that this large woman that I'd been so scared of was actually a tiny woman. But then in Primary I I'd had to lie on the floor and look up at her and she was huge.

We had a storybook. You got to choose your own cover for it; I had one with a basket of flowers on it. On Fridays you had to go out to the teacher's desk and choose a picture, which you would then cut out and stick in your book. The teacher would then draw lines beneath it and you had to write a story about your picture on them. We had to chant out our tables and be able to say them individually, too. There was a lot of rote learning that way. We were all expected to keep up; I can't remember anyone who wasn't actually able to do the work, only some who were slower. But I wouldn't necessarily have known; it wasn't our business to think of what other people might or might not have been doing. We were expected to get on with our own work, to see to our own progress.

**Iris Wilson,** born 1942: Aberlour

## Strictly no Doric: **1**

No, we didn't speak Doric in the classroom. If you did, you got a scolding and if you insisted on doing it deliberately, then you got a smack. It was very confusing when you went new to the school. It was very hard for all the kids, with the Buchan dialect and all that. The first week or two when you got to school, you'd be learning to read out loud – it was like a foreign language – it had to be in proper English, and ye couldna spik it. In the family or on the farm it was all Doric.

Miss Taylor had all the little ones: she used to go to the WRI meetings and tell jokes about some of the things they said. And this boy, Lumsden– his father was a shepherd, ye ken – and he went to school, you see, and he had on this suit and a little waistcoat and some men at the farm gave him this watch, and he said, 'Gad a'michty, Miss Taylor, is it nae near lowsin time yet?' She got great fun out of all that, but she explained the right way to say it to him. You went to school and it was completely different. You had to change your tongue, you see. You just learned it, just learned it.

It doesn't bother me. I can understand it in a way, not being allowed to use it because not everyone's going to bide in the little bit they were brought up in. You're going to be travelling and you've got to have a language everyone can speak, and that would have to be English, I think. The only time you got to use a Scots word was in the singing lessons when you had a Burns song or something like that. But for just speaking, oh no!

**Violet Cassie,** born 1920: Boyndlie

## Strictly no Doric: **2**

We didn't speak Doric in the class. We spoke it in the playground but, whenever you went in, you switched. It was a problem to start with. I can remember one boy who was reading and he came to the word 'bull' and he said, 'bull' ['u' as in 'umbrella']. 'It's not "bull," it's "bool!"' ' But when you think about it, for us it was 'bull'; that's the way we pronounced it. But he got a raging for it: 'No, not "bull", it's pronounced "bool". Now say it properly, say it properly!'

This boy, Lumsden – his father was a shepherd, ye ken – had on this suit and a little waistcoat. Some men at the farm gave him a watch, and he said, 'Gad a'michty, Miss Taylor, is it nae near lowsin time yet?'

There were a lot of things like that, with various words. When you went home, your father and mother would be speaking the Doric and they would be talking about the 'bull'. But when you got to school, you suddenly had to change it to 'bool'. I think all that was wrong. It was something we had to worry about that we shouldn't have had. Yet my Doric was just as broad when I left school as it was when I had entered it. In fact, I'm as broad now as I ever was. What really made me go back to it was 'Scotland the What?'. I just loved all that. They had the right Doric. But one advantage we had was that we could change when we had to. I did learn to speak proper English as well as my own language, and I could use it when I went out into the world. But we could have used them both in the school and we didn't. The Doric was treated as dirty, as something foul. 'Not nice!'

**Eric Brown,** born 1935: Bridge of Muchalls

## Strictly no Doric: 3

So it was what you would call an intimate school, yes an intimate school with the 'Missie' very much part of the ethos of what rural life was all about. Being in the estate at Dunecht, most of those going to the school would have been the children of estate workers and that meant everyone from the factor down to the most ordinary of labourers. All in the one school, together.

There was a great emphasis on correctness. Grammar and punctuation were important. My wife was taught over at Cluny and then became a shorthand typist. To this day, if ever she sees a comma or an apostrophe out of place, she loses the head. Loses the head with the affront of it all. 'Just look at that!', she'll cry out. It was all to do with the way we were taught at our primary schools.

I have only the one real complaint and that is the treatment meted out to our own Doric language. It was literally drummed out of us. When we were speaking in the playground it was one thing, but as soon as we entered the classroom door it had to change – completely. The only concession was, I remember, one poem by Robert Burns and another by Charles Murray – two poems in the whole of that time. I don't remember any Doric prose at all. Not in my whole time there. So it was Standard English – standardised English – for us right from the start. That was the rule.

I remember one lady who did come in and play hymns with us. We would be singing 'The Lord's my shepherd' and she'd cry out, 'No, no! Not "the Lord – thee Lord". She had the whole lot of us going from 'the' to 'thee'' and it just didn't sound right at all. She was over-emphasising in order to drum our own 'tha' out of us, and ended up with something that was neither Doric nor English.

I make a big play of the Doric situation now, but I don't actually think it was so very difficult for us to adjust at the time. Possibly, we use hindsight to make the whole situation more difficult than it seemed at the time. To speak English at the school, well, that was part of our expectation. Our parents would tell us, 'You're going to school now and that is

I do think a loss was involved. And now there's a great loss of the old words and of our ability to understand our own folk literature. That's a sad, sad aspect of the whole process.

where you'll learn to speak English'. It was part of the whole package – sums, writing neatly, speaking English. But I do think a loss was involved. And now there's a great loss of the old words and of our ability to understand our own folk literature. That's a sad, sad aspect of the whole process.

**Robbie Shepherd,** born 1936: Dunecht

## Strictly no Doric: **4**

At school we just switched from the Doric to English automatically. The first I knew that there were two languages was when Dr John Caldwell came to the house to do a house visit – now that's a thing that doesn't happen any more either! I was four. I remember being surprised to hear my mother using a different way of speaking when she was talking with him. I asked her, 'Fit why div ye spik like that tae the doctor?' And she told me, 'But that's the wye ye hiv tae spik tae the doctor!' When I got to the school I did the same when I was speaking to the teacher. I changed; we all did. There was no problem as I recall; we did it automatically. Then out in the playground we switched back again.

In fact, I would tend to overcorrect. Now, 'pints' – laces – and also 'points' at a game: I once went to the local farm for some milk and I found myself saying, 'A point of milk, please'. I had simply assumed that 'pint' must be a Doric word, not English. I also remember later as an adult talking with this French girl who'd been an assistant at Mackie. We were at the table, with Bob, who's from Keith, on one side with me sitting there and she on the other. As we were chatting away she suddenly started to laugh. I asked her why. She told me, 'It's the way you speak English to me and then, when you turn to Bob, you just use another language,'. I'd been doing this without even realising, it was that automatic.

**Iris Wilson,** born 1942: Aberlour

I asked her, 'Fit why div ye spik like that tae the doctor?' And she told me, 'But that's the wye ye hiv tae spik tae the doctor!'

# GOING TO THE KIRK

**Sunday, 14 February 2010**
The brae leading up to Cookney
Church and not a soul in sight.
The church building is now used
by an oil-related company.

# Visitors must wait

I left Banff and took up a teaching post in Edinburgh. My first winter there, I remember going to a church in the West End because I'd read that there was some famous preacher going to speak there. I went on the Sunday morning; I laughed to myself because this was the first time I would be paying my own collection and all from my precious salary, too. I got there early, saw the plate and put my sixpence into it. Just as I was doing that, a man stepped up and asked, 'Excuse me, but are you a member of the church?'. I was quite alarmed at his tone. 'No,' I said, 'I'm a visitor'. Then he said, 'In that case would you mind standing over there until the congregation is all seated'. I thought that was dreadful. I just had to stand and wait. He nodded and I had to slip quietly into the back. I can't remember anything about the sermon, I was so taken aback at what had happened. I'd never encountered anything like that back in Banff.

**Alexina Fleming,** born 1905: Banff

# A Brethren boyhood

I was born in Brighton Place, Aberdeen, in 1914. But my mother died when I was two years of age, directly after the birth of my sister. This meant my father was left with two young children to look after and so he sent us up to our grandparents in Craigellachie to be cared for. My grandfather was a carpenter and worked at the mills in Craigellachie.

The village was pretty well dominated by the Christian Brethren then and getting employment could depend on whether you were a believer or not. Now, I've nothing against these people, in fact I've followed the faith myself all my life, but I can tell you this: the Brethren who ran the mills were no different as bosses from anyone else and my grandfather was forced to work really long hours. He would start at six in the morning and not get home till after six at night. My grandmother used to say to me, 'You'll have to go to your bed at six in the evening because that's when we go, but you can get up when we get up and join us for our breakfast then'. And that would be three in the morning; my grandfather would rise then, take his breakfast and then spend time on the word of God before going off to the mill for a six o'clock start.

One of the leading lights in the Brethren in the village was the blacksmith. There was a little hall at the back of his workshop and he would hold gatherings there on a Sunday night. My grandparents took me to them. Then on the Sunday morning my grandfather would take me over to Aberlour to another Brethren meeting. We would travel in a pony and trap with five or six other men. I had to sit on the floor among their feet and look up at all their black suits and their beards. I can still feel the clip-clop, clip-clop beneath the floor of that trap as we made our way over the brae to Aberlour.

Life could be severe on a Sunday. There were heaps of beautiful, interesting books in the house and copies of the *London Illustrated News* that I loved to go through, but never ever on a Sabbath. That was for God's word only and I was strictly forbidden to touch them. But those early days in a Brethren household did plant the faith in me and 90 years later I still go to the International Baptist church in Cults.

For me the precise denomination is irrelevant; it's the faith that counts, however you come to it. My watchword is 'Love thy neighbour as yourself'. Impossible to live up to – we are all weak and frail – but it's what you must constantly strive to do. I believe that life is a constant test. I never forget what a great Baptist minister, George Balmer, once told me: 'We live our faith minute by minute'.

**Alec Milne,** born 1914: Craigellachie

**A scholar at heart**
Margaret Carmichael's father, the Reverend William Watson MA, BD, D.BLitt, DD, on his wedding day in 1910

# Life in a country manse

I was born in Oyne manse, 1915. My father was minister there for 41 years. He was a very educated man; he was a graduate of St Andrews University, with an MA, BD, and then he got his D.Litt. There was a great contest for the Chair of Systematic Theology at Aberdeen and he should have won it, but nobody could correct his Hebrew papers; nobody was up to his standard. But my father was a very shy man and he wouldn't push himself forward, so he had to settle for a quiet country parish. The disappointment was always with him, but at a place like Oyne he could at least get the peace he needed for his books. He would shut himself away in his study for hours on end.

Despite our father's calling we had a perfectly normal childhood. There was what we called the tack town opposite and all the children would come and play with us. We would run around our garden and kick up noise, much to my parents' annoyance. We got up to some awful things. I remember when our parents were out, we got hold of the garden rakes and fixed some rags to the ends of them and then soaked them in paraffin. We set light to them and we had these flaming torches that we could parade around. You could see the flares for miles around; they lit up Bennachie. We would play cards; we had all the games going. We also had a faithful family dog, Wendy. She was a lovely harmless creature and she had the habit of going into the fields and herding the sheep just like a collie. She never harmed them in any way but one day the farmer just shot her. She was brought back wounded and died in our arms.

Oyne in those days was the kind of place where everyone knew everyone. It had its share of worthies, oh yes. One of the elders in the church was nicknamed Honk Honk. He had a cleft palette and that's the way he would speak and that's the way he would sing. He was constantly falling out with the organist; she was an elderly spinster. They were both very set in their ways and both very determined. You'd hear then battling against each other in church: she would play one tune; he would be singing another: 'Honk honk!'.

Then we had a woman postie, not so common in those days. She would have to walk miles every day, half way up Bennachie and back. No post vans in those days. Part of her beat would take in this cottage at the foot of Bennachie. It was occupied by these two ladies – if that's the right term. These were Tibby and Maggie and they each of them had

**Maid of the manse**
A one-year-old Margaret with her brother and the family's long-serving maid, Maggie Dawn

**Desirable property**
The manse at Oyne which fetched £350,00 in 2007.

A beautiful house, but perishing cold in winter. You had to wear coats inside just to move from one room to another.

**The kirk at Oyne**
as it is now.

seven illegitimate children, all to different fathers. They weren't necessarily local men; they would roam far afield to get a new relationship going. But they never asked for a penny off the parish; as soon as they had borne a fresh baby they would up and be working the next day — domestic service and cleaning. Yet all those children did well enough; they went into nursing, became posties, got reasonable jobs.

Another character was the shoemaker, Slavery Bob. He would sit there sounding off about the world with a dribble of saliva coming from his mouth as he worked. He was a great beekeeper and would get into terrible rows with his neighbour. A swarm would appear over their gardens; he would claim it, she would claim it, and a great argument would break out. Once in a rage he picked up a skep of bees and threw it at her head with, 'There ye are; if you wint them ye can hae them!'.

Then there was Miss Smith up at Westhall. She would never take part in anything in the village; she was far too grand for that. She had a stretch of the Gadie that ran through her grounds and every day she would erect this notice: 'No fishing. Private property' and every night the boys from the village would come and throw it into the Gadie.

Oyne was a peaceful place, really quiet and peaceful. But there was the night when two boys smashed the window of the only shop in the village. There was no bobby in the village, but the pair were seen and were reported. They were tried in Aberdeen and both got the birch. They were about 12 years of age. The whole village thoroughly approved of their punishment. Nothing like that happened again, not after the birching.

The congregation was only a small one — about 20 or so. When I was born there were two churches in Oyne: the Free Church had its own, too. Now it's all long gone. I feel very sad that this is so. Ours was a big house, the largest manse in Aberdeenshire. It's just been sold — for £350,000. Sometimes a wedding would be held in the dining room. A beautiful house, but perishing cold in the winter. You had to wear coats inside just to move from one room to another. Mother did have a maid and she would come in at seven each morning and get the place going. One of my greatest childhood joys was coming down into the morning room for breakfast on a cold winter's morning and finding the fire blazing away and the breakfast hot and ready.

And you've got to remember the winters were harder then. The roads into Oyne could be blocked for days on end. When my brother was to be flown up to Scapa Flow in the war, the plane stopped at Aberdeen and the pilot announced that they could go no further because of the conditions. 'Fine,' my brother thought, 'I'll just stay the night at home'. He phoned up the manse. 'Could you tell me the times of the buses out to Oyne?', he asked my father. 'Well, the roads have been blocked for a fortnight now, so I doubt whether there'll be one tonight,' came the reply.

**Margaret Carmichael,** born 1915: Oyne

# The minister's daughter

The church played an important role in those days. My mother would take me to the Sunday evening services at the South Kirk, to the Sankey sessions they had then. I also had to attend Sunday School. This was just part of your life in those days; in time I graduated to playing the organ and to teaching Sunday school. The minister was the Reverend A. J. Falconer who was, I think, a very good one. He was a kindly man who meant well; his preaching, however, was marred by being delivered as a series of barks.

His daughter had something of an influence on me. She was a very elegant young lady and possessed of a bewitching singing voice. I loved her, but strictly from a distance. You would pass by the manse at night and look up and see the light shining in the upstairs bedroom and you'd think to yourself, 'There she is, at this very moment'. She had a little dog, which she would take for walks. It wore a bell around its neck and you would be in the woods and you would hear the bell tinkling away and know that within a minute she would there in front of you. Very exciting! But all that ensued would be polite little exchanges about the weather.

I never did get round to declaring my feelings for her. I was just a country loon, you see, and she was the minister's daughter, so fine and so elegant. She went off and got married to a chartered accountant and that was a very great blow indeed. She had three children and a long marriage. I attended her funeral at Torphins Kirk a few years back. I did once meet her in later life when we were both become middle aged; I noted that she had become rather fat… such is life!

**James Morrison,** born 1917: Torphins

> The minister was a kindly man who meant well; his preaching, however, was marred by being delivered as a series of barks.

# The brae was black with folk

We had to go to Sunday school; we all did; we were all expected to go. Our parents didn't go to church every Sunday, but did keep up an association with it. They would go on Communion Sunday. Church was an important part of the social life of the community. Most people had their 'own' seats for which they put in a rent. There was a very big congregation. The roads all the way up the hill to Cookney would be thick with folk going up to the service.

**David Chalmers,** born 1920: Cookney

> Most people had their 'own' seats for which they put in a rent.

# Blowing the organ at New Deer

The church has always played a familiar part in my life. We come from a line of adherents to the old Presbyterian kirk; I can remember my older relatives would keep to the old customs. At any meal they would keep to the habit which some people found embarrassing even then, but which to them was as natural as picking up the

**New Deer kirk**
where the young
Stanley Rothney once
blew the organ.

knife and fork: they would say grace. On a Sunday the members would jump on their bike and pedal over to the kirk in New Deer. If you missed a Communion Sunday then that would be reckoned as a sin near to damnation. So I grew up with the kirk as an unquestioned part of my life. I go to it yet.

It was the Free Kirk at New Deer that the family went to. In those days, before the electricity came in, the organ had to be blown by hand and, as a young loon, that became my regular job. I would have to take up my place in a little curtained-off corner behind the organ and crank a wooden handle, just like a pump for bringing up water. But that old instrument could be a thrawn old besom and things were always likely to go wrong. You had to keep your wits about you; the fact that you were only a young loon made no difference.

The organist was a local farmer's wife, Mrs Walker, and she liked to play with some panache. The real problem was to get the strength and speed of your pumping just right – if you put in too much air there was a real danger of the organ bursting; too little and the tune might die away altogether into a sad wheeze and leave Mrs Walker floundering. Even if things began to go only a breath or two out, you came in for dirty looks. The best was something like the 23rd Psalm to the steady tune of Crimond. You could do that and let your thoughts wander.

**Stanley Rothney,** born 1923: New Deer

# The Sabbath had to be kept

The power of the Church was such that the Sabbath had to be kept. The Second World War did change things in many ways, but before it the day was strictly for church-going and the Sunday school. And as an elder, my father was expected to observe the day as one of rest. But this could be very frustrating if the rest of the week had been wet and windy while the Sabbath dawned bright and calm and the sheaves were out there waiting to be gathered in. I remember one especially beautiful Sunday with my father just itching to get out to his crop. He waited till it was dark and the fee'd loon was back; then they crept out and got to work. There was a lovely moon up and they managed to get through quite a bit. I knew nothing about it and we were all sworn to secrecy afterwards. I can remember waking up and looking out into the yard and seeing the stack half built and wondering how on earth that had got there.

**Arthur Watson,** born 1921: Tarves

**Never on a Sunday**
Arthur Watson's father
at the hairst,
October 1931

# A lost soul

We went to the Brethren, up until my granny died. We used to go to the Brethren meeting hall; for me that meant Sunday School and the meeting at night. Very uncomfortable the seats were and the meetings seemed interminable. The preacher would say, 'Our God and Father' and I'd count the number of times he did that, just to make the time go faster. You were bombed out of your mind with boredom; no allowances were made for the young ones.

My granny would pray every night, by the side of her bed, on her knees. I can see it yet: red brocade curtains on either side, the bunnin bed. I slept with her; I'd be in the bed, she would be there in her nightie with its little collar, down on her knees. Her hair was in pleats down her back. She'd go through the whole family and bless each one of them. Then she'd finish off with: 'Please, oh Lord, look after the sinful soul who lies beside me this night'. This was me, her granddaughter. Right up until I was 16 I would be 'the sinful soul'.

I mind the night we got news of the death of my Uncle Robert in the war. He was in the Clydebank blitz. Word came through at teatime that he'd been killed. Father had to go down to identify his brother's body. They wanted to tell Granny the news, but Father said, 'No, not tonight'. I was sleeping with Granny and I can hear her yet, on her knees that night, asking God to bless her son Robert and to keep him safe, along with the rest of her family. I had to turn away and hide my tears. It wasn't till the next day, after breakfast, they told her the news.

**Isabel Harrison,** born 1926: Buckie

**A lost soul
– but looking none
the worse for it**
Isabel in her early 20s

My granny would pray every night, by the side of her bed, on her knees. I can see it yet: red brocade curtains on either side, the bunnin bed.

# A very religious community

I grew up in a very religious community. We were a Methodist family – still are – and Sunday for me meant the morning service, followed by Sunday School at two o'clock and then we would all go to the evening worship at six o'clock. The day usually ended with the Deep Sea Mission, so I would be at four religious events every Sunday. In between these times, we were expected to observe the Sabbath. The most you could get away with would be to stuff a tennis ball into your pockets, disappear over the dunes and join in a surreptitious game of football with a few mates – and even at that you'd take care to clear any sand off your shoes before you went back into the house.

All this sounds grim, I know, but at the time I didn't resent it. I quite enjoyed those Sundays, the Mission particularly. The Sanky hymns were fine rousing pieces and I would sing along with enjoyment. And although the religion we heard from the pulpit was fairly judgemental, I wouldn't have called it punitive. You've got to remember the fear that drink held in such a community. I was brought up in a strictly teetotal household; my mother would have fainted at the merest whiff of a barmaid's apron. My grandfather did buy a bottle of port at New Year, but this was only so he could toast in the New Year if any of his cronies called by.

> In Peterhead there were some 30 pubs and it was common for men coming ashore with their 'settle up' money to go into them, straight off the boat, and not emerge until they had drunk most of the housekeeping money away.

Drink was frowned upon and there was a good reason for this. Before the war Buchanhaven, like most such fishing communities, saw a real abuse of alcohol. At the harbour side in Peterhead there were some 30 pubs and it was common for men coming ashore with their 'settle up' money to go into them, straight off the boat, and not emerge until they had drunk most of the housekeeping money away. So the kind of wariness towards drink which my parents showed was a natural reaction to all that. All along the coast there were various temperance movements such as the Band of Hope and they would come out and play their flute bands in places like St Combs and Inverallochy.

All that has left its mark on me; when I came into Aberdeen as a student I found it difficult to bring myself to have more than half a pint on an evening out. Even today I will usually have to stop after at the most a couple of glasses of wine. I have this ingrained fear of falling prey to the demon drink and losing control.

These attitudes fitted in with the general values of the community – honesty, thrift, hard work were practised as articles of belief. They went hand in hand with a tremendous community spirit. People looked out for each other. If you made a pot of soup then you would also ask yourself whether there was any of your neighbours in need of a drop or two as well. Much of this stemmed from the basic facts of the fishermen's lives: on board, the crew have to be able to trust each other implicitly – life or death could depend upon the ability to help each other promptly and selflessly.

Each Sunday evening about 11 o'clock onwards you'd see this steady procession of men going down to the harbour, ready to get on board so that the boat could sail at one minute past midnight – no fishing on the Sabbath! The whole of the Sunday evening would be overshadowed by that event. Early on there would be visits to friends and relatives and the serving up of tea in the best china, all set out on a finely laundered linen tablecloth. Then at nine or so it would be back to the house to pack and to prepare for the trip. When the men walked down to the boat, each would have a small kitbag slung on his back and this would contain his little treats for the trip – his tobacco or fags, some sweeties, a bottle of lemonade.

**Andrew Dick,** born 1936, Buchanhaven

## The minister calls 1

Our minister was Mr Crichton. He was a very caring man and he was considered to be a real pillar of the community. He would regularly visit his parishioners; the day of his visit, oh boy, that was the occasion for a massive cleaning operation in the house. The polish was out and the candlesticks would be made gleaming. The best crockery would appear and the finest biscuits too. There would be polite conversation: he would carefully ask everyone's health; he would enquire as to how the children were getting on at their school; he would comment on the weather. If anyone was unwell, he'd be round like a shot.

Oh yes, Mr Crichton was someone you'd look up to and respect. The present minister is a super guy, but it's different now: the minister is more human and you can have a two-way conversation with him. It's much less formal; he's one of us, but then the minister was a man apart and there was a sort of barrier around him. If I met Mr Crichton in the street he would always stop and ask, 'And how are you, Jack? Is your mother well – and your father? And how is your sister getting on at school? And isn't it cold for the time of year' – and so on. Now the chat can be about anything, about the Locos' latest performance, anything.

**Jack Hendry,** born 1925: Inverurie

## The minister calls **2**

The minister would expect to be addressed as 'sir'. Sundays were strictly kept. In those days the minister expected you all to attend his services; he would come to the house and enquire, 'I didn't see you at the church this Sunday. I trust that you haven't been unwell?'. The routine was to walk the two miles uphill to Benholm, rain, shine or snow, and to do it in your best clothes and good shoes, whatever the conditions. Then back to Johnshaven for Sunday School. After lunch there would be a family walk and then church again in the evening.

The afternoon walk was a grand affair. You'd be dressed up in your very best and for me that meant kilt and jacket. You'd walk along the shore and greet all the other families politely. You might come across Miss Scott out for her constitutional. She was the grand lady who lived at the Brotherton House. You'd be required to give her a salute as she swept along in her long skirt with gloves and handbag and always to refer to her as 'ma'am'. 'Good afternoon, ma'am!' After all she more or less owned the village; each householder had to pay her a feu annually. She once stopped, bent down and asked, 'You're the Beattie boy aren't you? You're mother was once the Beauty Queen, wasn't she? I remember seeing her – name of Lily, wasn't it?'-except that she pronounced 'Lily' in a strange anglified way. 'Yes, ma'am, thank you, ma'am,' is what I had to say.

**Douglas Beattie,** born 1930: Johnshaven

## The minister calls **3**

The minister was a fabulous figure. The church was a great centre: oh, we'd all be washed and brushed up and off to church on a Sunday. You could see the big church building sitting there, at the top of the village. Now, sadly – and I can hardly credit this – all that beautiful interior, that place of polish and red velvet, has gone. I loved the ritual of the place. John Pool was the minister and he rode around the village on a big, glossy, black horse. He was just out of this world. Most people only had Clydesdales

> The minister would come to the house and enquire, 'I didn't see you at the church this Sunday. I trust that you haven't been unwell?'

**Still dominating the village – but now a store for furniture.**
Mary Harvie's 'splendid' New Byth Church

or a sheltie, but he had a great, shiny, black horse and he would go around us all, astride it.

He had had a son who had been killed in the war and his wife had gone slowly mad over it. We used to go and visit him; the manse held a real library and he would allow us to take down books from the shelves and look through them. He had a great big desk and he would give us tea at it. I think of that house then as something like out of *Jane Eyre*, with him sitting downstairs entertaining us to tea and a mad wife upstairs.

John Pool had a marvellous way of speaking about things. He was well-educated and articulate in a way none of my family could have been. Nobody else in the village could command a voice like the one John Pool had. I didn't particularly like what he would preach, but, oh the voice! I resented the message that we were all natural sinners, but I loved the way I would be taken off into wonderful places by what happened in his church.

It's now a sad sight. The church has become the store-room for an auction house. It's full of junk. The villagers have to go to Cuminestown now for their worship. The manse has been bought by an outsider, someone from the West of Scotland.

**Mary Harvie,** born 1940: New Byth

# EARLY CENTURY LIVES: 3
## Molly Massie

**75th wedding anniversary**
George and Molly Massie

**Cranfield, 1912**
With father, mother and brother George

# Seventy-five years married

He sat there for ages, but still no sign of the mother — until there was this scuffling kind of noise and the woman came out from beneath the bed. 'Ah canna kip it in ony langer!', she said.

We've newly celebrated our 75th anniversary, my Bill and me. My father died when he was 34. It was a sudden death, just after the First World War when there was this epidemic of flu. He came home ill, one Monday, and died the following Monday. I was just 10 years of age.

He worked on a dairy farm and every day he would go into the city to sell milk. It used to be called Cranbog, but when the next farmer came he said, 'Bit Ah canna see ony bogs aboot the place,' so he called it Cranfield. But one night a friend of his daughter was out visiting and she said, 'Ye can ca it Cranbog an ye can ca it Cranfield an ye can ca it fat ye like, bit it'll aye be Aul Crannie!'

The farm was out on the Potterton road so he would have to get up really early, about four or so, winter and summer, jump on his bike and cycle out to it. Then he would come into Aberdeen with his horse and cart. The milk was in churns and they would go round from door to door. His boy would pour it into the customers' jugs.

The usual was to pay on the spot, but sometimes a customer would run up a bill. I mind him telling that there was this woman who flitted, without saying where to, and still in debt. Well, my father got the new address from one of her old neighbours. It was a tenement over in Torry, so one day, after he'd completed his round, he went over and knocked on the door. A boy opened it and told him that his mother was 'awa at the shops'. 'Weel, in that case, Ah'll jist cam in an' wait,' my father told him. The boy showed him into the room. He sat there for ages and ages, but still no sign of the mother – until at last there was this scuffling kind of noise and the woman came crawling out from beneath the bed. 'Ah canna kip it in ony langer!', she said.

I wasn't a strong child and if there was anything going I was sure to take it and I was aye the last one to return to school. When my father died I took the flu and all; I was 10 weeks off the school. Even when I got back it was half days only for a while. I remember the first day back and how queer it seemed to be walking up the road once more. I came home and said, 'De ye ken, Mither, fan I pit doon ma fit I felt it wis gaen to gae up throo the corner o' ma ee'.

Soon after when the teacher was getting me into trouble for chatting in class – I've aye had a long tongue ye ken – she said, 'And another thing, when I'm off ill I don't get to take half days when I return'. This upset me; it seemed so unfair that I started to cry, and after that the teacher was as nice as anything to me. That same teacher, I remember, one fine day when we were hard at our lessons and the spring sunshine was lighting up the outside, suddenly told us to stop what we were doing. She went over to the window, flung it open and said, 'Now, children, just listen to that!'. The school was next to a field and there was a farmer at his horse, ploughing up and down and whistling as he went. What a bonny whistle he had! That's what she wanted us to hear, the farmer at his work in the fine spring sunshine.

My father's death was a great shock to the family. Mother never remarried. She had to bring up three young children by herself as best she could. No pensions, no benefits in those days, so she had to take whatever work she could find. She would go to people's houses and do their washing and, sometimes, their baking.

One place she went to was a farmer's wife at the Bridge of Don – an awful fine wifie she was, too. One time, the woman next door asked her if she could call in and do her washing too, so she did. But after she'd finished, the woman said, 'And wid ye dae a bakin, too?' She did, but wasn't happy about all this extra work. When she returned the following week she told the first woman what had happened. It had been a real big wash – the woman had a few sons and the baking came on top of that. Well, the first woman went to the other one and told her off: 'Ye jist didna thunk!' She'd never thought about what it was like to be a widow with three young children and her own home to run. And washing in those days was hard, hard work – no machines, no electricity, only the heating up of the boiler, the scrubbing board, the bar of soap and the mangle. And I doubt she got more than a few coppers for it all.

Like any mother in those days, mine was kept busy: baking, sewing, knitting, washing, cleaning – the work was never done. The children of the house had to start on household tasks very young. When my father was alive my brother and I had the job of polishing his boots. He had to be smartly turned out for the dairy deliveries. One day my brother complained: 'That quine aye gits the cleanest beet,'. 'Weel,' my mother said, 'there's ane wye tae fix that – from noo on she'll tak the left beet an ye'll tak the right ane.' So that's what we did.

But we did have some fun. We'd play ludo, cards and there was snakes-and-ladders. And we had a big gramophone with a horn. I'd listen to any music that was going. When we have a sing-song in the home [Haven Court, Stonehaven] I tell them, 'Ah canna sing ony mair, bit Ah can remember aa the words'.

After school I got a job as a maid at Ardoe House, Belhelvie. The lady of the house was Miss Harvie. She had a cousin who'd been a captain in the war; he'd lost a leg, but he could still drive around. My first wage was £5 for six months; I lived in and we were well enough fed. My job was to keep the house clean. There was also a cook and another housemaid, as well as a gardener.

Miss Harvie was nice to me, though it was the cook who gave me my orders. As well as the £5, the Captain gave me a pound and his wife a ten-shilling note. I was able to buy a bike. The cook and us two maids all slept in the one room: she got the single bed and we had a double one. I had to wear a white apron and be smartly turned out. I was always going around for fear that I'd be spilling something on that lovely white apron.

**At the teacher's house, Potterton**
Molly centre, with sister Margaret and young school friend.

Washing in those days was hard, hard work — no machines, no electricity, only the heating up of the boiler, the scrubbing board, the bar of soap and the mangle.

**Cranfield, 1918**
11-year old Molly with father (back row), mother (front row), uncle, cousin and sister Margaret.

Miss Harvie held a service for the staff in the kitchen and we all had to attend. You had to take your turn in reading out bits from the Bible. The Captain was very good about this: if ever we came to a difficult name, he'd just take over the reading without any fuss and help us out. He was a real gentleman. We were also expected to go to the church each Sunday. Once my bike got a puncture and there I was thinking to myself, 'Good, noo I winna hae to gae tae the kirk, efter aa'. I was just turning back when the Captain came by in his car and stopped. 'A puncture, Mary? Well, just put your bicycle behind that tree and get in. I'll see you get to the church; don't you worry about that.'

But I was only the six months at Ardoe House. I went to work on the farms and I ended up at Cranfield, doing the cleaning and the milking. The men would come into the kitchen. We'd meet them coming in for their breakfast just as we were going out to the byres. But on a Sunday we all had our porridge together. One Easter the men were talking about how they would be going into the town for their Saturday night out; I said, 'Weel, mind tae bring an Easter egg back fer me'.

Well, come the next Sunday, I came in and all the men were sitting there, and when I came to take my seat they all started laughing. I looked into my bowl and there was a chocolate egg, melting into my porridge. That wasn't all; I found other eggs lying around in other places waiting for me. They'd all got one for me. Later, when I arrived home for my Sunday visit, there was my grandfather standing at the door with yet another Easter egg for me. So, I'm telling you, I got plenty eggs that Easter!

We had a lot of fun, more than I could ever have had at Ardoe House. There'd be music in the evenings; some of the men played mouth organs or melodeons and we all gathered round the fire to sing along. But there was aye plenty work to do; everything had to be done by hand. There was the big concrete floor where all the muddy boots had been; I had to get down on my hands and knees and just scrub and scrub. You had to go into the yard and fill your bucket from the pump.

You had to do cooking and baking. One of our jobs was to make butter. There were big basins and all the milk was poured into them; You let them stand for a day and then

the cream was skimmed off and put into the churn for turning. We had to make pancakes and scones. You learned all that just as a matter of course; no recipes, just a 'pucklie this' and a 'pucklie that'. The men were aye well fed at Cranfield.

I slept in a room above the kitchen. I kept my clothes behind a curtain on a rail which made a sort of screen; I had to keep a nice dress for the kirk. We washed our hair at the pump in soap and cold water. No make-up; I was that bonny I didn't need any of that!

It was at Cranfield that I met Bill; he was a horseman on the farm. We'd actually been at Potterton School together, but we'd lost touch. Now here we were together again. We married: it was 1932. Our wedding was nothing fancy; we just got married at home. I wore my brown dress; there was a nice meal that my mother set out for us, but just for the families. And for our honeymoon, well, we were back at work the next day. We hadn't the money for anything else.

You can see the card from the Queen for our 75th anniversary: we got one for the 70th too and that says, 'Congratulations on your Platinum Anniversary,' but the 75th just says, 'Congratulations on reaching this remarkable milestone'. They've run out of names for the length of time we've been wed, I doubt.

What's the secret of staying together for so long? Look, I've no idea how all that has come about. It just happened. You have your ups and downs, of course, and you have to ride through them. We've had our disagreements, but we've aye managed to get over them. That's just life isn't it?

**Molly Massie,** born 1908: Belhelvie

**Fancy dress at Potterton School, 1920**
Molly is the milkmaid holding her stool, second row left.

GRAMPIAN LIVES: 1900–1950

# LIFE WAS HARD

'A pretty open society.'
The High Street, Strichen
around 1900.

# A country vet

Half the time he never got paid. Mother would tell him that he should at least ask for something in return, like half-a-dozen eggs or a chicken, but he would always tell her, 'Oh no, I canna do that! Folks are so poor these days'.

My father had done very well in his veterinary courses; he'd won medals at the Royal Dick College in Edinburgh. When the war broke out he went out to the trenches in Flanders as part of the Veterinary Corps and he would tell us how terrible the whole experience had been for the animals as well as the men – the noise, the mud, the flares, the constant sense of confusion.

After the war he settled in Strichen. Life wasn't easy for a country vet in those days. Farming in the 1920s and '30s was at a very low ebb and quite often Dad would come home and say that so-and-so's horse had died and the farmer hadn't been able to afford the cost of the insurance. 'Of course, I couldn't charge him anything,' he'd say. He was very soft hearted that way. He was very fond of all animals; at home we kept a whole menagerie – cats, dogs, rabbits, a guinea pig.

He never failed to answer a call, but in those days it wasn't like now when you take your cat or your dog to the vet's and pay on the spot. He would have to send out accounts and half the time he never got paid. Mother would tell him that he should at least ask for something in return, like half-a-dozen eggs or a chicken, but he would always tell her, 'Oh no, I canna do that! Folks are so poor these days'. And in those days when the vet had to see to the doctor's dog, he never sent in any bill at all. In those days, you see, professional people didn't charge each other.

Strichen was a pretty open society between the wars. We all mixed together although there were one or two people who liked to put on airs and graces a bit. The banker's daughter used to act a bit toffee nosed and then there was one lady whose husband ran one of the grocer's shops. She always made a point of speaking in this oh-so-nace posh voice – 'like thet, don't-you-know' – and with all the local usages wiped clean away, or so she liked to think. One afternoon, a woman from the village called on her and found she was entertaining some neighbours to a cup of tea in her kitchen. 'Oh do come in,' she cried, 'and join us. We're just taking our home-over cup of tea.' The rest of Strichen called it a 'hame-ower cuppie' and from that day on, people in the village would take great delight in talking about going up to Mrs S, in order 'to partake of her home-over tea'.

But really Buchan was a democratic area, much more than I've found Angus, where I now live. On the whole nobody thought themselves to be better than their neighbour. The estates and the farms were smaller and folk saw themselves as working together. Then there was the language: in my childhood all classes would freely speak to each other in their native Doric tongue – even the lawyers did – and that was a great equaliser.

Certainly as children we all played and mixed together. One family lived just across the lane from us. A big family in a small house, packed with us children. Practically every night in the winter, I would go across and sit with them all at the kitchen table under the paraffin lamp and play at cards or draughts or whatever. There was a bed in the corner of the kitchen and Mr Emslie – we all called him Jake – would be in it trying to get his sleep and we would be sitting there all together, shouting at our games and laughing and crying out 'Snap!'.

**Catherine Strachan,** born 1915: Strichen

# They left school early

We all got on well together, the cottar bairns and ourselves. I've still got one friend from that time. She came out of a large family: nine of them in two rooms – can you imagine that! The cottars married early, you see: the girls would go for it to get away from their work. They would leave school at 14 and go straight into service. Some of them were bad used by the farmers; some of them would end up pregnant. This friend of mine talks about it still; she had a bitch of a wifie as her boss. As for the boys, they would leave at 14 and go straight onto the farm. At that age they might be in charge of a pair of Clydesdales and would be sleeping out in the bothy, along with the men.

They just couldn't afford to stay on at the school, you see.

**Winnie Brown,** born 1916: Inverugie

# A private laundry

My mother ran a private laundry. Most of her business came from the big houses in Huntly, the private houses where the doctors, the lawyers and the businessmen lived – all the big shots.

There was an extension off the kitchen and that's where she did the work. That was a big business in those days, taking in people's washing. And a jolly hard one too, I can tell you! You had to light the boiler and then you had to fill it and stoke it and keep the thing going. You'd stand for hours and hours at the washtub, rubbing and scrubbing away. The boiler was in one corner and you had to go from it to the tub, backwards and forwards to fill it and to empty it. There were no pipes to connect the boiler to the tub; no one seemed to have thought of that. I think they just expected the laundry business to be hard work and it certainly was. We used bars of Sunlight soap to get the clothes clean, no fancy powders in those days but just these big bars of soap that came in boxes of 48. You had to scrub and scrub till your hands got red and raw. But they were aye clean; I'll tell you that.

Life was very hard for my mother. She had divorced my father and we saw nothing of him. Divorce was very unusual in those days; in fact, she was the very first lady to do it in Huntly. She would never speak of the reasons and as a child I knew very little about it. I was two when she did it. My father was a complete blank in my life; he had nothing to do with us and he never paid a penny towards our support. And no State handouts either, oh no, there was nothing like that! So my mother was left with two young children to bring up single-handed: my brother and me. I was only two at the time of the separation.

Mother worked hard; we managed to get by. Good honest, plain food. And hand-me-downs for my clothes, that's what we had. Mr Ewen, the tailor, he would take my aunt's cast-offs and turn them and take them up so as to fit me. I did resent it, but I was always turned out quite smartly, weekdays as well as Sundays.

As for holidays, well I can only remember one day's picnic outing to Banff and I was sick. We went by the train and I got very travel sick, and that was my big day out. I just

> We used bars of Sunlight soap to get the clothes clean – big bars of soap that came in boxes of 48. You had to scrub and scrub till your hands got red and raw. But they were aye clean; I'll tell you that.

hadn't been accustomed to travelling, you see. We did have some games in the house like ludo and snakes-and-ladders but strictly no playing cards, not at 54 King Street, oh no! They were sinful, you see. Discipline was strict, very strict: if my mother judged I had done anything wrong then out came the big size 10 slipper. I remember once telling my brother to sit on a bee and, of course, he got stung – and so did I, by the big slipper on my backside!

Helen Benzie, born 1919: Huntly

## Politics on an upland farm

I was born at Upper Jericho, Culsalmond, 1919. This was a small hill farm. Life was hard; my mother had to go out and hoe the neeps while I was still a wee bairn. She aye tellt me how she would wrap me up in a shawl and put me down at the end of the drill while she got on with the hoeing. She was aye hoping that someone would come along and pinch me, but no such luck! And when you look at me, you couldn't blame her, could you?

On the farm in the early 1920s, there was no money to play around with. Just human misery, it was. The Tories were in power and you know how much they did for the poorer classes. I've aye voted Liberal myself and could never understand how it was that some folk could be persuaded that voting Tory was the wise thing to do. Why, the Tory Party even managed to persuade my wife's granny to hand over a half-crown for party funds; the puir crater didn't realise what she was doing but that's the way the Tory party worked – they just exploited folks' ignorance. My own granny would aye get a hurl in the Tory candidate's car on Election Day so she could get to the polling station and cast her vote – but what she never told him was that once she got there it was the Liberal mannnie that got her cross.

I went to the Glens of Foudland School – the 'Glen Academy', that's what we called it. We did that to give it a wee bit of class, you see, our wee school up in the glen. But my own education was strictly basic. There was a map on the wall of the world and we had to pay attention to how much of it was coloured red. On May 24 we had to go outside and salute the flag – Empire Day. Then this big fat major mannie, Major Bisset, visited the school, all got up in his kilt, and we would have to stand there to attention while he addressed us with some inspiring words of 'Blah, blah, blah!'.

I swore that if I ever had children of my own I would do everything in my power to make sure they got a good education and Helen agreed with me on that. Our son is Professor in Gynaecology & Obstetrics at the University of Sydney. Our daughter took her MA degree, later gaining an Honours degree in English through the Open University. We've never grudged a penny that went to our two children's education.

There was a lot of class division in those days. I was actually dux at the Glen Academy, but there was no way the family budget would have let me carry on with my education,

My granny would aye get a hurl in the Tory candidate's car on Election Day so she could get to the polling station and cast her vote — but what she never told him was that once she got there it was the Liberal mannnie that got her cross.

so I had to leave at 14 and go out to earn my own living. If you had money then you got the opportunities; if not, then it was a matter of luck and family sacrifice. I remember there was this young chap who had no brains, but got to the varsity all right. He would fly around Huntly in his smart sports car, but could make nothing of his life. He was a fine enough lad, but no real use to anyone. His good education was wasted on him. All he was doing was to take up a place that some poorer loon could have made something of.

**Jack Benzie,** born 1919: Glens of Foudland

# Foraging for yourself

I was born at Crimond in 1920. See, I'm at the age when I can now speak about it! A working class family; my father was practically a jack-of-all-trades. He was very good with his hands. He was an engineer, a ship's engineer. In the First World War; he was there all through the war, in the minesweepers. Then after the war, his main job was in the quarries, them country quarries where they're making the granite stones for the roads. In between times, when the jobs were scarce, he went on the fishing boats, to Lowestoft and Yarmouth – all down the East Coast. He took whatever jobs were going.

My grandfather had a farm and he worked on that for a while and when the time came that there were too many of them at home, and the farm work was scarce – this was during the 1920s, remember, and times were hard, real hard; he had a lot of brothers, see, a big family, 11 of them there were – and then he would go from farm to farm and ask, 'D'ye wint drainin dane to yer fields?'. So, whatever jobs were going, he just did them. He went and asked for them. He was never on the dole or anything like that. And then at night – if we was needing my shoes repaired – he would mend them, and he did that right up to the time when I was working.

Whenever we went back to school, we always had new boots, but a new blazer, well that might be more difficult – unless the rabbits were plentiful. There were always rabbits to be found about the Mormond Hill and so they went in for a bit of poaching. Self-help, that's what it was, what you call foraging.

**Violet Cassie,** born 1920: Strichen area

> Whenever we went back to school, we always had new boots, but a new blazer, well that might be more difficult – unless the rabbits were plentiful. There were always rabbits to be found. Self-help, that's what it was.

# My life was all about work

I was born on a farm, near Tarves. My father was a farm servant in those days. Then we went to the Turriff area and he left farming and went to drive lorries. I was never academic and school didn't mean much to me. As soon as I got to 14 I was out the door. My life was all about work. All my life really, I've been a worker. We were very poor. I've seen me as a young boy, having to go up to the boss's wife to ask money for my mother to buy the groceries with. He just wasn't getting paid his wages – and they were

**John Duncan**
With Granny and sister Madge, Cuminestown around 1927

**Ready for anything**
John about to leave school and take on the world of work.

only £2 a week. There were no unions to help people like my father in those days.

I worked all through the time I was at school. We stayed beside the mart at Turriff. There was this woman who kept a little house beside it and she would make meals for the farmers and the lorry drivers who came to the mart. So I used to get up early in the morning and run messages for her. I would go to the butcher and the grocer for her. All this before I went to the school. I would get a penny, one old penny, per message. Then at night, I would go after school and polish her lobby, with Mansion polish. I was seven at the time. I remember one time this lady, she was catering for a dance and she asked if I would come along and help serve the stuff and do the washing of the dishes and she gave me a 10-shilling note. My mother was shocked: 'Fancy that – 10 whole shillings!'. To her it was riches.

There was a lot of poverty in the country districts then. I would see it when I went around the farms with my father and his lorry. The cottar house folk were really poor, awful poorly paid for all that they did. My own father had had it very hard when he was growing up. He didn't have a proper father himself; his mother was what was called a kitchie dame and the farmer there had knocked her up. There were three children altogether: two were lassies and my father was the boy. He had to help about the farm from the very start. When the hairst was on and they took on extra workers he couldn't even get a place to sleep indoors. He would just have to go and look for somewhere to sleep under a ruck or a hedge, anywhere he could. He actually got rickets because of the poor diet; he had rounded shoulders as a man.

I can't say it was as bad for me. I never actually went without. My mother always found something for me and I was always a big lad for my age, so I could work. I handed over any wages I got, but I would keep the tips for myself. That lady I cleaned the floor for would sometimes drop me a penny or two and I would spend them on a lucky apple or something – in the hope of getting another penny. I never resented any of this. My mother shielded me from the worst.

I didn't have the hard time my father did. I hardly saw anything of him, apart from the work. He had to work right round the clock, morning, afternoon and night. After school I would go down to the crossroads and wait for his lorry, so as I could go around and give him a hand with his deliveries. Sometimes I would wait there for a couple of hours, winter or summer. He just expected me to be there. I couldn't go off with my pals then, but I never resented it. I just accepted that that was the way things were.

The first house we lived in was over by the Green at Cuminestown. We had a dry lavvy and it just stank to high heaven. Mother did her best to keep it clean with disinfectant. It was just a shed at the bottom of the garden where my father grew tatties. They were great tatties though! We had no electricity – gas lamps. Look, you can see a cut on my finger and that's from when my mother was lighting the lamp and I was sitting by the fireside and she dropped the glass and it shattered. One of the shards flew over into my finger. That was more than 80 years ago and I've got the mark on me yet.

But, you know, I had a good childhood. I had plenty of pals. We would play football

and cricket. We would go for walks. On a Sunday we might walk over to Banff, and that was 12 miles there and back. We'd just jump into a field and pinch a neep or two and that would be our dinner. It was a business to survive because my father's wages were so very poor. But he was never scared of work. It's funny, but when I look in the mirror now that's who I see looking back at me, my father.

John Duncan, born 1923: Cuminestown

**Into the city**
The young message boy, Union Street, Aberdeen around 1935.

# A frugal existence

I was born in the parish of Old Deer, at a place called West Lodge, Pitfour, Pitfour being a large estate. My father had fought in the First World War with the Gordon Highlanders and was wounded three times in the trenches.

My mother had left school to go into the Big House at Pitfour, to work downstairs, but when the war came she graduated to the clerk's post at Mintlaw Junction, the post falling open with the absence of men off to the war. She was basically a hard working, capable country girl. She had attended Torphins School which, as was usual then, she had left at 14.

After her schooling, she'd started out as a lowly skiffy downstairs at Pitfour House, but she was a capable, clever woman and when in the First World War all the men were away at the Front and the railways were crying out for labour, she'd been able to land this post.

**'You can easily tell who was the doctor's or the minister's sons.'**
Look at the back row. Strichen School 1931. Stanley Rothney is third from right, back row.

Her days in the Big House had also given her a basic grounding in how things should be done: how to set out a table and how to address people. And the curriculum then was much more suited to the artisan class than all the airy-fairy stuff that came in later. At her school she learned baking and all sorts of domestic skills. She was also given a thorough grounding in the basics; her handwriting was immaculate and this stood her in good stead when she came to work for the railway.

She and my father met when he had returned from the war. The Rothneys are thirled to the land and my forebears would have all been agricultural workers of one kind or another. But by my father's generation, they were beginning to spread their wings a bit and to look to better themselves. I think that's why my father went into the railways; it wasn't well paid, but it was a good secure job. He received £2.10 weekly and, believe me, in those days there was a world of difference between a flat £2 and £2.10. He became a signalman at Brucklay, on the old Buchan line, first stop north up from Maud. All the rails have now been lifted following the Beeching cuts, but when I was growing up that line and Maud Junction seemed to me to be the very hub of the universe.

I'm the oldest in our family. I'm the first born of six children: two girls and four boys. This meant eight mouths to feed from the £2 10 shillings per week. To keep us all from starvation my father augmented his meagre income by taking the post of beadle at the Free Kirk in New Deer. The extra was enough to keep us all in footwear for the 12 months.

Life was very frugal. I grew up with the air blawin through ma breeks. The furniture was what you would call basic: our bedside cabinet was an old, upturned orange box and the divisions within the bedroom were made up by an old curtain that my mother sewed up. Washing was a feat of domestic improvisation. On Mondays after school I would be sent off with a box surmounted on an old pram chassis to scour the woods for sticks that could be used to light the fire for the next day. This was the week's washday. Mother would then go out into the yard at the side of the house and get the fire going between three big black stones with an large pot of water over it, for all the world like an old witches' cauldron. This she had to do all the year round whatever the conditions. There was no running water in the house, but we were privileged to have a tap outside, though its water was not fit for human consumption; for that you had to go and use the wooden pump that raised up fresh spring water.

Our diet was basic. There was a lot of oatmeal and plenty tatties. We also got a lot of fish. Hawkers would come to the door in some old car loaded with a box or two of herring they had picked up at Fraserburgh – but, really, as the signalman's family, we didn't want for free fish. The fish would be loaded on trains at Fraserburgh and they would pass through Brucklay and Maud. There would be 'fishers' – special fish trains thundering their way south with a load of fresh fish to sell in the markets of the big cities, like Billingsgate in London. But often enough, the fish would be loaded onto a truck or two of a slower, more local train that was due to stop at Brucklay, and then the driver or the guard would be likely to hand over a herring or two, which would be part of what they had picked up at Fraserburgh. On the quay and on the station near the harbour, there would always be plenty of fish slapping around and spilling over the open boxes; they were regarded as free pickings for anyone connected with their transport. The driver would then, like as not, string a few fish through their gills and say, 'These'll dae fer Alec Rothney at Brucklay'.

I was brought up in the Depression years of the 20s and early 30s. You only have to look at the photos of us all to see how poorly clad we all were. In the school photo at Strichen, you can easily pick out the doctor's and the minister's sons – they were the only well dressed ones. But poverty is a relative concept and when everyone is the same then no one feels especially hard up and so it was with us. We were poor, but we didn't think about it much. We just got on with what life threw at us, as our neighbours did and everyone else we knew around us – except, of course, the laird's family and those of the minister and the doctor.

**Stanley Rothney,** born 1923: Brucklay

## Any job going

My father came from farming stock and he was fee'd as a young man. In the First World War he'd volunteered into the Gordons and when he came back there was nothing else he could find but to take up the farm work again.

Then he tried the insurance business for a while. Then my mother's uncle invited him to join him in his contracting business. They would take on all sorts of tasks, like erecting the stands for the Games or, on one occasion, shifting the safe for the local banks. They would take their picks and shovels and dig out new water supplies, take on the task of shoring up the Dee, or join the gang laying out a new golf course – just anything for a job and a bit of cash.

> On the quay and on the station near the harbour, there would always be plenty of fish slapping around and spilling over the open boxes; they were regarded as free pickings for anyone connected with their transport.

**Joining the gang laying out a golf course**

Glenloshie 1921. Jean Lawrie's great uncles – Alexander and Duncan Fowler – at the end, left, sporting the pickiesae hats to denote their 'boss' status

That was all right during the summer months, but in the winter the work would dry up. In those days to take the dole was a great stigma, but sometimes he just had to. Mother would buy up food stocks in the summer to help tide us over those months. She would take on any small occasional job to do with her cooking and sewing skills. Often one of the faite iron [tin-plate; would-be grand] families would be holding a dinner party and they would ask her to come in and do the cooking for it. These were the kind of houses that really only ran to one little maid, so she would come through the back door, into the kitchen, quietly set about preparing a five-course meal which would be served by the regular maid and then she'd slip away again usually with a half-crown for her evening's work.

**Jean Lawrie,** born 1924: Birse and Aboyne

**Shoring up the banks of the Dee at Dess**

Jean's father is directly under the hook; Laird Davidson has the plus-fours

# From servant to secretary

Mum, she was 42 when I was born. She was the third youngest of a family of fourteen. She was born at Kinellar and at that time all her sisters went into service and her brothers, the five brothers, all went abroad. None of them ever came back. But in 1901, Mum left school and she cleaned her bike and cycled the nine miles to Aberdeen to go to Webster's secretarial classes. She insisted on doing that instead of going into service like the rest. She actually refused to do that, actually refused! Each day she rattled over the Tyrebagger and into Aberdeen. It wasn't a very good road in those days, but there were no motor vehicles to watch out for.

She then went into employment and, of course, got better pay than she would ever have got in service. She was at four different places in Aberdeen in her 17 years there. She was at the Central Mart at Kittybrewster. She was junior to the cashier there and handled all the money. At that time everyone paid cash – £20 for a bullock, £10 for a ewe – they just paid it out.

She didn't get married till after the First World War, 1919. She was married in Inverurie and came to the farm of Newcraig; she thought she was in for a life of leisure, because for the first four years things were good. But then came the collapse of 1923 and that halved the price of their stock when they'd only newly got on their feet. And she had two daughters by that time, because my sisters had been born by then. So she had no option but to put her hand to it. She had two housemaids when she first went into her own farmhouse. But they had to go. It wasn't just the cleaning either – you've got to remember that in those days the men who worked on the farm got fed in the farmhouse, they got three square meals a day in the house. So my mother suddenly had it hard.

**Alan Morrison,** born 1930: Daviot

> In 1901, Mum left school and she cleaned her bike and cycled the nine miles to Webster's secretarial classes in Aberdeen. She insisted on doing that instead of going into service.

# Fourteen in the family

My father started as a farm servant. I was one of 12, bang in the middle of them all, so he was needing a larger house for us all. That's when he took a farm over Lumphanan way and became a tenant farmer.

How they both managed it all I often wonder. All I know is it worked out all right at the time. Father was a good provider for us all. There was never a butcher's shop and never a coal merchant in Lumphanan that ever got our custom. He'd go out into the woods and come back with what was needed. It was a case of pheasants, hares, rabbits, grouse – you could call him poacher, I suppose, but it was all out of sheer necessity. He'd go out with his gun and come back with what was needed.

There wasn't running water in the house, never. We'd to go a quarter of a mile for our water. Ah well, just, that's what we had. There wasn't just water for the house to fetch, but for the animals, too. A never-ending task. We'd take hares down to the well and skin and wash them there to save the journey with the full buckets of water. It wasn't till after the war that my parents ever knew what it was like to be able to turn on a tap and see water coming out of it in their own home.

**'Fourteen bodies in one wee hoose'**
The Lawries at a family reunion in later life. George is front row extreme right. The occasion was Mr and Mrs John and Jean Lawrie's Golden Wedding, 1952.

My mother was an excellent home manager. She was a great baker – oatcakes, scones, pancakes – and all on the open fire with the girdle. We never starved, but I was meagrely dressed. As the sixth all I got were hand-me-downs, stuff that had been patched and mended time and again. We all had our jobs to do as we got older. Mine was chopping the sticks and getting them in. And we all had to take our turn in going off with the bucket to fetch another load of water.

You'd to walk three miles to the school – no other option. It was just a cart-track and in the snow – and we had real storms in them days – you'd be walking along on top of the snow when suddenly, 'pumpf!' you'd be falling through a drift and the others would have to pull you out and you'd get to the school with your clothes all soaked through.

My parents gave us all a good upbringing, oh aye. There were 14 bodies in the one house, but we all found somewhere to lay down our head. It would be a case of top and tail, all in the bed together. You kept warm! It all seems quite hard now, but at the time it never seemed to us that we might be suffering in any way. Everyone was in much the same boat. You'd go to the school in patched trousers and battered sheen, but you'd look around and see the others in the class were much the same. I mind once coming home with a full jotter and telling my parents I needed a new one – they just handed me a rubber and told me to get on with it. In those days such things weren't provided by the school; you had to buy all that. When the teacher held a wee competition, she would offer a jotter as the prize. I can't imagine any kid these days being thrilled by that, can you?

My father and my mother just had to work and work. He didn't even get much of a retirement. You could say he died of sheer exhaustion. He'd spent a lifetime doing as much as he could to turn a penny. On the farm he would take a broom dog to the sides of the fields to get as much under the plough as he could. He'd take this fork to pull out the roots of broom and that was real punishing work, I can tell you. He was done by the time he was 65 and no wonder.

You just had to use whatever came to hand in those days. The farm had wet, sour kind of soil; you'd sow in the grains and they'd aye be shifting. We couldn't buy in fertilisers so the dung from the cattle had to be spread over the fields. Father would go to the mart and come back with a 'leg horse': this was some old clapped-out horse that could just about be used for half a day's work at a time – it was too old and done for more, but he could get it for £5 and it would have to do. Then we'd go to the old ruined crofts round about and take the lime out of the stones. That was used as grit for the hens. Waste not want not. You'd go up the hill and cut down bracken and Father would build up a ruck so we'd have bedding aye handy for the cattle. Or I'd cut down ferns to get cover for the tattie pits. I'd go over the ground after the hairst with a smiler rake so as to get up every bit of straw I could – bedding again.

In the house, you had cement floors; no need for a hoover – a brush would do the job. You'd put a sack down and that would be your carpet. We had a caff saik bed – an old hessian sack full of chaff from the threshing mill – and we'd all wriggle into that. It was fine and warm – just the job as long as there were no thistles in it. There were so many of us that some had to just bed down on the floor in a shakkin doon.

When I think of the kind of society we live in now where folk just throw away clothes and food and without a thought to how they might still be used, well I often think that my parents could have lived oot o amang the fingers of the folk today – the stuff they just pick up and throw away as rubbish. Jean and I get quite amused when we hear Gordon Brown going on about 'prudence'. It's an old fashioned kind of message, but that's the way we had to live then – prudence, taking care, using up whatever's to hand. Nobody seems to believe in thrift or saving up now, but that's the way we were brought up. We've aye paid cash up front; now when they ask for your credit card and you tell them you haven't got one, they look at you as if you must be stupid.

I left the school at 13½. In those days you could get exemption that let you off the last six months before the leaving age. You had to stay at home during that time; those were the conditions. My parents were keen to get me away from the school as soon as possible, so I could help about the house and on the farm. None of the 12 of us ever got the chance to go on at school; the family budget just wouldn't run to it.

In later life only two of us went very far away: a sister went to Australia and my eldest brother went down to London, but the other 10 all got jobs all round about, mostly in farming or trades connected with the land in some way. Right up till our parents died we would always be there for them and for each other. There wasn't one of us but our parents knew they could turn to and there wasn't one who wouldn't give over a pound to another if the need was there.

**Jean:** One of the saddest experiences I ever had was when George's parents retired

'It was what a country boy did in those days'
George in 1950, aged 18

We had a caff saik bed full of chaff from the threshing mill and we'd all wriggle into that. It was fine and warm – just the job as long as there were no thistles in it.

from the farm and we were helping with the packing up. George's mother handed me the certificate which granted him his exemption to leave school early and do you know, she handed it over to me as if it was an honours degree. That was all he had to show for his years at the Lumphanan School; a certificate of exemption.

**George:** It was the lack of money and all the work that had to be done. School meant clothes to be bought, jotters and pencils to be got. They needed me at home as soon as possible to keep the farm going. They did their best with what they'd got. We were all given a good upbringing and with good homely food aye on the table. We were a loving family.

I got a job at the mill for £1 a week and my keep. The first thing I did was save up to get a Sunday suit. I went to MacKay's in Union Street and bought a second hand RAF suit; it cost all of £2. I was so proud of it that I would hang it up in the bothy covered in paper to protect it. The next was to get a pair of new sheen. I would polish and polish them till you could see your own face in the black leather uppers. Up till then I'd just had to go around in cast-offs; all I had was just what you stood up in.

**Jean:** When we got married and George's mother was round at the house, I opened the wardrobe door and she looked at what was inside and she said, 'Dae aa thae claes belang to oor George?'. In those days you just had the one change of underclothing which had to washed and changed, turn about. And George's mother washed his clothes right up till the day of his marriage. She would charge him for it. I remember when he got married she said to him, 'Mind ye owe me fer three manths' washin'. But she had no real alternative: he was earning and she had so very little for herself.

**George and Jean Lawrie,** born 1931 and 1924: Lumphanan

## It was hard on my mother

When I was eight the family moved to Glenlivet where my father became the grieve at Drumin Farm. Things went well for a time until he was struck down by TB of the spine; he was admitted to Woodend Hospital, Aberdeen, and spent 21 months there. My brother had to leave school at the age of 13 to help support the family.

My mother had to cook for five or six farmworkers and when the threshing came round I can remember as many as 18 getting a midday meal from her. She also had to milk two or three cows morning and night so as to supply the farmhouse and workers. My mother was a good cook; I can still see the huge black kettle hanging on the crook above the fire, so that there was always a welcoming cup for any callers. She did all her own baking on a girdle on an open fire – oatcakes, scones and pancakes – twice weekly. I remember seeing them all lined up on the kitchen table, dozens of them, but within a day or two they'd be all gone.

The farmworkers came in for their meals always spot on time and in order: foreman,

**A hard day's work**
Hoeing with his future brother-in-law and female labourer, Braes of Glenlivet in 1949

second horseman, tractor man, orraman, cattleman taking up the rear – and they left the table in the exact same order. Breakfast was at 6.30, lunch at 11.30, tea at 5.15 and always on the dot. It was important to have a good pocket watch, along with a good pair of tackety boots and oilskin leggings. Good timekeeping was the order of the day and lateness was just not tolerated. Breakfast would consist of brose, milk, bread and tea. Midday meal would be soup, beef and potatoes and pudding, though sometimes rabbit would substitute for the beef as they were in abundance on the farm and some of the workers would shoot them for food. Tea was usually porridge, boiled egg and plenty oatcakes, cheese, bread and scones.

With hungry men to keep fed the cupboards had to be well stocked. We were well catered for mobile vans down from Tomintoul or Aberlour and Dufftown. I can remember my mother coming in with an armful of loaves – no wrappers in those days. Oatmeal, milk and potatoes were supplied by the farmer as perquisites.

Through all this my mother visited my father in hospital every second Saturday. To accomplish this she had leave at 8.30 to get the service bus to Dufftown station; the train arrived in Aberdeen at midday and then she would get the tram to Hazelhead and then walk the rest of the way to the hospital at Woodend. The visit would last an hour before she had to set off on the return journey, without any time for even a cup of tea. Children under the age of 14 weren't allowed to visit, so I never saw my father all the time he was

**Carrying on the family business**
Charlie Gammack in his workshop, 2006

What a great thing the hoe was. The big farmers from the estates at Kinermony and at Ballindalloch, they'd come in and get half dozen done at the start of the season.

away in hospital. When he came out he had to convalesce for several months before he could resume his duties, wearing a spinal jacket. The fact that he was able to do this at all was due to the hard work my mother had put in to keep things going.

The irony of it all is that she died at the age of 52, struck down by cancer, while my father lived till he was 78.

John Goodbrand, born 1932: Glenlivet

# The saddler's shop

The first item my father sold when he came here was binder rivets and tacks. It was for a farmer who was repairing his own binder. 'Sixpence,' and it had to be entered into the book. As my mother said, 'We couldna hae started wi much less'. There it lay for maybe six months; bills were settled on the term dates, November and May. It's sad looking through the old books. 'Harness repair, one shilling'; 'Bus to Knockando, sixpence.' Small sad amounts- – and they all had to be entered into the book, done properly.

Then the war came and horses began going out. He expanded into the ironmongery side of things. He started out with bits and pieces – stable brooms, pots and pans, hoes. Over the years the saddler business went down and the ironmongery went up. But he had a lot of work for the estates, all the game bags and repair work connected with the shooting. Then, something like binder cloths were big business too: 500 a year in those days. It was hard, hard work.

There were very few cars in Aberlour, scarcely a vehicle of any kind to be seen. When I was a boy you could sledge right down the doctor's brae and across the High Street with no fear. But the High Street was full of shops. There were two tailors and two shoemakers. Everybody had their clothes made locally then. We made a lot of stuff too, repairing and leather patching heavy clothes for farmers. We would sew up the big heavy jackets. Then the zips came in and we had to sew them into the clothes.

I mind what a great thing the hoe was. The farmers would come in needing their hoes done. We had to drill the holes into the end of the poles; now an electric drill will do it in seconds. We did it by hand; a terrible slow job. All the big farmers from the estates at Kinermony, at Ballindalloch, they'd come in and get half dozen done at the start of the season. That kind of trade is done now, but then each farm would need its shovels, its brushes, its grapes. Another thing was the farmers coming in when their horses broke their shoulders. The work would rub the shoulders out; they'd go to the vet and he would tell them, 'Go and see the saddler'. We would alter the collars and get the pressure onto the right part of the shoulders. It was a disaster for the farmer if he lost a horse; horses were so valuable then on the farm – more valuable than the men, in some ways.

Life was hard. My father would say, 'Poor but honest'. Very true: some of those boys had very little, but were real genuine. A lot of what went on then would bring tears to

your eyes. Old Alfie McIntyre had a shop on the corner; like me he's a bit of a magpie at keeping things. He's kept books about the football club and you can read how the girl did all the washing of all the strips and she'd get just a shilling for it all. Then there's a letter to Sandy Farquhar, the local carter, asking him to scythe the football field for half-a-crown. And all this had to be set down properly on paper. So sad.

**Charlie Gammack,** born 1933: Aberlour

**'Scarcely a vehicle to be seen...'**
Aberlour High Street in the decade before Charlie Gammack's father opened up his saddler's business

# LIFE AT THE BIG HOUSE

'**We'd have got the sack...**'
Isobel Smith and Molly Ellis taking
their 'bit of fun' round the
back of Brucklay Castle

# The head gardener's son

My father was head gardener at Dunecht House. When he arrived, the place was more or less a wilderness, but Lord Cowdray and my father decided they would make the best garden in Scotland out of it all. And that's just what they did. All sorts of things happened: greenhouses went up, they brought in soil from Cumbria; nectarines and peaches were planted, fruits of all sorts. And roses, roses.

My father was a famous horticulturist. He showed all over Britain – Southport, Glasgow, even London, and he would win prizes at all of them, especially for his fruit. He was famous for that. They would plant apples and pears in pots in the greenhouses and turn the fruit every day, a quarter at a time just when their colour was coming up, so they caught the sun all the way round. They would water them twice a day. If the peaches ripened when Lord Cowdray wasn't on the estate, they would have to be packed into boxes with cotton wool bases and sent down to him in the south of England. There was a team of 17 gardeners in those days. There would be five in the greenhouses, seven outside, and five labourers who swept up the leaves and cut the lawns and generally keep the place tidy.

You could call it a disciplined life, but then that would depend on how you classified 'discipline'. Certainly you had to be careful to do things in the proper way. If you were out and one of the toffs came along then, as a kid, you didn't dare be seen by any of them; you had to get behind a tree or duck beneath a shrub.

Queen Mary used to visit Dunecht and she liked pink roses. We had to have all the rooms decorated with pink roses. We would have to prune them at such a time they would be in full bloom for her visits. And you had to be careful to pack anything unusual away, out of her sight. She would go around the rooms and she would say, 'Oh, I fancy that'. Then it would have to be given to her. I remember once as a young lad being called over to the Big House to pack up all these items into a big trunk, which she had 'fancied', to be sent away to her down in London.

Vice-countess Cowdray in her own mind had the power to go into anyone's house on the estate at any time of the day. She would just open the door and walk right in. Even if you were sitting down for a meal she would come right in. She was there to see how people were keeping their houses. If she saw anything she considered out of place she would report it to the factor and he would come round to discuss the matter with the tenant. But they would hand out Christmas presents and often give a £50 or so to any needy case.

The lawns were cut by a hand-pushed mower and you'd run a mower over the tops of

**Still keeping a bonny garden.**
Ronald Smith at home in Elrick, 2004, at the age of 90

**Dunecht House**
from an old postcard around 1900

the boxwood hedges and cut their sides by hand. All the paths had to be raked and raked. You wouldn't dare go on the paths at all; you'd go up the side on the grass. That way my father could tell if any of the gentry had been passing by. And the greenhouses, they had to be kept at exactly the right temperature. You could be sitting down to your lunch and the sun would come out, so you had to leave your food and go off to the greenhouse to open the windows and let the air in. Then, 10 minutes later the sun would go in and you'd have to go back and close them up again.

Everything had to be kept totally correct. You had to have the fires stoked up for the greenhouses: you'd go along at five in the evening and then back at 10 to bank them up. If a severe frost was on, you'd get up at five in the morning to do the same. It was a life of total service. You knew nothing else. You would be in and out of the Big House all the time and you'd see all sorts of things. You had to see to the decoration of the ladies' bedrooms with fresh flowers each day – carnations. There was this day when there were some high jinks on the go. Two girls came running down the stairs, with nothing on at all. There was no ducking behind a tree in that situation. But they just said, 'Good morning gardener,' and laughed. They were going to be thrown into the tanks outside; some of the gentry lads were chasing them.

We took enormous pride in all our work. I remember the digging: we used dung, which we brought into position by barrows. We would see which of us could wheel the fullest barrow. But, by God, if you spilled any dung on the paths, then you'd really be hauled over the coals. That was our pride in our own skills – to do something like that without making any sign of a mess. And when we dug over the borders, the foreman would be first in line, then the first journeyman, then an apprentice and so on. There might be six of us at the work. If you didn't keep out of the road, then you'd get your fingers dunted by a spade. You had to learn how to do everything properly and at speed. You had to be so particular about everything you did.

I know it was all very subservient, but it was also a very interesting way of life. There

> It was a life of total service. You knew nothing else. You would be in and out of the Big House all the time.

**Isobel Smith at Brucklay Castle**

Her living quarters can just be seen peeping up above ground level

was always something new. You might be growing a particular seed, you'd see it germinate, you'd prick it out, watch it grow up, go into flower. If it was a new variety, then you'd be really interested to see how it would turn out. That needed real skill. I was very proud to work at Dunecht. I was proud of my skills, proud of my training. You were proud to go down to a show in the south and come back with an award. At one time we could be regarded as one of the leading estates in Great Britain. I remember the time we went down to the Shrewsbury Show and returned with the prizes. We beat all the rest in the whole country.

I will always stand up for the estate system; they looked after you.

**Ronald Smith,** born 1913: Dunecht Estate

# We lived downstairs

I left school at 14 and went straight into service at Brucklay Castle. There was never any suggestion that I'd stay on at school. My father's attitude was, 'Na, na, ye're fowerteen noo an it's time tae earn sam money'. It was a strictly religious household at the castle; they had their own vehicle, a kind of little bus, in which they would take all the staff off to church at New Deer. You had to go every fortnight; on the other Sunday it would be your turn to stay behind and prepare the lunch. As a rule they would only employ Free Church members and I was Church of Scotland. But the minister's wife gave me a nice character reference and assured them I was a good Presbyterian and so they took me on.

The castle kept a large staff. There were the two tablemaids, two housemaids, a kitchen staff of three, three gamekeepers, a chauffeur, handyman, three gardeners. In its heyday it was a lovely place with beautifully kept grounds and gardens. There was one man who seemed to do nothing but cut the grass; we named him the Grass Man. Then there was the Home Farm and this provided the house with eggs, butter, cheeses and fresh milk each day. It was just a world on its own.

The castle was in the hands of the Dingwall-Fordyce family. They were a very quiet, even shy family – the lady, the brother, and another brother who was a major in the army and wasn't always there. They were all unmarried, so there were no children. They hardly ever entertained and preferred to bury themselves away. In her younger days Miss Dingwall-Fordyce had held a little sewing circle in the castle, but you had to be a person of some standing in the community to be invited – people like the minister's wife, the dominie's wife, never the likes of us.

My first job at the castle was in the kitchen, peeling the potatoes, shelling peas and preparing fruit and berries, which they grew themselves, for jam making. My working day began when I got up at five to set and light the fire in the kitchen; then I had to make a cup of tea for Cook and take it to her in her bed. We lived in a room that was right in the basement; we had a window which was at the level of the grass, next to the billiard room. We were 'below stairs', you see. The head tablemaid had her own room, as did the head

> There were the two tablemaids, two housemaids, a kitchen staff of three, three gamekeepers, a chauffeur, handyman, and three gardeners.

housemaid, but we had to share. It was pretty austere: bare boards, mats on the floor.

When things were slack in the kitchen, my job was to help the housemaid in her cleaning and scrub the floors. The castle had great long passageways and a large winding staircase which had brass rods to grip the carpet and all those rods had to be polished till they were gleaming. I was what was known as a 'between maid', someone who would go wherever I was needed. I was never allowed to sit idle. We all had to wear a smart, well-laundered uniform – a plain blue dress with a white apron and a white cap over our hair, and black stockings.

There was a strict sense of order and I was at the bottom of the staff. The idea was to give good service, prove yourself to be a reliable and capable servant and so work your way up to maybe the position of head tablemaid. You were expected to behave yourself at all times. There's a photo I've still got of myself and Molly Ellis, the under tablemaid, and we're seated on a motorbike which we found parked round the back of the castle. It was just a bit of fun, but if her ladyship had seen us it would have meant instant dismissal – unladylike behaviour! We did manage to have a laugh together when we were on our own, down below, but once we were in the house proper then that was quite different and we had to walk around with a serious expression on our faces and speak in low voices. If we met any of the upstairs ladies or gentlemen then we were expected to melt as much into the background as we could and only speak when spoken to. It would never be more than a 'Good morning, Ma'am'; never any chat.

The hours were long and you only got one half-day off each fortnight. Even at that I would be required to do the lunch dishes before I could get away, so it would be near

**'Fit why div they need aa that mony fowk...'**
Isobel, front centre, with some of the Brucklay Castle staff, mid 1930s

We did have some fun: when the head gardener came in to confer with the laird, he would hang his cap up on a peg and we would hide it and have a joke with him about where it could be when he came back.

three o'clock before I could set off on my bike for home. I would have to be back by night; the doors would be locked at nine prompt. I can remember those lonely bike rides back, all up the long drive with the wind blowing in the trees and me struggling to be on time, before the head tablemaid closed the door on you.

In what free time we had we would sit in the servants' lounge and chat together, doing embroidery, or playing cards. We did have some fun: I remember that when the head gardener came in to confer with the laird, he would hang his cap up on a peg and we would hide it somewhere and have a joke with him about where it could be when he came back. He was an old man, all bent over; it was rumoured that he would put a hot water bottle on his back so as to get going on a cold morning. We had little in-jokes of that kind.

We were well fed. Down in the kitchen we would get some of what was being prepared for the dining table upstairs; none of them were particularly big eaters, so a lot of food would come back down again. I learned how to perform a whole range of kitchen tasks. We had to butcher the sheep from the estate and we had to skin rabbits and gut fish. I also learned how to do things properly in high society. I saw how a table should be laid, how the cutlery should be all lined up on each side, the dessert spoon on the inside and never along the top.

My father would say, 'Fit why div they need a' that mony fowk tae look aifter them?'. But you've got to remember that in those days gentry expected to be waited on hand and foot. That was the way of life they had been brought up to. The discipline came easy enough to me. In those days you were brought up to it. At school you had to obey the teachers and never answer back. At home my father's word was law: if he said 'Jump', all you would say was, 'And how high, Father?' No, we were brought up to respect any adult and if they were in a position of authority, like the minister or the headmaster, then you looked up to them. So going to the castle and having to work for a laird and a lady was just a natural development of what we were used to.

The hours were long and the work was hard, but I don't regret starting out as a maid in a large country house. I was taught the proper way to do things and I became a good cook. Besides, I'd been brought up to never sit idle. If ever he saw me with nothing to do, my father would call out, 'Oh, ye canna jist sit aroon like that, lassie. Find yersel samthin useful tae dae'. Even in my old age, if I'm ever sitting idle then I feel guilty and I'll go off down to my daughter's in Ellon and do a spot of cleaning.

And now what has happened to Brucklay Castle and all that grand way of life? After the war the upkeep became too much and the Dingwall-Fordyce family sold it off; there was a big roup and all the contents were sold off. I often wonder what could have happened to all that fine silver and the lovely pieces of furniture. Later, the roof was taken off and the building allowed to fall into ruin. It's a way of life which has completely disappeared.

**Isobel Smith,** born 1922: Brucklay Castle

# Life on an upland estate

I was born at the Lodge of Glenbuchat on the 11th of May, 1923. It was in the middle of a snowstorm, so I'm told – in May. My father had to clear the way of snow for the doctor to get through. My father was the head keeper on the Glenbuchat estate.

We had a good diet. Being head keeper that was one of my father's perquisites. He could go up the hill and shoot a hind for our own use. We had rabbits, white hares. Father kept a cow – he had a little croft along with the job; always fresh milk. So a good healthy diet. And there were plenty of travelling vans, too. They would bring you everything you needed. If it wasn't on the van that particular week, then you would say the word and it would arrive shortly. Davidson kept the shop at Glenbuchat and his van came twice weekly. He was a general merchant and you could get everything through his shop – screws, nails, and drapery. If you asked for it, he had it.

We were well looked after on the estate – for the time. You've got to remember this is all a very long time ago now. Things have changed incredibly now; since the war the changes have been absolutely amazing. There was no such thing as a five-day week for the keeper then; he could work seven days straight and still never be done. I'm not saying he was a slave exactly, but life was hard. But at that time the tenant farmer would look up to him because he was seen as the representative of the laird.

For the woman of the house life was very hard. Everything had to be done by hand. The washing and the cleaning. No hoovers then, only a brush and shovel. When you look round this room that we are sitting in now – the fitted carpet, the TV in the corner, all the furniture, the change is…well, it's just a different world, a different world altogether.

You had to entertain yourself then. The outdoors was our entertainment. I did a lot of fishing when I was a boy. I'd fish for trout in the burn. Then my father taught me to shoot and I abandoned the rod for the gun. Rabbits, hares and deer. I suppose I was 12 when I shot my first hind. That was a great moment. I could show you the very spot where I did it. You can see it yet: when you go up the Balloch road towards the lodge you see a wood behind the lodge and then, just beyond the edge of the wood up on a hill, there's a patch of bracken. Well, the hind was standing in that bracken. It was well set up for it. I brought it down with the one shot. A very proud moment. I was on the brink of, well, if not adulthood, then adolescence. For me it was a moment of coming of age.

I remember the first rabbit too: at the lodge; by the light of the moon, the full moon. There was a lot of snow on the ground, a lot of light and you could see this rabbit standing in it, absolutely still. I asked my father if I could shoot and he said, 'Go ahead'. I got him!

What I'm talking about here is a whole way of life. It was a very good one – for me. I was quite content with my childhood. I often wonder, though, whether my mother wasn't lonely. She might go for weeks without seeing another woman. She never said anything, but she must have found it lonely. You've got to remember the only means of transport was the bicycle. When I was a boy there were only two cars in the Glen – the laird had one, of course, but he was only a seasonal visitor. One belonged to the shop, the other to Mains of Glenbuchat – and that was it, just the two cars.

**Billy Duncan,** born 1923: Glenbuchat

**'I can see it yet…'**
Glenbuchat Lodge where the 11-year old Billy shot his first rabbit

**Roping-in the stag**
Alex Duncan, Billy's father and head gamekeeper before him, at the Glenbuchat estate at work in 1930. Lt-Col. Milne, his employer, is to the left.

# The Aboyne set

**'In good service'** Jean's mother taken with her uncle, Alex, Fowler, when working in Dumfries before the First World War

My mother had been in service and had travelled all over the south of England. Before the First World War she'd been down in a big house in London. While she was there the family who employed her sent her to cookery classes, very expensive classes too, with the result that she learned a wide range of culinary skills, well beyond the normal home-made stuff. She was in what she liked to call 'good service', that is she worked in the big houses which the upper classes kept at that time.

My father came from farming stock and he was fee'd as a young man. After she and my father married they took a cottage in Birse, just across the Dee from Aboyne. Aboyne in those days was a very fashionable place for the gentry and the rich to keep a big house in; it was quite normal for them to come up for the summer and then go back down to their London residence in the winter. She took in boarders. Because of her experience and her training she was able to get good business from the big houses. Often she would be sent the grandchildren and their nannies. People would come back year after year; she had an excellent reputation. It was just a cottage, but it had an inside toilet – a real luxury at that time. But no bathroom; she would heat buckets of water on the range and then take them up the stairs to fill a hip bath for her boarders.

We got to know Lady Outram, of the publishing family. Sir Francis had a large house in Aboyne. They were a strict Plymouth Brethren family and held prayers every morning. They were very strict with their staff, too; the maids were kept in their place. They got the tea-leaf sweepings to drink. Lady Outram lived to be a very old lady and till the year she died she would send me Scripture Union publications and a little gift each Christmas.

There was this maid, Lizzie Green, who had come up from Glasgow to work in the Outram household. The local postie took a fancy to her and started calling around at the back door just to see her. Sir Francis got wind of the amount of time the postman was hanging around his house, so one day he went down to the servants' hall to see what was what. Sure enough, when he entered, there was the postie sitting at the big kitchen table with Lizzie chatting

**'The important thing was to be seen'** The Marquis of Huntly and guests at Aboyne Games around 1910

away to him. She looked up, saw Sir Francis glaring at her and immediately fell into a faint at his feet. It was all put on, of course, but it was enough to allow the postie to scoot off while Sir Francis was fussing around his poor sick maid.

There was a big class distinction in Aboyne society in those days. There was a huge gap between the ordinary working folk and the people who resided in the large houses and kept staff. Many of them, like the Outrams, came from well established old families and were used to practising the ways of grand living but there were others who had newly arrived on the scene and maybe didn't have quite so much of the true blood in them as they liked to pretend. These were what my granny used to call the fite iron gentry, the ones that weren't of the true steel.

Yes, there was plenty of snobbery, but also plenty of genuine society in Aboyne in those days. All sorts of rich and high-class folk ran large houses. There were a lot of old tea planters who had made their money out east and were now retired to Royal Deeside. There were the Mitchells, the tobacco people, and there was Miss Usher from the beer family. There was a kind of regular season to Aboyne life then. People would come up in the late summer for the shooting; they would take a beat on the Dee for the fishing and then there was the Aboyne Games. The great thing was to reserve seating for yourself and your guests and make sure a report appeared in the papers: 'The house party of Lord Such-and-such were in attendance at the Aboyne Games on Saturday last'.

The big houses would entertain each other on a regular basis and guests would come up from the south. They brought their staff with them: there would be cooks and butlers and maids, but the great thing was to have your own chauffeur in uniform. Often he would have to double up as a gardener; the really grand folk were those who could afford to have a gardener and a chauffeur. One of the big annual events was the grand jumble sale that was held at the end of the season, just before they were disappeared south again. This was the occasion when all the big houses would donate the stuff that they weren't going to take with them; the proceeds would go to the Nursing Association to support the district nurse. The locals would take the chance to stock up on clothing; there would always be plenty of children's stuff that the big house children had grown out of. My sister and I got some beautiful summer dresses that way. There would also be what were called 'penny bundles', that is bundles of old scrap material and ribbons tied up for sale. The idea was that these would go to dress up dolls, but there were plenty of old ribbons that appeared on the hats of the women of Aboyne, believe me!

**Jean Lawrie,** born 1924: Aboyne

**The Aboyne guests**
A picnic to Glenshee in the mid 1930s. Jean's father and grandmother are at the back, her mother front row, second left.

Guests brought their staff with them, but the great thing was to have your own chauffeur in uniform.

**Glentanar**

Lady Glentanar, her
daughter, Miss Jean,
Pierre Fouin and
donkey

# The butler's son

We lived in the stable yard, at the top end and just around the corner. It was a rather more salubrious residence than those of the other employees, possessing as it did its own walled garden, lawn and a gate with a corkscrew surmounted on it. The estate supported a large number of staff; in its heyday there had been over 200 of them; even in my time there were something like eight gardeners, three footmen, a hallboy, cooks, stillroom maids and so on.

There was a social hierarchy at work and we were all aware of it, very much so. My mother was a trained tailoress, but she'd been in service as well. After the First World War she'd been working for some Jewish families in London and had also been abroad with them, to Prague, Cannes, Nice. So both my parents had rubbed shoulders with aristocracy and were familiar with their way of life. When we used to go off on holiday to France, we would stop off at the North British Hotel in Edinburgh, where my father would order lobster. He would also flourish a big cigar. That's the way in which the holiday would be launched, a millionaire's way of doing it. He was familiar with wines; the laird had a wonderful cellar, one which had a widespread reputation. Father would take me into it; he'd switch on the light and you'd gaze out over row upon row of bottles, all covered with cobwebs. Another memory is coming upon all the staff seated for lunch at a long table, with my father at its head and, at the other end, the housekeeper.

Everyone on the estate was conscious of who they were and what rank they occupied in the scheme of things. As a child, you'd hear the laird approaching and hear his loud confident voice and you knew to dodge out of the way. He was actually my godfather; he'd been invited to this because of the closeness in birth to his own Jean, but I still found him a rather frightening character, a loud voiced gentleman whom everyone in our family called 'Lordy'. Their talk was full of 'Lordy is doing this or 'Lordy is going there'. He'd been to Eton and saw himself as the leader of the social set on Deeside. He was kind enough to us all, in a paternalistic fashion. In my early days I would be brought into the nursery to play with Jean; I'd be taken out on the donkey by Lady Glentanar. But even here, the order of things had to preserved: Jean might be my playmate but she had to be 'Miss Jean' always, never the plain 'Jean'.

The estate really came alive during the shooting season; that's when the whole atmosphere lifted and things were really humming. Then Lord Glentanar would be in residence and you'd see his flag hoisted up on the mast. That's the time when you tended to creep around the estate; the policy for us kids was to look out and to listen and if you spotted anyone of importance approaching you'd dodge behind a bush or back round the wall. At other times we'd stroll around as if we owned the place.

When he was in residence everything had to be just so, the drives continually raked, the cars washed and gleaming each day, every last weed along the flower beds lifted. You'd see the students who were employed as beaters about the place; you'd see the gamekeepers all dressed up in their fine green cloth suits. John the piper would march around at 7.30 in the morning.

My father and mother did find their submissive roles difficult at times. Mother had been well educated and was well read. She was very fond of classical music. She didn't really get close to any of her neighbours on the estate and she would follow her own very regular and quite independent routine. She was very house-proud and would spend the mornings making sure everything was spic and span and in its appointed place. Then for the afternoon she would change into a skirt and tailored coat and take her daily walk. This was a strict two miles up the road to the Black Ship pool on the Tanar and then back again.

Father was very aware of condescension, of when he was being patronised and not being given his due. He knew exactly how his seniority among the servants should be evaluated and resented it when it didn't come. His hours were very long: he would start at eight in the morning and often not get back till 10 at night. He couldn't leave until he was certain that everything was absolutely in order for the next day. His final task was to supervise the washing and the drying of the silver and then to ensure that his lordship's clothes were correctly pressed and laid out for the next day. The shoes had to be polished till they were gleaming.

My father's domain was on the other side of the padded door, which separated the servants from Upstairs, and within it he was at its head. The butler, the housekeeper and the cook could regard themselves as the senior servants and held that everyone else was below them and had to give them due deference. They all accepted their place and no one challenged the set order of things. The key to getting on at Glentanar was conformity and loyalty. As long as you observed these proprieties then you could be confident you would be looked after. Not until 1945 and the return from the war did this begin to change. Then some people had had enough of being ordered about by so-called superiors who, because they came from a different background were automatically considered to be above them but who were, in fact, often incompetents.

But before the war, to be employed on the estate carried some kudos. You might not be well paid but you had security, you had a provided house, you got your milk, your coal, your sticks for free. The Depression might be raging in the outside world, but here you were looked after. If you kept your nose clean and did as you were bid then you were set up for life. And at the end of it all, the estate would find you somewhere nice to live out your retirement. To be dismissed, however, was a real disaster: not only would you lose your tied house, you would have to find your way in the outside world with no references to support you.

Looking back, I can see this was a very special and privileged way of life – but very much of its period and its place. I wouldn't have brought up my own family in that way, but I've no regrets that I was. It was a period when you had to learn how to be

My father had a saying, 'The Laird may own my body but my mind is my own'. He would give his service as a butler efficiently and professionally, but he would keep his true thoughts to himself.

deferential, to hold your tongue. I see my own desire as an adult to have my say and to make sure my voice is heard as a reaction to those days, as something I'm still working out of my system. I sit on committees and am taken aback by the hypocrisy you see, by the extent to which people will go to hold their tongue so as to avoid causing upset, at how things don't get done.

My father had a saying, 'The Laird may own my body but my mind is my own'. He would give his service as a butler efficiently and professionally, but he would keep his true thoughts to himself. He couldn't agree with much of what he saw around him; he'd seen too much of the world for that. He was furious at the unthinking way in which people would vote Tory. Our local MP was Lord Kemsley and he would ask them, 'Now, why would you vote for a baronet to look after your affairs?' and they would answer, 'Oh, but the Laird wouldn't like it if we didn't!' For him the proper way was to vote for what you thought right, not for what your employer wanted.

**Pierre Fouin,** born 1928: Glentanar

A full account of Pierre Fouin's life, both at Glentanar and later, may be found in his *The early life and times of a Glentanar Exile*. [Librario, 2005]

# Growing up on the estate

I wouldn't say that it was an over-ordered or hierarchical society – I've a great respect for the laird system as I experienced it at Dunecht. My father was always the last one to get any money in the village – he'd send out his bills every six months and by then he'd often forgotten whose shoes he'd been sorting, anyway. But then, money wasn't the only currency we used: if, for example, he was needing some sticks, he'd just have a word with the forestry lads and next day a load would be delivered to the door; if he wanted a day's fishing, he'd just chum up the head gamie the night before and then he'd get his day's fishing. There was this great spirit of helping one another. The estate looked after you. If any of us kids were likely to land in trouble, we'd be checked by the knowledge that somebody would be having a word with our parents.

You walked everywhere. I was never in a train until I joined up for my National Service. Never in a train till then! I remember getting on and walking up and down and finding this café half way along where you could get a drink. 'A grand affair this!', I thought. But then, I had to change trains and there was nearly a bit in the P&J to tell the world, 'Homesick Dunecht loon throws himself off train in despair'. You see, I didn't realise this second train had no passage-way and I just opened the door to the carriage thinking I'd explore it a bit more and nearly fell out. So that was my first experience of going on a train.

But then, there was no need for travelling out of our community. There was so much that was happening at Dunecht. There was cricket, there was football, there were all the normal outdoor things that bairns play at, there was fishing down at the burn. You were

**If my father wanted a day's fishing, he'd just chum up the head gamie the night before. There was this great spirit of helping one another. The estate looked after you.**

never inside – you were always out playing with your pals. The local environment, that was our play station. We were never bored. And if I did go inside it was because I had studying to get done. And if I wasn't doing that, Mother would make sure I was never bored. She would have us all knitting. I got knitting at the school. The first thing I did was a dishcloot, with size one needles, these muckle great needles and string. We all had to do it.

I can't understand the vandalism and the talk of 'being bored' nowadays. In this computer age, there are so many things they could be doing. Our way of life meant that we were brought up to be content with what we had. And there was a striving on the education side as well, a striving to be as good as you possibly could be. These two elements combined meant that we never felt ourselves to be idle. I also had to help my father in the shop. He had what he called his 'finishing machine'; after he had repaired the boot he had to wax and polish it and that is what my brother and I were expected to assist with when we got home: 'Right, loons, pit doon the school bags and cam ower here'. It was a treadle machine, operated by foot, with all the buffs attached to it. Our job was to get the foot power going – he was doing the skilled work, but we were supplying the power. The family firm at work.

People all felt the same. I now realise how much Mum and Dad did for us on their limited income. Now it amazes me, looking back. Mum made most of our clothes and Dad the furniture – he was very good with his hands. I had no cause to think I was somebody, some little cocky boy, off to Gordon's with my bursary. After all, my parents could never have afforded to send me to Robert Gordon's College and it was the good education I'd received at my small village school which saw me passing the exam for an Aberdeen Endowments Trust bursary that made the whole thing possible.

In the village, at that time, we'd be in and out of each other's houses all the time. The forester's son or the painter's daughter – we were all in it together. Every family had its own valued role to play, its own part in the community. You were kent as the 'soutar's loon' and that was you. People are amazed when I say that we had a cricket team. That was the legacy of old Smith the gardener – he was at one time trained at Sussex Park; Lord Cowdray and Smith wouldn't employ anyone unless he could play cricket. So that was the start of that. The cricket team I joined was all the folk from the estate. Really, we had everything on that estate.

The estate was very self-contained. The estate offices were next to us, the hall was alongside it, and the estate had its own shops, granite built, and housing a smithy, a mason, the painter and so on. They were all there together and so the social life, the way of life we led, was all tied in with the community.

**Robbie Shepherd,** born 1936: Dunecht

# EARLY CENTURY LIVES: 4
## John Ritchie

**The golden age of Moray Firth fishing.** A group of Buckie loons, around 1900.
(BUCKIE HERITAGE CENTRE COLLECTION)

**'Whitehills was all fishing then'**

The harbour crammed with vessels, around 1900

**Not a fishing boat in sight**

Whitehills 'marina' harbour, 2010

# We never had to lock our doors

My father was a fisherman. There were six of us – five boys, one girl. I was the third, right in the middle. Whitehills was all fishing people then. In those days, the young folk in the village could only go with each other. I remember there was one lad and he started courting a girl from Macduff and that created a real commotion: 'Dis he nae thunk that ony o the Whitehills quines are guid enough fer him?'

I once got my lineage made up. As you go back, you discover that this person is your second cousin, that one's your third cousin and so on. You can always find a link. Nearly the whole village would be your relatives, one way or another. There were just a few family names: the Watsons, the Smiths, the Ritchies.

Once a man came into the village and asked if he could see 'Mr Cruickshank'. Three or four men looked up and said, 'Na, there's nae a Cruickshank in Whitehills'. But then one said, 'We've got a Crooky, but we hanna got ony Shanks'. There was someone called Jimmy Crooky, you see. Now that was a T-name. We all had T-names. If you wanted to ken anybody, if you asked for John Ritchie, well, there might be three or four of us with that name, so we were given these T-names to distinguish us. Stripey, Smokey, Tufty; we were all given these different names, you see. I was Reedy. My grandfather had red hair and so he got this T-name and it came to me. I thought nothing about it; it's just what everyone called me.

Then there were only fishing folk in Whitehills. Now the Low Shore is full of holiday homes and the Whitehills folk have moved to bungalows up above the shore. Whitehills is a village of bungalows nowadays. But the house my grandfather lived in, that was no more than what you'd term a but-and-a-ben. There was the kitchen with a bed in the wall, a bung-in bed we called it. The floor was just sand. Just two rooms. How six lived in it, I don't know!

In that time there was no sanitation: you had to carry the water from the well. But we had our own ways. We had to go out to the rocks with pails to get rid of our waste, but we were clean. That's one thing the fishing folk made sure of – that they were absolutely clean. Saturday was a busy day for the housewife. That was the day to make sure everything was spotless; the fire was black-leaded, the floors were swept.

This was to get ready for Sunday, you see. Nothing was done on the Sunday. Sunday was for the church. It was the same when we went down to Yarmouth or to Lowestoft: on a Sunday the Scots fishermen wouldn't go to sea, even though the English did. We worked all the week, but never on that day. We would lay down our pipes, our tobacco and our

knives; we'd take them out of our pockets before we went to church. You'd never go into the church with such things.

I left the school to go to sea as a fisherman, but I was never happy about it. I never did get to like it. I suffered from seasickness every time we left harbour. But I had no choice. To begin with I passed to go to Banff for my secondary education, but when I got to 14 the education had to stop. No money in those days, no money to do anything. I've seen me go to the school and some of the boys might have a penny – that was real money then. There was a baker's by the school and you could get a bag of broken bread for our penny. The boy with the penny would go into the shop, come out with his bag and he'd open it up and shout out, 'Help yourselves, boys'. It wouldn't be like that today – everybody would buy their own bag – and it wouldn't be something like broken bread either!

It was the same at home. People didn't lock their doors then. We all felt safe. There was none of the stuff you get nowadays. No vandalism in our day, just petty stuff, at Halloween and New Year, just pranks really. Everybody knew everybody else. Now it's a completely different generation; people don't know each other any more; they can't trust each other now. In our day if you were going off somewhere you could get anyone to look after your goods – if you tried that today, you'd find when you got back they would have sold them.

I went to Whitehills School to begin with. Whitehills was quite a big school: six teachers. But it wasn't like it is now: you got the same teacher for everything. You'd start off with some religion, then there'd be arithmetic, reading, writing, spelling, dictation, with some woodwork or navigation later in the day. The one teacher for everything, all day long. One teacher in one room, from 9 till 4. You couldn't get the teachers to do all that now.

At Banff you got languages. I liked the school, all the days I was at it. I was sorry to leave. Circumstances forced it. At Banff I had Latin. But after the second year there I had to leave. I'd go back to the school tomorrow, I would, most definitely. I was never bored.

That man
taught
everything:
navigation,
woodwork,
everything.
Everyone
said if
you had
Mr Wilson
you'd pass
all your
exams; you'd
be all right.

Whenever I got home the first thing I did, I'd take out my books and do my lessons. I found it all very interesting.

I liked the teachers well enough, too. They treated us fairly. I never got the belt, never needed it. Some of the pupils would be ruffians, they would take their rulers and flick paper and stuff about the room. But Mr Wilson, he fairly looked after things. I'll give you an occasion. We were in his class this day and we got this sum; it was a pretty stiff sum and none of us could get the answer to it. At 11 o'clock it was our interval. We crept back into the room while he was away for his fly-cup. One girl went to his desk; she lifted the lid and looked for the answer, but that was the moment Mr Wilson came back into the room. He opened the door and he just stood looking at her and we just sat there looking at him looking at her. She got the answer and wrote it down and he just stood there looking at her. Then he spoke. 'Weel, wifie, have you got all the answers now?'. That was all – and that was more than enough punishment. She was scared out of her wits. I can picture it still, the girl with her head in the desk, our teacher over by the door and us just sitting there, wondering what could possibly happen. 'Weel, wifie, have you got the answers now?'

That man taught everything: navigation, woodwork, everything. Everyone said if you had Mr Wilson you'd pass all your exams; you'd be all right. The teachers had to take big classes, 40 and more. Teachers nowadays would cry out about such numbers, but in those days it was easier in some ways. The children would come to school far better prepared for it because of what they got at home. We listened to what our father and mother said. Now the parents don't take the same interest – they're both too busy with their own work.

In our day you always knew when you got home that the mother would be there and there would be a meal on the table. That was one thing about the wives in those days – they would always be at home. They had to be; there was so much for them to do. No washing machines in those days. I always remember that when it was washing day, I couldn't get out to play until I had turned the handle of the mangle for my mother.

Teachers were held in respect then. If any parent said, 'I'll put you up to the teacher,' well, that was a big thing. Oh yes, there was great respect for the teacher. The school was the school; you went there for your education, not to play around. But there were a few dunderheids. I remember one day one of them pinched the master's strap and threw it away. But he came in and he said, 'Don't worry, I've got another one'. He didn't ask what had happened, he just said, 'Don't worry, I've still another one – and I intend to use it'.

I enjoyed it even more at Banff. You got languages there. I liked that. I forgot them for many years, but now they are starting to come back. All the things I did at school, they are coming back to me. French: I can count in French: 'un-deux-trois-quatre-cinq'... Then there are the poems we chanted out: 'Maitre Corbeau sur un arbre perche'...I can recite it yet.

In the playground we just played the ordinary games – running, throwing a ball, tackies. We all got on with one another well enough, though there was a bit of feeling with the Banff children, with the Banffers. One time a ship carrying a cargo of coal got washed up on the rocks at Whitehills and the Banff people came over and took the coal. We called them 'Banffers poochers'.

All this is so long ago. People look back on it now and think we belong completely to a different age. Folk wouldn't do the things now we did then. People were happy with what they had. We were pleasant to one another. If you had two-pence to buy a piece then you'd share it all out. And when you were out playing and you got hungry you'd go up to any of the houses and the wifie would come to the door and ask you, 'Weel, John, fat are ye wantin?' And you'd tell her you were hungry and she would make up a piece for you and then you'd go back to the playing. We thought nothing about it; it's just the way we all lived together. In Whitehills it was like a big extended family. No one locked their doors. There was no hankering after other things. We were happy with what we had.

Nobody at that time knew whether they were poor or not. There was nothing to measure such a thing by. We had the same as each other and we thought it enough. The first time I went to Lowestoft on a boat I got £30 for my four months trip. I came home and handed it all over to my mother. She wouldn't take it; she said, 'But this is your first real wage, you just have it'. She put it in the bank for me – when I got married 20 years later the £30 was still there.

Apart from the war, I've lived in the same one area all my life. Now my own family is all away, but I'm still here, in the home in Banff. I had an operation on my back: my legs got cramps and I had to go into Woodend for an operation to relieve the pressure of the nerve from off the spine. It did help, but the surgeon told me I would always feel it. Now I find I'm fine when I'm sitting down, but if I try to stand without support then I would just fall down. But I still drive my own car. I go off on a trip round Whitehills of an afternoon, just to look at the old place. I'm in my nineties now, but I've no problem driving the car.

**John Ritchie,** born 1910: Whitehills

> Nobody at that time knew whether they were poor or not. There was nothing to measure such a thing by. We had the same as each other and we thought it enough.

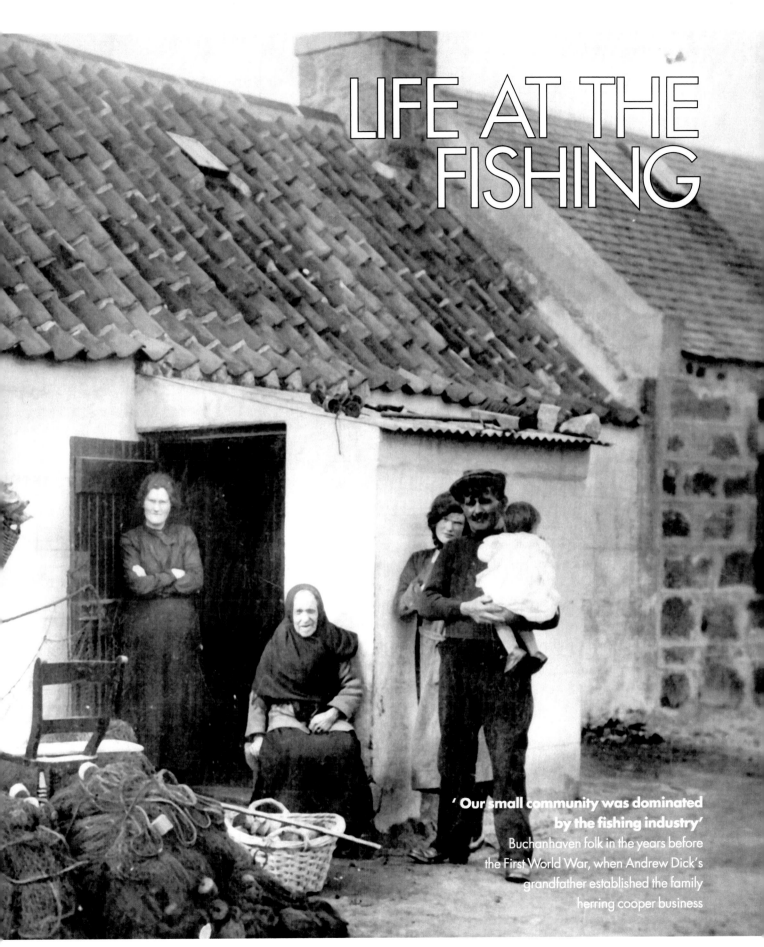

# LIFE AT THE FISHING

'**Our small community was dominated by the fishing industry**'
Buchanhaven folk in the years before the First World War, when Andrew Dick's grandfather established the family herring cooper business

**In the room where she was born**

Isabel Harrison and her plate collection at 139 Main Street, Buckie in 2006

At the school there was this division of us all into three classes, three social classes: the toonsers, the fisher folk and the country bairns — and that was our order in importance.

# Four generations in one street and all at sea

I was born in this very room; May 23, 1926. Four generations in this street and all of them at sea. My father was a fisherman till 1929; that's when the boat was lost. Then he went into the Merchant Navy. He used to go on long trips abroad. I'll tell you why he stopped them. He came home this time and mother was out in the washing shed. I was by myself in the house and this strange man walked straight in. I went running outside, crying, 'Mummy, Mummy, there's mannie in the hoose!' She came in to see, and the strange man was my dad. He'd been away so long, for a whole year, out on the deep sea run. I was only five and I'd forgotten all about him. He was so upset that he says, 'Ah'll niver gae awa sae lang agin, na niver!' From then on he would only take the short trips, along the coast. What had upset me the most was that he had actually kissed her, this strange man.

Up till the last year I used to go into the schools and tell the children about what it was like to grow up here, before we had baths in our houses. I've told you about my bath, have I? My dad brought it home from down south. It came out of a luxury liner that was being broken up and he got it for £1. Still there to this day – a good pound's worth. It's got these high sides, made that way to stop the water spilling over the side when the ship was rolling. It's a fixed bath in the bathroom through there. Before we got it, you had to take your bath in a tin bath in front of the fire. When he brought the bath home he had to make a new room for it.

In those days, up the stairs, there was just this one living room; the rest was a loft, for the storing and the laying out of the nets. So he got this bathroom made out of the space. We had a toilet put in, too. As the youngest I was the first to have a pee in it; mother, father, sister and brother all gathered to watch it. A great thing for that time, an inside toilet.

If you'd been in this room 70 years ago, when I was a child, you'd have seen a recess bed over there by the wall, and two cupboards and a coal fire. That's called a hanging press – I now call it my glory hole. When we had to mend the nets we'd have the fire lighted. This is where they would take their rest and have their tea. Everything in the room had to be for a purpose; we were all very practical.

Life was hard. When the Depression started in the 1930s it was very hard. When my dad's boat was lost, it wasn't insured because they hadn't been able to find the money for it. They lost the lot. People forget how tough things were – and it's not so long ago, really. They had just shot their nets off Smith's Knoll, but the weather suddenly changed, the wind swung right round, and that was it. She went down stern first, but everyone was saved. There was a lot of that in Buckie in those days. When a boat is lost it really hits you; everyone in the community is affected by it. Oh, it really hits you; they're plenty sore hearts for days and months to come.

There was hardship. I ken for a fact that our clothes were given to other families who were worse off. We aye got warned that if ever you spotted something on another child that had once belonged to yourself, you must never, ever, say anything about it. You knew that your clothes would be given away, that there were always folk ready and willing to take them.

At the school there was this division of us all into three classes, three social classes: the toonsers, the fisher folk and the country bairns – and that was our order in importance. We got on well enough among ourselves, but we were treated as different by the teachers. If you were brighter than a toonser, you would get marks taken off so that they'd be at the top. By toonsers, I mean the children of the shopkeepers, the tradesman, the minister, the doctor – what you might call the middle classes. Yet if it hadn't been for the other two classes they wouldn't have had a job at all. The teachers might try to hide it, but they'd speak to the toonsers in a different way from the rest of us. My sister and the headmaster's son were really on the same level, but she'd get marks taken off so that he stayed ahead. She was very bright, but there was no way she could come before a toonser. Yet, as my father used to say, 'Withoot us, the toonsers wid be naewhere'.

But we were happy; this street was a wonderful place to be a child in. In the summer time we were never off the beach and in the winter we'd play under the street lamps. We always had to be in at a fixed time. I was a 'ten-to-eighter' – the railway was at the bottom of the garden and that was the time of the train; when I heard it clattering by, I knew I had to be in. My sister was older and she was a second bedder and had to listen out for the nine o'clock train. This was a marvellous place to live; a brilliant community spirit and loads of kids to play with.

**Isabel Harrison,** born 1926: Buckie

**Outside the Buckie Fishing Heritage Museum, 2005**
Left to right: Peter Flett; Willie Mair; Allan Fraser; Isabel Harrison; Frank McCleod.

**Queen Street, Gourdon around 1900**
The shop which Margaret Duncan's mother later kept was on the site of the two-storey house with the child on the pavement.

**On the doorstep**
Margaret Duncan's mother with her two older sisters, Gourdon, 1928

# My father was lost when I was months old

I lost my father at sea when I was eight months. When the ship went down, it took all the personal effects with it; all I have of my dad is a small bottle with a ship and a model of a quayside in it. Some old seaman had made it for him.

I had two sisters, so my mother was left with three of us to bring up. She'd no real education, but she was a determined woman. When she became a widow she simply baited a line for a fisherman and got paid for it. Then, when I was five, she opened up a shop and made a great success of it. It was a general store which sold sweeties and groceries and tobacco and it was in great demand. She worked from the moment she got up till late at night. The shop was next to our house; you'd go through the front door and to the left was the shop, to the right the living quarters. Often there would be someone knocking at the window late at night. You'd go and there'd be this fisherman: 'Jean, Ah'm awa tae the sea an Ah've fargitten ma fags. Cid ye gi me sam?' She'd put on her dressing gown, open the door and hand over the cigarettes with a 'You can pay me later,' and off the fisherman would go to his boat with the fags in his pocket.

I started serving in the shop when I was seven. I'd come home from school and go straight into it, behind the counter. We made the first ice-cream in Gourdon and my sister and I would go round the village and sell it from a cart. Gourdon was built around the fishing and the Selbie flax works. There was a big fleet: the harbour would be that thick with boats you could walk from one side to the other, from boat to boat, across the decks, without any need to use the pier. But prices weren't high and life was hard. It's a dreadful thing to say, but it was the war that brought prosperity to Gourdon. The younger men were called up to serve in the navy and only the older fishermen were left. Prices soared and the shop did well. Whenever a van came with new stock, you'd see a queue form; before that van had left the village everything it had brought would be sold out. Why, you could have taken a stone and rolled a piece of paper round it and someone would buy it, they had so much money to burn.

But Mum was a very hard working and unselfish person who did a lot for others. She taught us always to see to others less fortunate than ourselves; we might have lost our father but we were some of the luckier ones: we had clean clothes, food on our table and a roof over our head, whereas there were plenty who didn't have any of that and it was our duty to give them a helping hand, and not to talk about it afterwards.

This was the real Gourdon way. I think that living so close to each other, down there at the foot of the brae away from the outside world, made you like that. Besides, fishing folk do the same kind of work together and share the same kind of dangers and hardships. You never bothered to knock at a door; you'd just open it and give a cry, 'Are ye in?' and then walk straight inside. We all knew we had to help each other through the hard times.

**Margaret Duncan,** born 1928: Gourdon

**Getting ready for the fish sale**
Gourdon quay, around 1950

# A hard life is what we expected

My father was a carpenter, down at the slip at the boat-building in the village, but he'd go out at the fishing when work was slack. That was how he met my mother when she was at the gutting down in Yarmouth at the end of the season. She was a Shetlander.

Isbel, my wife, was away to the kippering when she was 13. Thirteen just, and she'd be working 24 hours a day sometimes, when a lot of herring came in. For that she got a shilling an hour. But it was wartime, jobs were scarce and that's what the young girls round here did then.

The house I was born in is still there, just down the brae from here. It was no more than a but-and-ben with an open loft upstairs and a sheddie outside. A fire and a pot – that's what we had for cooking and for hot water. No toilet; you had to go out to the rocks to do your jobs. When I was three my father took me down to the shore and showed me where to go. We had a bucket in the shed as well. When we were first married we still used a fire boiler. Isbel would go down to the beach and look for odd bits of wood and old shoes, anything that would burn. This was to heat the boiler so she could get her washing started. In those days everybody threw their rubbish onto the beach; what stuff you would get! Always enough to feed the boiler.

It might have been a hard life, but it was what we expected. We thought nothing about

**'Awa tae the kippering'**
Isbel Flett (extreme right) with workmates at Yarmouth around 1950

## The well earned fly-cup

Isbel Flett (second row, third right) and the guttin crew around 1950

## A filthy job

Fishermen tarring the rope in Buckie around 1900

it. The other day I was looking at this diary I keep up the stairs, an old Boys' Brigade diary. The 12th March 1943 and it says: 'Got berthed on the *Springfield*'. That was my first boat; we went away in May for the summer fishing. I can mind when I got the berth: I asked my parents if I should go and they went down to the harbour to look and see what kind of a boat it was. A lot of lads of my age, they were all going to sea as well. We were all speaking about the berths we'd got; they would talk about the coiling boxes, the lockers they had for stowing the ropes in, and how they would have to coil the ropes in them. Great four-inch ropes and new tarred and your hands would stick to them and you'd get blisters with it all. But this was the life of the sea and you just had to carry on with it.

You started off as cook. You'd get herring every day. It was your job to clean them and then fry them. There would be 30 herrings and a crew of 10 and half of them never got right fried. You just accepted it all. You'd get the same stuff for a month on end, though we did try to get loaves in each week. Talk about hygiene! You'd cut a sheaf off a loaf for each man and then, if anyone wanted more, he'd just go up and cut another piece – and his hands would be none too clean! And the butter: this was just a big lump set out on the table and so was the cheese. The men would just cut bits off. Sometimes you'd see the rats' teeth in the cheese; you just cut round that bit and carried on. And we had these hard biscuits to bite through. It's all hard to believe now, the way we lived.

My father was dead and buried and I never even knew. He was 50 years of age. We were fishing off the Faroes on a steam trawler, 380 miles north of Aberdeen and I trying to earn some money to get married with. Rough, rough seas and all for £1 a day. He died on the Tuesday and I didn't find out about it till the following Monday when we were coming back into Aberdeen. They kept the funeral back to the Saturday, but my boat still hadn't come in. They just had to go ahead.

Believe you and me, it was a complete shock. I was second engineer; we were two miles off Aberdeen and I was on deck in the wheelhouse. I was looking through the

glasses at this trawler, which was passing. The skipper had been talking to this other trawler on the wireless and he looked up and said: 'Hey, Peter, Ah've git a message fer ye. Your faither's deed an buried'. That was the way I learned. But on the Sunday I was also in the wheelhouse and the skipper was down below talking on the radio and I could hear these voices speaking about some message or other. I reckon he kent it then, but he never told me. He was afraid I'd have to be put ashore and that it would spoil his trip.

A trip would last 16 or 17 days. You'd come into land, unload, get one clear day and then be off again. You worked all the days you could and didn't take a holiday unless it was something really special. In '51, when I was married, I was bringing home £6 to £7 a week.

The first boat I was on had a three-cylinder paraffin burner and when the engineer lit it up, the stink was quite sickening. You'd be sick before you'd even left the harbour. Not everyone would get sick but I did, just about each day. It took me years to get over it.

**Peter Flett,** born 1928: Findochty

# A quality life

Our small community was dominated by the fishing industry, absolutely so. Most of its men would have been on a boat at sea, or serving a boat at sea, or handling the product of a boat at sea. I can't think of any family which didn't have a fisherman or a marine engineer, a cooper, a curer or a kipperer. Apart, that is, from one or two wee shoppies – but then they depended upon the fishing for their trade. The whole of Buchanhaven was fish, fish, fish. In retrospect you could see it as grim, a grey and stoney place. But it didn't seem that way to me then; the rows of fisher cottages, the little harbour, the streets of granite gussets – they were the most natural things in the world to me.

Our people liked 'quality'. The fisher household would pride itself on having good quality things always available for the visitor, or to put on show in the cabinet. My

**'Nae mair fishin'**
Peter and Isbel Flett at home in Findochty, 2006

**Whenever anyone came to the house for a cup of tea, she would set out the table with the best china, the best linen, the best cutlery. These would be presented on a proper tablecloth, all starched and spotlessly white.**

mother, whenever anyone came to the house for a cup of tea, she would set out the table with the best china, the best linen, the best cutlery. These would be presented on a proper tablecloth, all starched and spotlessly white. When I came to work in Inverurie and got invited into a home for a cup of coffee and found that I was being offered a heavy mug of the stuff to perch on my lap, why I was just flabbergasted. My mother, now, would have served it up with due ceremony, not just plonk it down in front of a visitor like that. And there would have been a nice slice of homemade fruitcake, or a loaf with butter spread on it and some shortbread she'd made specially.

This quality thing was inherent in the fishing community. We might not have very much in the way of material goods, but what we had must be of sound quality; nothing cheap, nothing flash. Exactly the same with clothes. You had your navy blue serge suit which was kept for Sundays;. When it began to shine up a bit, it became your 'going ashore' suit – the clothes you wore when you were going on shore at Yarmouth or somewhere like that on a Saturday – in other words, your second best. I can remember how each Hogmanay my father would make a big thing of going into Peterhead, of going 'doon the toon', to buy my mother's present. This would be something like a pair of slippers. But often he would also return with a brand new rug to be laid out on New Year's day, there in front of the fireside for the whole world to see.

Possibly this insistence on quality was related to the poverty and the pride of the community. We didn't have much, so what we had had to be good and it had to last. These were the days before men were paid a regular wage and just relied upon a share of the profits from a trip. A bad fishing season could bring real shortage. Sometimes men, once they'd paid their grub money – the bill for their keep on board – could find themselves with almost nothing and the winter coming on. Then there would be a lot of shooting, not for sport, but shooting for the pot. My own father went out regularly. They'd get permission from some farmer to go out into his fields and hope to come back with a rabbit, a hare, the odd pheasant. In return they would maybe hand over half a barrel of salted herring. The poverty we all shared was probably responsible for the high sense of community spirit among us. If one household had enough for a pot but the neighbours didn't, then like as not, that pot would be shared out among them all.

The women must have a hard and worrying time of it. Many's a night they would have heard the wind rising up and lie there fearful for their men out on a stormy sea. Death in such a place was a regular enough event and a whole boat could go under with all her crew. The community was very supportive of widows and orphans. Religion undoubtedly helped, too: church groups offered material as well as moral comfort. I remember just after my grandfather died, and I was still a boy, this old fisherman made a point of telling me, 'Naebody iver wint tae Andra needin a pun and cam awa withoot it'. Now, I never knew any of that; such acts were performed quietly. Those words told me something about my own family and of the place I lived in; they made me very proud.

**Andrew Dick,** born 1936: Buchanhaven

# Just a wee bit of fun

I was brought up in small village almost totally devoted to the fishing business. This meant learning to have a sense of thrift right from the start. My mother kept a Post Office savings book for both my brother and me – sixpence a week or so throughout my childhood. And we were expected to contribute to the family income, too. One source of income which the whole family could join in was the buckies. You'd collect buckies off the beach in a bucket and then put them into a large jute sack which stood on the green above the shore. You'd wait till the sack contained a bushel and then it was tied up, put on a bike and taken up the hill, the mile-and-a-half to the station, for despatch right the way down to Billingsgate, London, where they'd be sold as winkles.

A number of people in the village would take in *The Fishing News* and pass it around, so that by the end of the week practically every household had been given the chance to peruse its columns. It was a vital source of information on all things fishing – the comings and goings of vessels, the size of their catches, local sales and dances. On its back page you'd find a series of adverts and this would enable you to decide where to send the buckies. One of the smallest was placed by this Billingsgate firm, but we were attracted to it because it promised to send you up a prepaid label which you could stick on the sack. You'd send off your buckies and then a week later a postal order for ten-and-sixpence would arrive – riches!

But life for us boys was far from being all work. We had the freedom of the village and the shore to roam about all day long and work out whatever amusements we could from what we found there. We all took up fishing. To begin with this meant taking a bamboo cane or a straight branch from a tree and raiding your mother's sewing box for a piece of cotton thread as your line. Then you'd go to the end of the pier and try and catch any small fish you could.

One of our ploys was to build a raft from any likely bits of wood we could get hold of. Once we came across some old 'backs' of tree wood and strapped them together. To give our wood some buoyancy we picked up some old large tin cans from the NAAFI supply base at the end of the village and used them. We first took off their lids and hammered them to the underside of our craft and then jammed the cans into them.

We were away, out into the harbour. But the fishermen took exception to our little raft bobbing around among their boats and threatened to destroy it, so we decided to sail it out to a sheltered cove we knew of some 400 yards along the shore. But to get through the harbour mouth meant sailing the raft over the partly-submerged rock which stood across the entrance channel. This could be done if the tide and the waves allowed it, but we miscalculated so that just as we were above it, moving up and down with the swell of

**The complete family**
Jim Wilson, right, with parents, brother and boat. Sandend, 1946

**'You could just about jump from my bedroom into the harbour'**
The Wilson's home is the larger gable-ended one to the right. Sandend 1950s.

**'At the herring'**
Yarmouth 1925. Jim Wilson's mother is middle row, third left.

the sea, a wave fell and we suddenly found ourselves balanced precariously astride the rock. There were three of us on board, so the weight wasn't evenly distributed and one of us – me, of course – nearly got tipped off. Just at the vital moment another wave came and righted us, but I can still remember the moment when I thought I was a goner. I couldn't swim, you see.

None of this stopped us in our tracks, not for a second. Now if I even see my own grandsons straying out of the garden I'm gripped with terror for them, but in those days we were fearless and, generally, the adults left us to our own devices.

We did go indoors sometimes. Everybody had radios. I used to listen to *Dick Barton* and to Radio Luxembourg for the latest pop music. Then there was *Children's Hour* with Tammy Troot, the *McFlannells* on a Saturday evening, at teatime, and Scottish country dance music. Another thing was that we used to tune into the radios of the fishing fleets out on the Firth. I remember my father buying this special box – it was like the digital boxes that nowadays you fit onto the top of your TV set – and he sat it on top of the radio and he'd tune into the frequencies of the fishing fleet. He'd twiddle around and pick up news of how the fishing was going, when the boats intended to come in again to harbour and so on. I used to listen in as well.

But mostly we were out and about. Our house butted directly onto the green which led right onto the harbour – I could have jumped out of my bedroom skylight and landed in one of the boats that would be parked up on the shore there. The beach gave us our games equipment, so to speak. All kinds of stuff would be washed up onto it and the households of the village used to dump their bits and pieces of rubbish there. For us it could be a treasure trove. For example, you'd get old boots and shoes; their soles might have gone, but you'd find the tongues would still be in good shape and we could extract these and stretch them out for use as catapults. We'd line up old bottles and cans and hold target competitions. I was no more than a moderate shot, but some of the lads became sufficiently expert to bring down a seagull or two.

We had masses of games, a million local games. One was called Leario. If you can imagine it, in a little fishing village like Sandend, there would be all the houses in little rows with alleys in between, narrow little alleys, plenty of places where we could jink in and out. We'd divide ourselves into two sides – the hunters and the hunted, so to speak. If you were caught you had to go to this dell, but then a team-mate could come and sneak up and rescue you from it, by shouting 'Leario!'. And we played football along the streets, with tennis balls, all along the street.

There were a lot of small fishing boats in the harbour and all kinds of things for us to do on a Saturday in the winter-time when the boats were back home. The boats would be pulled up out of the water, onto the fringe between the harbour and the road – we called it 'the green'. They used to get a block and tackle and attach it to the boat and had sleepers to run the boat up on. All along the street there'd be these chains that were built into the street and the idea was to attach the block and tackle to a chain and so pull it up and secure it, away from the water. These were built into the roadway where we played and for every yard that the boat was pulled in, there would be created four or five of extra rope at the end. So if they pulled up the boat maybe 30 yards or so then there would be over 100 yards of corresponding rope, rope for us young lads to grab hold of, and then we'd run along an alley between the houses and tie the rope to something like a water barrel. So when the boat was pulled back this object would now be attached to it and go bouncing along. It was just a wee bit of fun.

We had all kinds of pranks that we used to play like that. A lot of the houses had for their guttering these water spouts and we'd take a bit of lighted newspaper and put it into a spout. We'd light it with a match and pop it in and this would create an up-draught which would suck in all the air and make a big whooshy noise. Whoosh! It would frighten the life out of the people inside. Another thing was if you had a fishing line and it had a hook and sinker on it, you could go up to a house and attach the sinker to the putty of a window and the creep away and tug on it. This would make tapping sound on the window, like someone chapping at the window for attention. Great fun.

Jim Wilson, born 1938: Sandend

> We'd take a bit of lighted newspaper and put it into a spout. This would suck in all the air and make a big whooshy noise. It would frighten the life out of the people inside.

# Birth, death and marriage in a Mearns village

When I was a girl the village was a maze of narrow alleys and cottages. These were very simple affairs: usually just earth floors and two or three rooms. They would shell their mussels, live and sleep all in the one room. When I was very small, there was no running water in the house; father and mother slept in the same room we all lived in. Me and my sister, my grandmother and my parents had these three rooms

My grandfather's favourite saying was: 'Kip the fire burnin in yer hearth even if the cupboard's empty; people'll see the smoke frae yer lum, bit they winna see inta yer cupboard'.

and that was it. There was a black-leaded grate in the living room for cooking. Eventually when I was eight, we got a sink and a toilet put in. Up till then we'd used a chemical toilet.

There was a lot of poverty. My grandmother would tell me how, when my grandfather was away at sea for several days, she would have no money in the house and the food would be running out. Then she would just go down to the rocks and gather in buckies to sell to Buckie Jock to get the necessary food for her family. But they were also a very proud people. My grandfather's favourite saying was: 'Kip the fire burnin in yer hearth even if the cupboard's empty; people'll see the smoke frae yer lum, bit they winna see inta yer cupboard'.

As well as the fish, the village had a flax-spinning mill which employed 70 or 80 at its peak. A lot of the young women went to work in it. When it first opened in the late 19th century, it was run by the Gibb family and they proved to be harsh employers. Mother always claimed that the bosses were responsible for ruining half of the village because of the way they treated their female workers, with work so tight and the general feeling being that you had to obey those in charge. The boss lived in a big house at the top of Johnshaven and treated his workers as personal property.

Conditions were so hard that in 1913 the union – the Dundee Flax and Jute workers Association – called them all out on strike. The firm was ready to settle and a meeting was to be held in the Templars Hall, but the girls refused to enter it. Mr Gibb attempted to address the crowd, but the women simply drowned him out and followed him down the street, catcalling. Feelings ran very high and eventually the mill was forced to raise the spinners' pay by one shilling a week, making the total wage 11 shillings for a week's work.

Then the Burness family took over and things improved considerably. But as was the way of the time, working conditions were still hard. My mother worked there for a while and she would talk about how the overseer would go around shouting, 'Keep your ends up or you'll be down the bloody road!' There was no gentle persuasion in those days. They would start at six and go on to eight, with just a half-hour break in the middle of the day.

My mother looked after Granny to the end, despite all her many afflictions over the final eight years or so, and I looked after my mother. There was no placing an old relative

into a home then. But, of course, people didn't move away then; you had your extended family around you. Now the young move off and Johnshaven's become a dormitory settlement, full of people who come to it as strangers because it's a nice picturesque spot to live in and because housing is so much more reasonable than it is nearer Aberdeen. You can get a decent-sized house here for the price of a flat in the city.

So that was a measure of living standards in Johnshaven. But folk were always ready to help each other out. My grandparents had a fish business and they would take any fish left over at the end of the day's trading and give it to the poor of the village. A couple of years ago, out in the street, I was stopped by this old woman: 'Ah jist wint ye tae ken hoo very guid yer granny wis tae us aa fan Ah wis young. We were a large faimily an not very weel aff, bit she aye made sure we git samethin to pit in oor moos at the end o the day'. And when I was a girl my mother would make a big pot of broth and send me round all the old men who lived by themselves to make sure they got something for their lunch.

My granny was left school and into work at 11. She was sent to work in the fish house down at the harbour. She'd be working all day long, up to her elbows in ice and cold water, barrelling and salting the herrings. She was a little, hardy woman who worked and worked. In those days that's what you had to do – work till you went out in your coffin. There were no benefits then. I had a great-grandfather who died working in a quarry when he got caught up in an explosion. He was 78 at the time and still having to do a day's work.

There was a lot of superstition. If the men were about to go to sea and caught sight of the minister, they would turn back. He had to learn to keep to the house when the tides were right for the fishing. And you could never say the word, 'pig'; you had to use the term, 'curly tail'.

People were also very conservative. I remember how my grandfather, who died in

## Trouble at the mill

Johnshaven 1913, with the striking mill hands pursuing their union rep after the abortive meeting at Templar's Hall.

Campaigning mill hands rally at the harbour.

> The men did nothing about the house, nor with their own children. That was strictly women's work. Often you'd see the women baiting lines while they were trying to rock a cradle with a foot.

1944, refused to have electricity put in: 'Na, na – nane o that electricity – we'll a be gassed in oor beds!' A woman was meant to leave school, marry and bring up children. I remember once running home from school: 'Granny, Granny, the teacher read my essay out to the whole class'. And she said, 'Whisht, lassie, dinna you gae tellin onybady samthin like that.' Women weren't for education, you see. She never voted in her life; politics were for the men; she would stay at home and trust them to make the big decisions. People like her never bothered much about what was going on in the outside world. When my great-granny's sons were called up to the First World War, her attitude was: 'Fit's aa this waur gat to dae wi ma sons? Fit why don't they pit the Kaiser and the King inta a field and lat them fight it oot atween them? Ah'll follow fa-iver wins'.

No, she was conservative and so was much of the village. There was the feeling that society was ordered in the way it was and that it would be best to leave it that way. There was the gentry, there was the minister, the doctor and the dominie and then there were the ordinary working folk, like themselves, and that's the way it had to be. Those who were in power were so because they knew best: they had the experience and the position to look after everything properly.

The men did nothing about the house, nor with their own children. That was strictly women's work. When their husbands were home they had to be waited on and when they were away at sea the house had to be kept going. Often you'd see the women baiting lines while they were trying to rock a cradle with a foot. Certainly, the men did have hard lives out at sea, but when they were ashore they expected to be waited on hand and foot and then go off to the pub. No woman would never ever be permitted to accompany him. Drink was for men only.

My mother had to do everything about the house and often on hardly any money. She had to black-lead the grate, do the washing outside in an old stone boiler, which had to have a fire lit under it; she did the mangle and used a scrubbing board. She had to cook, to bake and keep the house clean and tidy. She knitted and sewed – and she looked after me and my sister and her own mother, too.

The man of the house was its lord and master. My mother would tell how her own father simply had to lift his finger to get instant obedience. Once she and her sister were down at the harbour playing and Grandad was chatting to a man over on the other side of the quay. Suddenly he called out, 'Hannah! Jean!' and lifted his finger at them. They instantly stopped what they were up to and ran round as fast as they could to where he was. When they got there, all he said was, 'Noo ye may gae an play agin!' He'd simply been demonstrating to the other man the power he had over his children.

When my grandmother came to be married she was already nine months pregnant. My great-grandfather's first wife had died early and the sister-in-law had come to look after the two children from that marriage. They lived together as man and wife and had eight children, but under Scots Law at that time a man couldn't marry a dead wife's sister, so their own children were classed as illegitimate and were never christened. Now my grandfather's mother was very religious and wouldn't allow her son to marry a woman

who wasn't baptised. Not only that, she insisted that all the brothers and sisters must be christened as well. By the time all this was done, my grandmother was due to give birth. Sadly, the baby died and she had to arrange a funeral service. So within the one week she experienced her own christening, marriage, a birth and a death.

Death was treated as part of everyday existence then. Old folk would keep a box under their beds and in it there would be a white nightdress ready for their own lying out. I can remember my granny had one and every summer it had to come out to be given a wash and iron before it was put away again. Once when I was a small child she took her nightdress out, hung it up against herself and told me, 'Won't I lik bonny in this fan Ah'm deed'. That sent me screaming from the room.

The lying out would be in the house. People would come, knock at the door and be invited in have for a last look at the body. They would be offered a glass of whisky or sherry and taken over to the coffin. The face would be covered by a flap and this would be carefully pulled back, so that the visitor could gaze into it. I remember one of our neighbours insisting she wanted none of this when her time came,. 'They'll be nane o thae peep shows fan Ah'm gane,' she'd say.

My granny had a hard time of it at the end. She lived till she was 88, but for the last eight years she was in a sorry state, becoming blind, deaf and suffering fits of madness. But mother looked after her at home till the end. That's what you did then – no putting the old parent into a home. That would have been regarded as a cause for shame. I remember my granny would say, 'Ye'll nae pit me intae the Poors Hoose, wull ye?' That's what going into a home was associated with then, the Poor House.

**Joann Beattie,** born 1946: Johnshaven

**Still very much involved.** Cecilia Penny and young eco-warrior at the opening of the Eco Park, Stuartfield School, 2000. The plaque on the bench has her name on it.

# CHARACTERS AND COMMUNITY

# Shops meant service

In Fraserburgh you'd see lovely shops, oh lovely shops there were! The shopkeepers took great pride in doing up their windows; they had them done up to perfection. I used to love looking in at them; they were as good as anything you could see in Aberdeen. My own father was a florist, greengrocer and confectioner, and he had his own shop in the centre of the town. It would be piled high with fruit, boxes of vegetables, sweets and lots of flowers. He also sold coffee; he would buy in the beans and he would grind them for the customer on the spot; you could get any blend you wanted. It filled the shop with a wonderful, lovely smell.

Nothing was pre-packed then. It annoys me nowadays that you have to buy a packet of something; you take it home and you find that half of the things in it aren't suitable. In our time you would sell everything loose, exactly the number and the weight the customer wanted. Our shop would buy boxes of grapes and raisins and prunes, from California mostly. We also bought lots of dried fruit – peaches, apricots, apple rings and so on – from a wholesaler in Aberdeen such as Peglars or Knowles. You name it, we had it. And the flowers in winter wouldn't come from Holland as they all seem to nowadays; we'd get them up from the Channel Islands and, when the season was right, from other parts of Britain. My father ordered them by telephone and they would be up in Fraserburgh by rail that same day, sometimes within an hour or two.

We prided ourselves on being able to get whatever the customer wanted. Boots the chemist had this boast that any medicine that was needed would be in the customer's hands within 24 hours and we were much the same. It was all done by speaking to people, over the phone or direct. Now it's all computers and that's what they blame if anything goes wrong: 'computer error', they call it. But really it's the people who feed the computer that's at fault. They just don't seem to care, not when they've a machine to blame. Oh, you should read the stinking letters I've had to send off to companies over all the things that go wrong nowadays.

But then we believed in service, personal service. If you made a mistake, even one wee error, you could be sacked on the spot; now they can be thousands of pounds out and it doesn't seem to matter. There's not the same pride in the work; they just stick out their hands for their wages, that's all they're interested in these days. I mean, where are the manners now? If you came into our shop you'd have the door opened for you and got a chair to sit on. Courtesy and obligement, that's what you had to offer, each and every customer received it. If a customer complained, that was enough: you could get the sack, simple as that.

Shop assistants were trained; they knew how to address a customer and make them feel important. And they knew their stock, too: they knew where everything was stored and kept. They knew that you mustn't place eggs near the soap; they knew where the fruit came from and what was in season and what would be coming into it the next month. Why, my father would turn in his grave if he could see the way that bananas are just thrown down any old how now; he would have his hung up in proper hands.

But then folk just don't take the care they used to. What a waste goes on nowadays. Folk just fill their bags, they go home, they put the stuff in the fridge and then forget they ever bought it in the first place. The amount that goes to waste nowadays is criminal; in my day you had to budget for every single item and then make sure you used it properly. You see, money was scarce then: you had to choose between a loaf or half-a-dozen biscuits, you couldn't afford both – and you certainly couldn't buy in a couple of packets that might get stale and throw them out a fortnight later.

In those days Fraserburgh, in the fishing time, would be filled with girls who'd come down from Shetland to follow the herring and do the gutting. They would stay in the outhouses at the back here and they'd have to fend for themselves. On a Saturday they would stop their work late at night and that's when they would come by to get their food in for the weekend. First they would call in at the butcher for a wee bit beef and a bone; then they would come along the street to my father's shop. They would shout in, 'Surely you're not shut yet, are you?' Late as it was, my father would let them into the shop and would sell them two carrots, a half neep, two leeks and a bunch of parsley, all for one penny. That's what was known then as a pennysworth of vegetables and it would be for their Sunday broth.

Service, that's what I'm talking about. All the shops practised it then, and staff would stay on at the same shop year after year. My father would get in a young assistant straight from the school and she would be there for years, right up to the time when she got married. The centre had all the shops you could possibly want – grocers, butchers, fishmongers, fruiterers, drapers and chemists. And every corner seemed to have its own wee shop and they would sell everything, from paraffin to sugar.

My father worked a very long day in the shop and we were brought up to work too. When you came in from school there would be the dishes to wash and dry and your father's boots put out for you to polish. I was doing all this when I was at infants' school. There were the linoleum floors to be scrubbed and then the range had to be polished. Every Friday night the house had to be cleaned and dusted from top to bottom. And you'd be expected to run any messages to the shops. We were brought up to be useful.

We were also brought up to respect money. No credit for us in those days; if you wanted something then you had to save up for it or go without. These credit cards will be the ruination of the country! Even now I refuse to have one; I still like to go to the Post Office and collect the pension each week; I like to see the cash in my hand.

**Violet Johnston,** born 1909: Fraserburgh

# Carry on poaching

I loved to keep myself fit. Physical training, you'd call it. I'd play football; I'd do some hammer throwing. That and the running. Most evenings I'd run round to Kinneff and back, about six miles.

But I was always getting into scrapes and injuries. I must have been about 13 and this fellow who was working with my father at the smithy, he said, ' Fit aboot comin tae the

> I could get 15 to 20 rabbits for a reasonable night's work and then I'd go to the local butcher and he'd buy them, no questions asked. I'd make more at my poaching than I got from my wages at the smithy.

**George Carr's father**

at Barras smithy, 1930s.

pictures at Bervie the nicht?' I'd never been to a cinema, so I was fair taken with the idea. But I had to attend to the cow before I could get away. I went out to the byre and because I was in a hurry I fed the cow first, which I shouldn't have done. Then I gave it a shove to move it over, but she wouldn't go, so I gave her another push and she came back on me. My arm got pushed against the wall and I felt something go. I went into the house and told my father, 'Ah think Ah've broken ma airm, Dad'. So there were no pictures for me, after all, just the doctor. It wasn't till several years later that I saw my first film, a cowboy film.

I broke that arm a second time. I used to ride my motor bike to Aberdeen on a Saturday night. You'd race along; no helmets but no cars either, not on the roads in those days. Anyway, this night I took a corner a wee bit fast and came off. My mate, who was riding pillion, fell on top of me and that did my arm in again. When I went to the doctor he felt it all over; then he called the other doctor in: 'Feel this arm. There's nothing but muscle on it. I've never seen an arm like it'. The work at the smithy had done that for me.

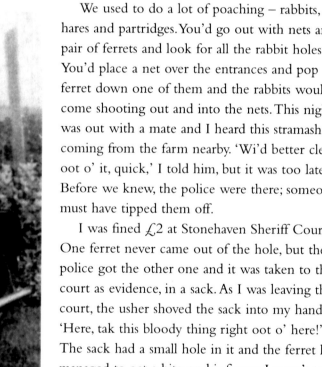

We used to do a lot of poaching – rabbits, hares and partridges. You'd go out with nets and a pair of ferrets and look for all the rabbit holes. You'd place a net over the entrances and pop the ferret down one of them and the rabbits would come shooting out and into the nets. This night I was out with a mate and I heard this stramash coming from the farm nearby. 'Wi'd better clear oot o' it, quick,' I told him, but it was too late. Before we knew, the police were there; someone must have tipped them off.

I was fined £2 at Stonehaven Sheriff Court. One ferret never came out of the hole, but the police got the other one and it was taken to the court as evidence, in a sack. As I was leaving the court, the usher shoved the sack into my hand, 'Here, tak this bloody thing right oot o' here!' The sack had a small hole in it and the ferret had managed to get a bite on his finger. I wasn't too sorry about that.

**The proceeds of crime**

A 16-year-old George Carr on the motorbike he bought from his poaching 'earnings'

The fine did nothing to stop me. Just carried on. Rabbits were an important part of the diet then. I could get 15 to 20 for a reasonable night's work and then I'd go to the local butcher and he'd buy them, no questions asked. I'd make more at my poaching than I got from my wages at the smithy. Nobody eats rabbits any more, but everyone did then – including the sheriff, no doubt. Poaching was just accepted as part of country life.

**George Carr,** born 1916: Barras

# Toon dirt and country yokels

Torphins in the summer always seemed to be bathed in sunshine, broken only by the odd storm that would roll around the hills and had the effect of terrifying my mother.

Our garden seemed to be bursting with produce: fruit and vegetables of all types. My mother would take the gooseberries, the strawberries, the brambles and the plums and turn them into jelly on the open fire. She would then pot it up in two-pound jars.

We had four beehives in the garden as well and from these we would get beautiful runny honey that dripped out of the comb sections. Against the north wall was the henhouse; the occupants were fed on kale and oats from the garden and they supplied us with fresh eggs in return.

I didn't get pocket money as such. I would earn it by manning the putting green clubhouse where I would sell tickets at twopence a round; my pay was twopence for every shillingsworth that I could sell. This would usually be to the summer visitors who filled the village then. I would love to have been fitted out in the tasteful grey suits and shorts which they seemed to wear.

Our house had a cottage at the bottom of its garden and every July and August my parents would pack us all, lock stock and barrel into it, so that the house could be let out to summer visitors from the city. It was the railway which brought them out; in fact, it was the coming of the rail in the 19th century which had put Torphins on the map – till then it had been little more than a clachan of agricultural houses.

These visitors would come out and stay for two, even four weeks, so that you would see them around the place day after day and observe how they behaved themselves. The father would go off each morning in the train to the city, leaving his family to disport themselves around the village, on its tennis courts and putting green. To us they were 'toon dirt', but the compliment was certainly returned because they seemed to look down on us as primitive rustics. They were uppity and loud and had every appearance of considering themselves to be more sophisticated.

One of our regular visitors was the Mearns family who owned a pub back in Aberdeen. At its head was Colonel Mearns who'd served in the Indian army and strolled around uttering a gobbled high-class form of speech of which 'Jimmy' was just about the only word I could make out. He spoke with this perpetual pebble in his mouth. The whole family seemed so refined that it gave me a sense of social inferiority.

Then there were the Hutchisons who comprised the baker and his three sons, each of whom journeyed into town to attend the Aberdeen Grammar School. They would come back to Torphins and stroll around in their blazers and nice grey flannels. They played tennis. I did too, but whereas they sported the appropriate gear, I only had my usual corduroy – sturdy country wear and eminently practical, but somewhat lacking in elegance. Moreover my father insisted I always wore boots – not tackety ones, they were for the farm labourers' sons – but boots nevertheless. 'Little Duke' they were called.

**James Morrison,** born 1917: Torphins

**Twopence a round**
Visitors from 'the toon' on Torphins putting green, 1931

Our house had a cottage at the bottom of its garden and every July and August my parents would pack us all, lock stock and barrel into it, so that it could be let out to summer visitors from the city.

# A country doctor starts out

**Dr Beatrice Sellars** in 1931 at her retirement after 38 years service to her Aberlour practice

She walked through a blizzard to a gamekeeper's near Knockando. She walked up the brae — some hike! She delivered the baby; it wasn't a breech after all.

I came to Aberlour in 1942; my first posting. I found it a very friendly place. I put some of that down to the Sellars [the doctor family]; they were so very friendly themselves. People would come in to ask about a problem, like a pregnant daughter, and be taken into the house for a cup of tea. That would never have happened in Elgin.

But we all did a lot of walking around then. I often had to go on foot for home visits, even in the Forties. I used to have to carry on with the visits in the most awful blizzards. I got off the little train at Carron and walked home, carrying out my visits on the way back. I had to climb up that steep brae all the way up to Dailuaine Terrace. First I had to call in at Carron House, then go to the distillery, then up the brae. Then I had to call in at Edinvillie, but the road was by now completely full and I had problems following the route. The men were all away at the war and there was no one to clear the road. I got to Nellie Shewan's shop and turned off up the road to Edinvillie. I thought I'd try to cut across the paddock there, but off the road and into the fields, the snow was even thicker. I got stuck. Eventually I got back to the Benrinnes road; I found a tractor had been along it and I could walk in its tracks. When I arrived I found my patient, a rather simple girl, was up drinking a cup of tea. They thought she'd had pneumonia, but really it was only a bad cold. I then had to walk all the way back to Aberlour, but I did manage to get a lift in a buggy and pony at the top of the Dowans brae for the last bit.

We had terrific blizzards in those days and the doctor just had to walk it. On that same day I had accompanied Dr B on the train to Carron. She had to go up to a gamekeeper's at the foot of the Dowan moor, near Knockando. She walked up the brae to it – some hike! She delivered the baby; it wasn't a breech after all. Then she had to walk back to the station. The gamekeeper never even offered to go with her for at least part of the way. She had delivered his child, wearing a purple blouse and a tartan skirt belonging to his wife while her own clothes were drying out before the fire. Afterwards she said that was the only time she had ever been really frightened in the snow.

The National Health Service started in 1948, while I was at Aberlour. A lot of people don't realise this, but most of the families were insured through something or other, like the Shepherds or the Foresters. But this only gave them the mixture and no flavouring – the basics. Penicillin came in while I was there, too. To begin with you had these tablets in an ampoule and you would fill the syringe with sterile water and dissolve the tablets in it. Nobody actually went without treatment. Dr B was very good about that. If their bill was getting too large for comfort, she would talk it over with them and come to an arrangement. They might pay her in kind, so to speak. One of the gamekeepers would keep her dogs in rabbits; another, who had a shop, would pay in biscuits. Dr B wasn't really worried about getting paid in such cases, but she thought it better for people if they did contribute something. One family – this was the biscuit people - claimed they had difficulties, yet the whole family had a season ticket to attend the cinema in the Fleming Hall.

I'd say that the word 'independent' is the one that sums up the people of Aberlour in those days. I remember being over at the factor's house for tea when the phone rang. Mr McKenzie stopped eating his egg and went to get it unhooked from the wall. It was the

laird at the castle. People would come to the doctor ask about a problem, like a pregnant daughter, and be taken into the house for a cup of tea. That would never have happened in a bigger place, like Elgin.

We used to do such a lot of home visiting – in all weathers and for all illnesses – and now they hardly do any at all. The doctor was an important figure in the community. We were all very much part of the local scene. I would defend Dr B to the very hilt for all she did for them all.

# The piper

Before the war I was working on the farms. It was at the feein markets at Huntly that I first got the notion for the pipes. You see, the army would always be in attendance, playing the pipes and on the lookout for new recruits and I would listen and fair enjoy the sound they were making and just the whole spectacle of the thing.

I was posted to Kirkwall in the early days of the war. That's where I first got into actually playing the pipes. A lot of the men were posted south to Aldershot and this only left two or three pipers. The regiment was in the way of playing to the public; the pipers would gather at the steps to St Magnus Cathedral and the folk would come round to listen. It was our way of saying thank you for all the great hospitality we'd been receiving from the Orcadians. So the pipe major asked for volunteers to take the place of the pipers who'd gone away and I put my hand up. I'd never played the pipes before, but I took to them at once and you could say I've never looked back. I've now been playing non-stop since those Kirkwall days, getting on for 70 years – and I've no plans to put a stop to it, not yet a while.

For me it's been the pipes all the way. If you asked me to play a tune just like that the chances are I would have to tell you I'd forgotten it, but when you're out with the band you just slip from one to the other automatically, no bother at all. I must have hundreds of tunes running through my head. I'm 90 years old and I still play my part in the band.

In August 1948 we formed the Huntly Pipe Band and it's still going strong – we'll be

**The young piper**
Jimmy Horne in the Gordon Highlanders in the Second World War

**Seventy years later an still blawin**

Jimmy Horne, at the age of 90, celebrates 60 years in the Huntly band. Also in the picture are Hamish Dean and Clarence Gould

celebrating our 60th year in August. I was a founder member, the only one of them still left and still playing. We play in the Square here and we also appear at the various games, at Aberlour, at Dufftown, at Nethybridge. I can still keep up, though these days I do notice where all the little slopes are that you have to march up.

**Jimmy Horne,** born 1919: Huntly

## Living history in Laurencekirk

I was born in 1921, in this very house, upstairs in one of the bedrooms. My father was a shoemaker. At that time there were three shoe shops in Laurencekirk. They were all the same set-up: shoe repairs and sales.

My grandfather died the year I was born and my grandmother when I was three. I remember her as this figure sitting in her chair in Garvock Street. But there are stories about them both that have come to me through my father. My grandfather was born in 1839; he left school when he was 12. Apparently, so the story goes, my grandfather went to school only in the wintertime. In the summer he had to go to the cattle. This was a common job for children then. The area round Laurencekirk, a lot of it, had been newly cleared for farmland. It was drained and ditched, but it couldn't be enclosed easily. There were no stones suitable for making dykes, so in many cases it was the children who had to take the cattle out to pasture and keep them out of the grain in the summer time. The children would be kept off school to work on the land for much of the year.

My wife had much the same story. Her great-grandmother had been employed as a child to do the same thing on a farm over at Marykirk. She used to take a toy with her, a homemade doll out of rags – a cloutie doll it was called – for company. Well, one day she

> My grandfather was born in 1839; he left school when he was 12. He went to school only in the wintertime. In the summer he had to go to the cattle.

put it down beside her and a cow started chewing on it. The cow choked and damn near died; that was the end of the job.

There's also a story about my grandmother in the family. In 1849 the railway was being constructed through here. My great-grandmother had two of the navvies as lodgers. They didn't work on Sundays and one Sunday they asked my grandmother, who was just a girl still, to go to the Western Hotel to get a bottle of whisky. She had to tell the hotel that the whisky was required for 'an unwell man'. She got the whisky, the men were happy and gave her a penny to herself. She was delighted, but her mother was furious. Whisky on a Sunday and getting a child to fetch it, too!

**Arthur Bruce** born 1921: Laurencekirk

**Living history**
Arthur Bruce in 2003, still living where he was born in 1921.

# Life in the glen

Was I lonely? Well, my father as head keeper kept 25 dogs and whenever you went out to the kennel yards they would jump up at you and be all over you. There weren't many other kids to play with, but I'd go off down to Rough Park with my mother every week to fetch the messages from Shand's shop there. Vans would come round regularly: baker, butcher out from Alford, the grocer's from Heughhead. He would come by on the Saturday and I'd always be given a sweetie by him. Personally, I assumed it was a gift, but later I realised that he was adding a twopence to the weekly bill to cover it. An early lesson in the realities of life.

A lot of the year was taken up with the rearing of pheasants. You used to go round to collect broody hens and take them home and set them on hens' eggs to see if they would take to it. Then you'd introduce them to the pheasants' eggs. The funny thing is that hens' eggs will hatch out two days quicker than the pheasants', so we'd be left with all these orphan chicks, so to speak, which we put into an old wooden cartridge box by the fire. When they grew up they imagined that our house was their own home and they would just come in through the door and wander about the place and leave the usual mess on the floor.

I had a snare and got a couple of rabbits now and then. I liked to go fishing. When my dad was up repairing the butts ready for the shooting season I'd go up with him and take

**Beaters at West Tornahaish in 1937**
Kenneth McHardy is eighth from left holding a flag.

**The Flea Pit, East Tornahaish**

A shooting party in the Edwardian era. Kenneth McHardy's grandfather, Alexander McHardy, head gamekeeper, is second left (in tie) back seated row.

my rod or a bit of string and catch a little trout. I remember my father taking a newly caught trout and splitting it open; he laid it on a flat stone and lit some heather and cooked it for me, out there on the hillside, straight from the water. Nothing like it!

So I was an outdoor lad. I had a lot of freedom to roam around, though you would never go into the policies around the Big House. That was taboo. But often I'd go out with the underkeeper who lived in the bothy beside the Big House and took his meals with us. We'd snare rabbits or feed pheasants – whatever the time of the year was.

In the glen our summer holidays didn't start till the first of August and that was so the boys would be available for work as a grouse beaters when the season began on the 'glorious 12th'. We had four or five weeks at it and got five shillings a day. Usually by working for two estates you could make thirty shillings a week, vital money, because it meant that we could all get new boots for the winter. Most of us also managed to purchase a five-shilling watch from the Bellabeg shop.

Kenneth McHardy, born 1927: Candacraig, Strathdon

## Class distinctions

You see there was a lot more in the way of class distinction when we were growing up. Far more than there is now, mercy yes. There were aye people you had to look up to in the community – the dominie, the doctor, the policeman and the banker too. I remember when the gamekeeper would be someone people looked up to. He had a lot of power, you see. If he didn't take to one of his under-keepers, he could just pass the word on, 'I don't think he's the right sort of chap to be working here', and that would be the kiss of death. You had to take care to keep on the right side of the head keeper, all right. He was the laird's representative, don't forget, and the laird might only come up to his estate during the season and so he would rely on his head keeper and the factor to keep things in order, as they saw it.

The policeman was another one we all had to look up to. I mean, we were all terrified of the bobby. If we did wrong our parents would threaten to tell the bobby and he would come and take us away and lock us up in the cell. The station at Strathdon had cells in those days and there might be the odd visitor to them, but nothing more than a drunk on a Saturday night – but to us kids the idea of that cell was enough.

We were kept in our place: never to be cheeky, never to speak back to the teacher, or to the dominie. Oh yes, you never spoke back to anybody, not if they were an adult. It was just our way of life.

**Mona Duncan,** born 1927: Strathdon

> We were kept in our place: never to be cheeky, never to speak back to anybody.

## A place where everyone knew everyone

Mintlaw was then the kind of place where everyone knew everyone. It was all local businesses then. There were a good number of shops. There was Farquhar's Emporium, That shop had hard, scrubbed, wooden floors and a wooden counter. There was a chair to sit on while you waited to be served and the floor around it was hollowed out where generations of heels had been. Then there was a jeweller's and a watchmaker. Mr Morris owned a tailor's and also sold fancy goods. There were three Miss Morrises, all maiden ladies: one kept the shop, another the house and the third taught. They would sell toys. They had wooden horses and carts, priced at 2/6 for the large one, 1/6 the small one. I remember going in with my penny and asking for a 'penny horse and cart'. No such animal! Then Miss Cummings had a draper's shop and there was a butcher, a baker, a shoemaker, a bank and a hotel. Really, Mintlaw was a self-sufficient place. We had no need of Aberdeen at all. And I shouldn't forget the blacksmith, Donald Mutch. He was very good to the children; I loved to go and see him working at the horses.

In those days there wasn't the big roundabout you have now in the centre. We called it 'the Square', but it was actually diamond-shaped; it was where some of the shopkeepers had their gardens.

It was the kind of place where you knew everybody. When I left school, I would go round with my father in his pony and cart selling potatoes. I got to know practically the whole village. And Miss Jemima Brown at the end of the village kept a little dairy and supplied the place with milk. She kept her cows in the field at the outskirts of the village. Of course, there weren't milk bottles; you had to go with your can and get it filled up from her cart.

**Georgina Adams,** born 1929: Mintlaw

**The Square, Mintlaw**
As it was when Gina Adams was growing up

**Different class**
Joyce Collie's maternal grandfather, Rector Mr Philips, with his Inverurie Academy staff, 1919

# Inverurie snobs

My mother was the daughter of the rector of Inverurie Academy, James Philip. My dad, however, was just a loon from the Colony. This was the scheme which had been put up to house all the workers who had come out from Aberdeen to work in the Loco Works. His father was employed as a brass finisher on the engines there. When his turn came, my father was quite happy to follow in his footsteps. He was a gem of a lad – everybody said that – but he had little in the way of ambition. He asked for nothing more than a job alongside his pals in the Loco works.

All this was very West endy/East endy. My mother was very much of the big schoolhouse, while my father had been raised in one of the workers' tenement houses. The locals tended to look down on them and their inhabitants. If you told any of the older folk in the town that you lived there they would sniff and say, 'Oh, so you're frae the Colony'. There was no mistaking what they meant by that.

What redeemed my father was that he was a superb cricketer and captained the Inverurie team. They won championships under his leadership. All this made him an acceptable member of the community among the higher echelons of Inverurie society.

But in his boyhood a form of snobbery did exist. He was blessed with this most gorgeous voice, whereas my mother could scarcely hold a note. He was so brilliant that when he went to a church service and they heard his voice, all the old ladies would be queuing up afterwards to try and persuade him to come along to their choir. But when the Musical Society held its auditions, she was the one who was offered a part while he was rejected. He was a Colony loon, you see, while she was the rector's daughter.

My mother was a beautiful young woman. She had two sisters, but she was by far the bonniest. When people talked about the three of them, they would refer to her as 'the bonny ane'. So it was quite a catch for a lad from the Colony to take her as his wife. They met at socials. Later, she would be invited to events in the town and would have to turn them down because my father hadn't been – such occasions were for the sons of the doctor, the minister or the hoteliers, not for the likes of him.

Dad's education was quite good: like my mother he'd been to Inverurie Academy and gone into the same system. This was: if you were smart, you could stay on and go for your highers; if not, leave at 14 and get a job in the Loco works. James Philip went to see my granny and told her that her son 'was definitely bright' and that he should stay on and go for the bursary competition and a place at university. She told the rector that he could stay on if he wanted to, that she would scrape and save and make the necessary sacrifices, if that is what he really wanted. But he would have none of it: ' Ah'm nat gaein te stay on wi aa thae snobs'. He was for going off to the Loco Works with all his pals who'd be leaving school for jobs there.

**Joyce Collie,** born in 1929: Inverurie

When the Musical Society held its auditions, she was offered a part while he was rejected. He was a Colony loon, you see.

# Inventing the hitch plough

In those days the blacksmith was very much at the centre of any rural community. You needed a blacksmith's shop to be within walking distance of the farm, so they were dotted all over the country. But they've all gone now. Things change.

Even the smallest farm, they all had its pair of Clydesdales and they all needed shod regularly. Every day there seemed to be horses, horses about the place. Dad, just by hearing a horse being led down the tarmacadam road outside, knew exactly what kind of a job he would be having to do on it. It was like a mechanic knowing from the noise of a car engine what the problem was.

**Bridge of Muchalls smiddy 1933**
Nina's father on left, journeyman on right. The three-year old Nina can be glimpsed at the house door, with her grandmother.

In the smiddy house the workshop lay just across the close, so I had its sounds all around me. Dad got in an engine that ran all the time to give him the power to drive his boring machines and lathes. When I got married and left home to go up to Gartly I can recall how quiet and eerie I found it. One day I can remember going out of the house and saying to myself, 'But it's awful quiet and it's not a Sunday – something must be wrong'. Then I remembered where I was, over 50 miles from Muchalls, and I laughed at myself. You see, the beat of that engine was a constant background to my early life.

**Rescuing the smiddy henhouse**
The great flood of 1958

**Bridge of Muchalls School 1938**
Nina is extreme left (with bow); the teacher is Mrs Brown.

As a girl I wasn't encouraged to go into the workshop – it was far too busy a place for a child. You see, Dad became more than just an ordinary blacksmith when he invented his hitch plough. The ground round about was very stony and when the first tractors came in the farmers had a real problem with it. The old horse-drawn ploughs had just skimmed the surface, but the tractor was cutting down deeper and hitting all these stones. Something would break and the whole operation had to come to a standstill. The farmer would have to reverse back and lift the plough as best he could over the obstacle. Ploughing was a stop-start business. My father would see so many broken ploughs coming into the workshop that he got to thinking about a solution to the problem. He finally hit on this hitch arrangement so that if you hit a stone, the plough would spring back and then, if you just drove slowly onwards, it would slip down again, on the other side of the obstacle.

His most successful plough was a three-drill ridging plough, used for setting up drills for planting potatoes. This was different from the plough which turned the soil, but it used the same type of hitch.

His hitch plough was unique. He patented it and did very well out of it. For years he was kept busy through his invention, because he made it on site. Mum and I were called in to lend a hand. We did some of the painting. Then he got a trailer to fix on the back of the car so we could deliver this machine all over the North-East. It went all the way up to Invergordon; we would take them down to Muchalls station for despatch. Some of them went on the boat from Aberdeen to Orkney for use up there.

He was just an ordinary country blacksmith, but he was a naturally inventive man. He thought all the time about how he could improve the local farmers' work. He was hearing so much about their grumbles and complaints and he would think their problems through. I can remember the day he hit on his great idea; he came in one morning, clapping his hands together and shouting out, 'I've got it! I've got it!'.

Nina Smith [Ogg], born 1930: Bridge of Muchalls

# The baker's round

When my father came back after the First World War, he became a baker's vanman. He did deliveries all around the area. He was a hard man, a strong man. His hand was as hard as a pillar-box – as well I knew – and so was his

nature. Everyone admired him; he had the respect of the whole community.

Father would start his day quite late, about 9.30. He'd go out to the van and check it all over, the oil, the tyres, the water. Then he'd drive it over to Keith and into the ironmongers to fetch a bag of nails maybe, or some staples, then onto the butcher to pick up a few parcels of beef. All these he built up at the front of his van. Then he went to the baker for his loaves, all freshly baked, and his van would be steaming with them as he set off. He'd go off out into the country and you wouldn't see him again till 10, 11 at night. Mondays were Grange, Tuesdays Drummuir, Wednesday Mulben And so on. Strathisla Bakery of Keith, that's who he drove for and he did it for 33 years.

His job was to deliver the shop's bread, but on the side he'd take all the little messages folk had given him the week before – that's where the nails and the beef came in. He'd go to the garage for a box of wet batteries and he'd go into all the wifies' houses, scrape off the terminals and collect the old batteries, exchange them for fresh ones and then take them to the garage for recharging for the next week. In those days everybody used them for the wireless and they depended on him to keep them going. He had time for everyone; they all trusted him with their little messages.

The money he got from them would be his hip pocket money. But often it wasn't money at all: he'd return with butter, a rabbit, eggs galore. Barter was as common as cash in those days. The money for the bakery was put into a separate bag; I'd get leave to count it out for him and put it into piles of pennies, the wee threepenny bits and all the pound notes and the ten bob notes.

The bakery knew about all this. They regarded him as a trusted employee, a real asset to the firm. He worked for Alec Patterson and even to this day his son will tell me, 'Your

### The baker calls

Ian's father with customer around late 1920s. His was the first motorised delivery in Keith, replacing the old horse-drawn vans.

Ian's father with another customer at the van, 1935

**Mr and Mrs Baker and sons**

Ian's parents with two older brothers, Alex and George

father was aye clean and smart, a credit to the firm'. As his father used to say, 'Geordie's aye the skipper o his ane boat'. The van was his vessel and he was allowed to steer it whichever way he wanted. He'd go out in all weathers and he never let his customers down. In bad weather he'd take chains for the tyres and he'd get through somehow. People could rely on him.

I was brought up very strictly. My father could be a hard man that way, not cruel but hard. I remember one day my mother was in the hospital and I had to go out with him on his rounds. It was getting late and I'd had enough; I was just seven years old and I was wanting home to my bed. We drew up at this big house and the woman came out to the van. She saw I was a bit girny and asked me, 'What's the matter, little man?' 'I wint hame tae ma bed.' 'Oh, and what do you want to be when you grow up?' she asked, thinking to wake me up a bit. 'A meenister,' I replied. 'Oh, and why would you like to be a minister?' she smiled. 'Well, a meenister disna hae to work aa the oors o the day and night. He can jist walk aboot his gairden in an aul pair o breeks an min' his goats.' She gave me threepence and patted my head. But as soon as we were out of sight of the house, my father stopped the van, took me out, pulled down my breeks and gave me a damn good hiding. How was I to know the house we'd stopped at was the manse and that the woman who'd been asking those questions of me was the minister's wife? I had the marks of my father's big hand on my flesh for days afterwards.

**Ian Stevenson,** born 1932: Keith

# For us life held no dark corners

A country community where everyone was dependent on each other. In the harvest, neighbours would gather round to help: they would come to us; we would go to them. It was called 'neiperin'. If there was a snowstorm, my father would get the Fergie out and go round to help anyone who was in need of digging out. We had fearsome winter storms in those days – what you get now is just peanuts in comparison. When I was at Newmachar School, my father would come to the school with the horse and sledge and take all the kids who were going our way home. There were no phones, but somehow the message would get through, 'Louis Rennie's comin!' and sure enough, I'd come out the school and see my father there and he would pile us all into the box cart placed on the sledge with straw on the bottom and deliver every child safe and warm back to their own houses.

There was always plenty going on. There was the Women's Guild and the Rural for the farmers' wives. There were visiting drama groups which would tour round the North-East and which were always a great draw. You'd go to the hall at Whiterashes or Newmachar, and the kids would sit on the benches, with the parents sitting behind – that made sure we behaved all right. In this way I saw *Mill o' Tiftie's Annie* and *Jim Fleeman* - all the great old pieces. The acting was very dramatic. I remember during *Mains' Wooing*, the actress beseechingly crying out, 'Oh, I'll never marry Mains!', and even then thinking it was a bit melodramatic. But I took it all in.

The farmers' kids would use the backyards to put on concerts to raise money for the Red Cross during the war. We'd use our garden gate as the entrance and charge money for the neighbours to come in. We sang, we danced, we did tricks. We made up our own little plays.

That kind of activity was part of our lives – dancing and stories and singing. It's something which really sprang from the community rather than something we learned at the school.

We enjoyed music. I would cycle the three miles over to Miss Annie Knight at Newmachar for a weekly piano lesson. I also attended dancing classes and learned everything from tap to ballroom. The country dances, usually following a concert with local talent, were great communal events with the whole family going. The children would be expected to sit quietly and watch, sipping at their lemonade and then fall asleep and have to be carried home.

Later when I went in to Aberdeen for the university, I mixed more freely in the big outside world. I would go down the farm road to take the bus, often in wellies because of the dubs, then I'd pop them behind the dyke and put on my high heels for the day in town. I travelled in daily, except at weekends when I would stay for the hops – I loved dancing and never missed the chance of a dance.

There were few dangers for us. I was seldom scared. You knew you could go to any door for help and that you would get it. Our parents would want to know where we were off to and if you were coming off the bus and, if it was dark, one of them would be there to meet you, but that was about it. The community was filled with familiar people and familiar places. It held few dark corners for us at all.

**Cecilia Penny,** born 1932: Newmachar

My father would come to the school with the horse and sledge. He would pile us all into the box cart placed on the sledge with straw on the bottom and deliver every child safe and warm back to their own houses.

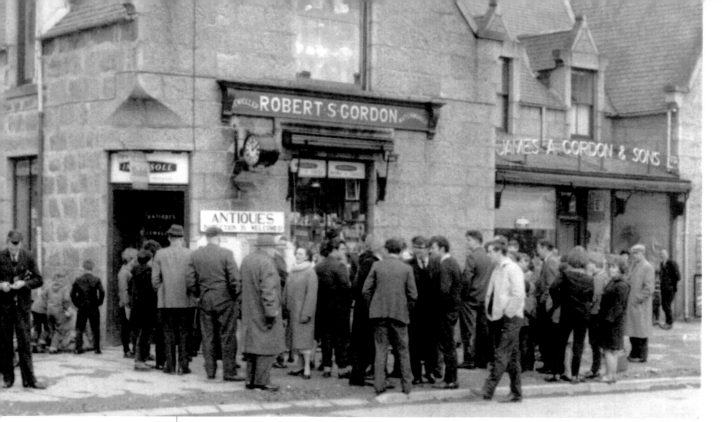

**Opening his new shop, Alford 1963**
Robert S. Gordon, Antiques, Watchmaker and Jeweller. Robbie is on the left, wearing a hat and with his back turned.

# The watchmaker's art

Watchmaking, in those days, was a very interesting trade. The ethos was that the job had to be right, absolutely right, no matter how long it took. That was a difficult system because the standard charge for an alarm clock, say, was five shillings to be overhauled and a chiming clock 25 shillings and you could spend one day, two days, three days, four, and all you could charge was the fixed amount. It's not like a garage where they charge by the time actually spent on the job. But for us the fee was secondary; the important thing, the only thing, was to make sure it was completed properly. That was drilled into us from the very first day of our apprenticeship. Pride in our craftsmanship was the priority, not making money.

Our routine was to start at 8.30 and keep the front shop open till six at night. On Saturdays it would be till 7.30. The farm servants' routine on a Saturday was to come down to the village, do their weekly shopping and then off to the pub for a drink before the return home. That's when they would bring in their watches for repair. We also dealt in fiddle strings, razor blades, bagpipe reeds; and most farm servants smoked the pipe then so another big thing was pipe lids. I mind when the Wilkinson safety blades came in; my goodness, they sold like mad and for the first year supply couldn't keep up with the demand. You took on candlestick repairs, cigarette case hinges, jewellery of all sorts – the only thing I drew the line at was false teeth.

Back in the 30s all the farm servants all wanted their very own silver case pocket watch. They would buy a double-cased one and it would last a lifetime. If the dial was white enamel it would cost £4.10 and if it was silver it would be £5.10. So that was more or less the first fee gone, but they had to have it. They would hang the watch down their trousers by the pints off their boots and when they wanted to consult it they would haul it up and fish it out. They didn't put the watch in their pockets, because they would have got too dirty and covered in chaff there. They would have it on them all day long out in the fields and sometimes the balance staff would get a knock and then you had to turn a new one for them. But these were sturdy, good-going watches.

Those watches weren't just a status symbol; out in the fields the labourers had to keep track of the time. They worked to a strict timetable: start early at 6.30, stop for 90 minutes at 11.30 to eat and have a bit of sleep and then on to lousing time at five. The cattle had to be fed and maybe milked two/three times a day and a dozen other tasks seen to. Timekeeping was important.

The farming folk were fine people to deal with, excellent folk. It's a two-way thing; it was aye drummed into me that if you look after your customers then they won't go past you. Do well by them and they'll keep coming back. We mostly dealt with cash; they would pay on the spot and what they looked for was good solid quality: watches and clocks that would last a lifetime. I remember once talking to this man who'd been working with white goods, but was now getting into our trade and he told us, 'I can't believe the way you boys operate, just can't believe it. In our trade we handle goods that have a lifetime of maybe five, seven years – planned obsolescence, that's what keeps us ticking over. But you lads try to sell stuff that's meant to last forever. How can you make a living doing that?'

In some ways he was right: we live in a throwaway society now where people like to buy simply because they're looking for a change, or want to keep up with the neighbours. Go to any charity shop and the items you'll see being handed in is amazing.

It was a different world altogether then. The ordinary farm servant had little scope for luxury. But the farmer folk went in for good solid quality goods, the kind that could be handed down through the generations. A lot of the ones round here had an old grandfather clock that had come to be seen as a family heirloom. The typical old farmhouse would have a 'Sunday' room which was kept for Sunday best and for high days such as a christening. There you'd find a seven-piece suite, with maybe a chaise longue, a couple of master chairs and a set of four that could double up as dining chairs. On the mantelpiece you might find a pair of wally dugs, or a brass lion, or cat or two. Pieces of Seaton pottery were also very popular – salt jars or a bread bin. On them you'd see an inscription – 'Miss MacConachie 1897', or some such – they made popular wedding presents so a lot of the houses had them, mostly for show rather than everyday use.

If it was a bigger house, one of the mansion houses, then you could find some Wemyss Ware from Fifeshire. This was a firm that would make up a suite specifically for you, so to have one was a mark of real distinction. Then round here lots of the kitchen floors were laid out in the green Coreen slate that you could get from a quarry near here. This was really thick, heavy tiling; I once heard of a floor that was set out in it and then the new house built around it, it was that prized.

So what the farmers appreciated was good solid items, made to last. By jings, it was a hard life on the farms and there was no room for lightweight stuff. The farmer's wife was kept busy with feeding the men that worked the farm, with the hens and the butter and the cheese-making and then, in the evenings, the knitting and mending socks. So she looked after the bits of jewellery she had, usually given to her for a special occasion such

The typical farmhouse would have a 'Sunday' room. There you'd find a seven-piece suite, with maybe a chaise longue, a couple of master chairs and a set of four that could double up as dining chairs.

as a twenty-first or a big wedding anniversary. A lot of them had pieces made up in rose gold, or an in memoriam brooch, a lot of them in Whitby jet. Round the back there'd be a cut-out section with a wee frame so when somebody died, a lock of their hair could be placed in it. Round her wrist she might have a gold bracelet and a gold watch, both in nine-carat gold.

Her husband, the farmer, if he was quite well to do, would wear a bowler hat and drive a pony and trap to the mart on a Tuesday or the kirk on the Sunday. He'd be all dressed up, gloves and a collar and tie. My own father would kit himself out like that; for the kirk he might have a soft hat, but for a funeral it had to be the bowler. That's when the Sunday watch would come out, attached by a gold chain and kept in his waistcoat pocket. They all wore waistcoats then and in the right-hand pocket you'd find the watch and in the left maybe a compass or a seal. This would be a nice piece of jewellery with a bloodstone and a cornelian on its sides. Later the ladies would get hold of them and turn them into necklaces, with lovely drops.

Back in the 40s and the 50s our customers weren't into fashion. If you'd told me then that one day you'd be able to buy a watch for £3 which would keep time to within a couple of minutes in the year, why, I wouldn't have believed it! That's why there's no watchmaker apprenticeships now; when something goes wrong people just buy new. People are much better off now and they have many more goods, but are they any happier?

**Robbie Gordon,** born 1933: Alford

# The crack shepherd

My great-grandfather was James Gray, the shepherd. He would look after other people's sheep over the winter. He would also drive flocks miles and miles across country to various marts. At home I have a photo of him taking a flock from Grantown-on-Spey all the way to Huntly *(see p273).* He stayed overnight in Aberlour and the photo shows him with a large flock on the grass in front of the parish church there.

He had a very good name as a shepherd and took his skills to other parts of the world. In the 1890s he took his wife and the three oldest children – there were 13 altogether – over to a farm in Queensland. He sent them back after a couple of years and the following year he himself returned. But then later he set off to Oregon to look after sheep there for a spell before finally returning to Huntly.

I remember meeting an old man who lived out at the Bin Hill. He asked who I might be and when he learned my name he told me that he certainly remembered 'Aul Grey' and what a fine shepherd he had been, one of the very best. I've a cousin in Banff who has some letters that were sent to my great-grandfather from various people whose sheep he'd looked after over the winter, thanking him for the splendid job he had made of it. And here I am telling you all this and I know nothing about sheep.

**James Gray,
1840–1932**

with his dog Jet

Yet I do feel I'm a son of the country around Huntly, even though all my own boyhood was spent in the town there. Partly this is because I was surrounded by so many uncles and aunts who'd come and visit and talk of the old days endlessly. My great-grandmother acted as the matriarch to the family and they would all congregate in her small house in Castle Street. Collonach, out in the glens, was where the family had lived and farmed before they moved into Huntly and it would always crop up in their conversation.

There were relatives who would come back from Canada and they would make a sort of pilgrimage back to the place. I've also got a photo taken at my great grandparents' silver wedding at Collonach back in 1907 and all the relatives and neighbours are gathered around. But really there's very little to see now – maybe a line of 10 trees which come back on themselves and would have enclosed the nine houses of the clachan, and piles of old stones which would have been the walls. That's all that's left of the nine houses; the whole place has been incorporated into the farm of Wellheads, which is a huge 1,000-acre enterprise. This cycle of small-scale farming being overtaken by bigger and bigger farms is one that has been repeated all over the North-East.

**Patrick Scott,** born 1937: Huntly

Uncles and aunts would come and visit and talk of the old days endlessly.

**A great place to grow up in** Findhorn lads appreciating the 'sand and the sea' in the 1930s.

# The bobby's son

The police house was a substantial one. It had a cell and this was frequently in use, especially at weekends. The usual crime was a spot of drunk and disorderly, or an affray. Father would arrest them and throw them into the cell and lock the key to leave them to sober up overnight. This could take some time and you'd hear them yelling and banging about into the early morning hours. When the morning came round my mother would go in with a tray with the prisoner's breakfast; I think she got 1/6 to cover the expenses.

In those days the policeman had a bit more freedom in how he went about dispensing justice and my father wouldn't be afraid to mete out a bit of physical stuff. What he always maintained was that if you hit someone on one ear, you had to be sure to do the other ear too, so as to give a swelling to each side of the head. That way it might not be noticed.

In those days the local bobby was one of the pillars of the community, alongside the minister and the dominie. He would know everything that was going on. My father had a large beat and only his bike to cover it. He'd go up to the distillery; he'd go inside and chat to the manager and get a dram, but when he came out he was careful to look through the bags on the bike just in case anyone had been popping in some stones so as to give him a heavier load for the return journey.

It could be tough being the only son, believe me. He brought me up quite strictly; it wouldn't do for the policeman's boy to be seen stepping out of line. I got by by adopting 'I never saw anything' attitude and at Findhorn that worked well. Some kind folk might get in touch with my father if ever they saw me doing anything wrong, like riding without proper lights on the bike, but generally I was left alone. The policeman's family were such a part of the whole community that I was completely accepted into it. In fact, Findhorn as a whole was a wonderful place to grow up in. I'd go down to the jetty any day, sit there and know that sooner or later someone would come and take me out in their boat. There was the sea, the sands, the boats and, in the distance, the hills – a lovely, lovely place.

**Fraser Sime,** born 1937: Findhorn

> My father always maintained that if you hit someone on one ear, you had to be sure to do the other ear too, so as to give a swelling to each side of the head.

# We could put a face to every door

I lived all my childhood in Fetterangus. I had two brothers and one sister. You could say that life then in the village was a pretty simple affair; we had few of the amenities children take for granted nowadays, but we did have lots of fun. I can remember the days before electricity came to our houses; I can remember the candles. You would have a candlestick; you'd sit in the bathroom with it; you'd light the match and then you tried to let it burn right down till the stick became completely black. You would then lick your hands, press them together and if the black mark came out perfect you could make a wish and know it would come true. I'd do this and I'd hear mother hammering away at the door and going, 'Come out of there. You'll burn the house down!' She'd smelt the smoke and knew what I was up to.

We had plenty of freedom and space. There were few about in those days, so the street could act as our playground. And there were no strangers to be wary of or warned about: everyone knew everyone else. In the 1940s there were only 350 inhabitants; my brother and I would sometimes sit in our room and go through all the houses and count them all. We could put a face to every door in each of the streets.

Fetterangus had a whole heap of shops in those days. There was the post office, a

**Granny Elrick feeding the sheltie** which with Tom Mennie, used to deliver the milk in Fetterangus, 1910s.

**A rainy day in Fishie** The opening of the Fetterangus Hall, 1896

After a bad snowfall Dr Dixon would do his rounds on skis, coming out along the roads and across the fields.

draper's, a couple of grocery stores, a hardware place, a souter's shop, a baker's, even a tailor's where you could see them sitting cross-legged on the floor sewing away. But that was nothing to what there had been in my mother's time when she was growing up in the village. She could reel off lists of them: a watchmaker, chemist, butchers and several little shops that old women would run from their cottages, selling home-made stuff such as toffee, biscuits and lemonade.

The church played a huge part in my childhood. My mother was the beadle for 31 years and her father had been beadle 40 years before her. I would attend the Sunday School from two-fifteen to three, then there would be the main church service from three to four, followed by choir practice from four to four-thirty.

The minister would get tea from my granny and then he would return to Old Deer. Often we would keep him company as he pushed his bike the couple of miles along the road. This was Dr Kemp, a very well respected, fine looking man, quite elderly and white haired. He would cycle everywhere and would go off on his bike for a round of golf at Peterhead

My mother worked hard as the beadle to keep the church in good order. Before the communion she would scrub the floor twice over and I would help her. Once while she was busy in this way, I climbed up the ladder that led up to the clock, right up to the little

window where you could look down on the street way below. I would shout out to any passer-by, 'Hello there,' and they would look around startled for where the voice could possibly have come from. Mother gave me a smack for that, 'You'll break your neck, so you will'.

The only time I really came to any harm was once when we were playing hide-and-seek and I was ducking down behind a hedge and got a cut from some sharp glass there. I went home and got some gauze bandaging on it, but it wouldn't stop bleeding, so my father decided to take me to Dr Dixon's surgery over at Old Deer. 'He's not going to put stitches in me, is he?' I was terrified. But he rubbed something into my hand before he got to work, so I survived. However, I do remember him coming to the house to take my brother's tonsils out. He did it on the kitchen table; I can mind peeping in at the window.

Dr Dixon was another great character that everyone looked up to. In the winter after a bad snowfall he would do his rounds on skis, coming out along the roads and across the fields from Old Deer to Fetterangus that way.

So that was my early life in Fishie. I wouldn't exchange it for anything or for anywhere else, never.

**Margaret Simpson,** born 1939: Fetterangus

## A Fetterangus wedding
June 3, 1926. Uncle Peter Elrick marries Isabella Grant (Auntie Bella); Margaret Simpson's mother, aged 16, is the bridesmaid, and Uncle Sandy is the best man; her grandparents are in the front row. The minister is the Reverend Robert Kemp, Old Deer.

**Retired, but still a gardener**
Dod with his dahlias and beloved
Yorkie, Mikie, in his home at
Ythanbanks, Ellon

# EARLY CENTURY LIVES: 5
# George (Dod) Forbes

# The fourteen-year old fee'd loon

**Dod with his two oldest children,** Margaret and Doddie, 1944

There were six of us. We all had to leave the school at 14 and go into jobs on farms. I became a fee'd loon on a farm at Slains. Now, some farmers were good and some not so good – in fact there was quite a lot of them just greedy, always trying to squeeze a bit more out of you. I met both kinds, I can tell you. Anyway, my first fee was for – well, I'll tell you what I got: nae very muckle! It was £7 for a whole six months work, plus my food and board.

This was at a farm which had five horses. There were two pairs and one single horse and my position was to look after the fifth horse. I was the orra loon and I had to do any odd job going. My first one was neeps and sheep. I was required to go out on the back of the cart in the winter to feed the sheep in the parks with neeps. The worst of it was when a large neep would get caught up in the cutting machine; then I would have to get my hands to it and pull it out, all among the muck and the dubs. 'Neeping the sheep' they called this job.

There were two horsemen, there was a cattleman and the farmer himself acted as the shepherd. I was at the very bottom of the pile – the orra loon, just: that was me! You started work at six. That was in the summer; in the winter you'd get a long lie in – till six-thirty. The horsemen had to be in an hour before you so as to feed the horses. At 11 you'd get a couple of hours off, but that wasn't to give you a rest: it was to feed the horses again and give them a break. You'd work on till five-thirty: at times of the hairst till later than that. Speaking of good farmers, at some farms you'd get a piece at the hairst, but then the next farmer might give you nothing at all. What we usually got was a scone and maybe a bottle of skimmed milk. Once I was out at the hairst and it came on to rain. The servant lassie was just coming out with our pieces and we were really looking forward to them, but then she was ordered to go back in with them. The rain meant we would have to break off the hairst and no hairst meant no piece.

I stayed in the bothy; the others were all married and had their cottar houses, so I was there all by myself. It was winter, but as for the cold – well, you just had to get on with it and not heed it. I got my food in the kitchen. If the weather was good, then in my spare time I'd jump on my bike and meet up with the loons from other farms and we'd get a game of football going in the park. On the dark winter evenings I would maybe get hold of an old newspaper, or a past copy of the *People's Journal* and read through that. I never got hold of new news, only the old sort. But most times I would just go to my bed.

My first fee only lasted the six months because, in the summer, the sheep would no

> Some farmers were good and some not so good – in fact there was quite a lot of them just greedy, always trying to squeeze a bit more out of you.

longer be needing neeps, so I had to look for another post. My £7 had to be spent on boots and clothes; there was nothing over for any luxuries, I can tell you. In any case, I was too young to go to the pub or to have tobacco. And I didn't even think about quines – too young! To me, at 14, they were just a different kind of animal altogether.

That changed, I can tell you. A year or two on and I started going to some of the dances in the country halls. It would be a case of loons lined up on one side and quines on the other and you asked up a different one each time. After the dance you'd ask some lassie that you'd had your eye on if you could see her home and then you'd hope that she didn't stay too far away. You might get a kiss as your reward. The lassie had to be really bonny if she was to be worth a six-mile walk.

My next farm only lasted three months for me, because I got the sack from it. My job was to work out in the fields, hoeing the neeps and so forth. But one evening the farmer asked me to stay on: would I see to the cow? Now, it was his wife who normally did the milking, but she was expecting, so this time he asked me to bide back till eight o'clock so I could do it for her. But I'd arranged to go off and get a game of football with the loons from another farm so I just told him, 'No'. I knew he would be not best pleased, but I never thought he would sack me – but he did. 'You winna milk the coo? Weel, in that case ye can jist bugger aff!' He gave me £5, which was half the fee, and off I went. It was summer time and I managed to pick up work elsewhere, helping with the hairst.

**From the family album**

School shots taken in successive years. Dod Forbes is second left row (vertical) at ages 7, 9 and 11. In the other rows are brothers Fred, Bill and Jimmy and sisters Bella and Mary. Bill lived to 98, Bella 99 and their mother 104. Dod is now 96.

## Farming in the blood

Dod's grandfather (extreme right) as horseman at Drumwhindle in 1890s

Yes, I was getting a whole £10 by now for my six months hard labour. But what else could I do? Out there in the country then there was very little work for a young lad straight from school. There were hardly any apprenticeships to be had and the farming wasn't paying well either. Well, you kent they couldn't be getting much themselves when you saw how little they were giving us – at least, I hope that was the reason. I know that for a hundredweight-and-a-half bag of corn, they would be getting no more than 10 shillings. They didn't have the money to buy in feed for their cattle either; it was a question of growing your own – the hay and the oats and the straw that came from the farm. And they couldn't buy in fertiliser. We just spread the muck from the byre over the fields and there was certainly no shortage of that. There's aye plenty muck on the farm! But there was no machinery: horsepower and manpower, that's what kept the farms going before the Second World War: manpower and horsepower.

I got to like working with the horses. It's a job that needs understanding and experience. You can't just rush in and treat each horse the same; you have to get to know them and their own little ways. Take the clips – these are the young horses that had to be broken in to the work of the farm. You couldn't just place a harness over its neck and

shove the new horse between the shafts of a cart and expect it to pull away. It all has to be done gradually; you have to build up the animal's trust.

You start off with a sleeper for it to pull around the yard and slowly you work your way up to the cart. It can take about two months to work through the whole business. You have to be ready to talk to them, to make them feel comfortable; you have to approach them gently from the side with their feed, not full on because they find that threatening. Even then you have to be prepared to take a few kicks. Be good to your beasts, that's my motto, aye be good to them. Even now when I'm well away from the farm work I keep a wee Yorkie dog and my daughter, Evie, she'll tell you that that animal comes first, even above her.

So that was my life then. Going from fee to fee and working all the days out in fields. And when it was wet, you didn't get off either: you had to stay behind in the byre to get on with some such job as sorting out the twine for the sheaves. You just had to be getting on with it: up for six, work, work, work till lowsin time and back for supper, and then lie down on your bed and rest up. After all, if you'd been harrowing all day and walking behind a horse and trying to keep up with that, then you didn't feel like doing much else

You couldn't just place a harness over its neck and shove the new horse between the shafts of a cart. It has to be done gradually.

> The farmer would reach into his pooch and get out your arles and press it into your hand. This was a half-crown piece and once you'd accepted it, that meant that the bargain was sealed and you were his for the next six months.

except take to your bed, believe me. Sleep – work – supper – sleep: that was my life during these days. You just had to keep at it. Do the job till it's finished and when it's done, it's done.

We did all this on brose and porridge. I take it yet. There's nothing better than getting your wee bowl filled with brose and then the kitchen deem comes in with the boiling kettle and pours it over the oats and then you get some cream to top it up with. That was awful fine and it still is. If you were lucky you might come in after your work and find a bowl of cream left out for you in the byre. Skimmed milk, in those days, was kept for the pigs and the hens.

We didn't see much in the way of meat or poultry – maybe only the odd rabbit the farmer had shot. I can tell you a wee story. I was at one place and we were all at our supper. The farmer and his wife were getting a chicken ben the hoose and we were getting some chicken broth out in the kitchen. Well, one of the lads was a real hallyracket kind and as the chicken was going through, can you think what he did? Well, he leaned over and broke off a leg, just like that. The next we knew, the kitchen maid was getting the sack from the farmer. He demanded to know which one of us had been responsible and she had refused to tell him. For that it was instant dismissal. The farmer could pay her off and know that there would be no shortage of other young quines coming forward to take her place. The reason she wouldn't tell was quite simple: she was sweet on the hallyracket lad; she knew he would be sacked at once if it had been known it was his doing.

I didn't see much of the outside world. I did get into Ellon, just twice a year for the feein mart. A day or two before that fell due, the grieve might be coming round and spierin what your intentions were; if you heard nothing from him then you knew you would have to be looking for somewhere else. On the Tuesday before the next term started, you'd go into Ellon and hang around Market Street and it would be full of farmers and farm servants. You'd knock about till someone came up to you and asked, 'Are ye lookin fer a fee?' If you said 'Aye', then he would reply, 'Then Ah've gat samthin that'll suit ye jist fine' and he'd take you over to the farmer.

Once you'd sorted out the terms, the farmer would reach into his pooch and get out your arles and press it into your hand. This was a half-crown piece and once you'd accepted it, that meant that the bargain was sealed and you were his for the next six months. There was no contract; you never even shook hands, just the arles. If you was lucky, the farmer might take you into the bar and give you a pint – and that was the only time I would ever have a drink, apart from New Year, of course. Couldn't afford any.

Unmarried men stayed in the bothy. If there were other men like you, then you just shared a bed. There was none of this stuff about liking to sleep by yourself; we just had to get on together and that was that. Besides, it was much cosier if you had another body beside you. You had your kist, which you took from farm to farm, and that's where you kept a change of clothes. You got them washed once a fortnight when you took them back to your mother to see to. You wore the same clothes for 14 days running – semmit, socks, drawers and all. For our own washing you would have a basin in the corner and you might get a bucket of heated water through from the kitchen. You'd have to share that with the other three and you'd take over your sark and do your best to scrub your bits and pieces with a block of Lifebuoy soap. But that was just the body above the waist; you never bothered with anything further down. The only time you'd ever get your whole body into the water would be when you could get into the sea in the summer and that was at Collieston.

You might get your Sunday off, but that could only be after the horses and the cattle had been attended to – they didn't take the day off. A horseman would get one Sunday in two off while the other horseman did it. Apart from that and the two mart days and New Year, that was it. Christmas was just another working day for us. But what could you do about it? Just get on with it. The whole farming year fell into a routine; each job had its own proper time: the neeps in, the corn in, the neeps to be hoed, the foons for the stacks to be sorted, the hairst to be gathered in, the thrashing to be done, the neeps to be caa'd in through the winter and then the ploughing and the harrowing and start all over again. It was a routine, a round of the same old jobs. And that was our life.

*George (Dod) Forbes,* born 1914: Slains

**Dod's first new bike**
Chapelhall, 1950

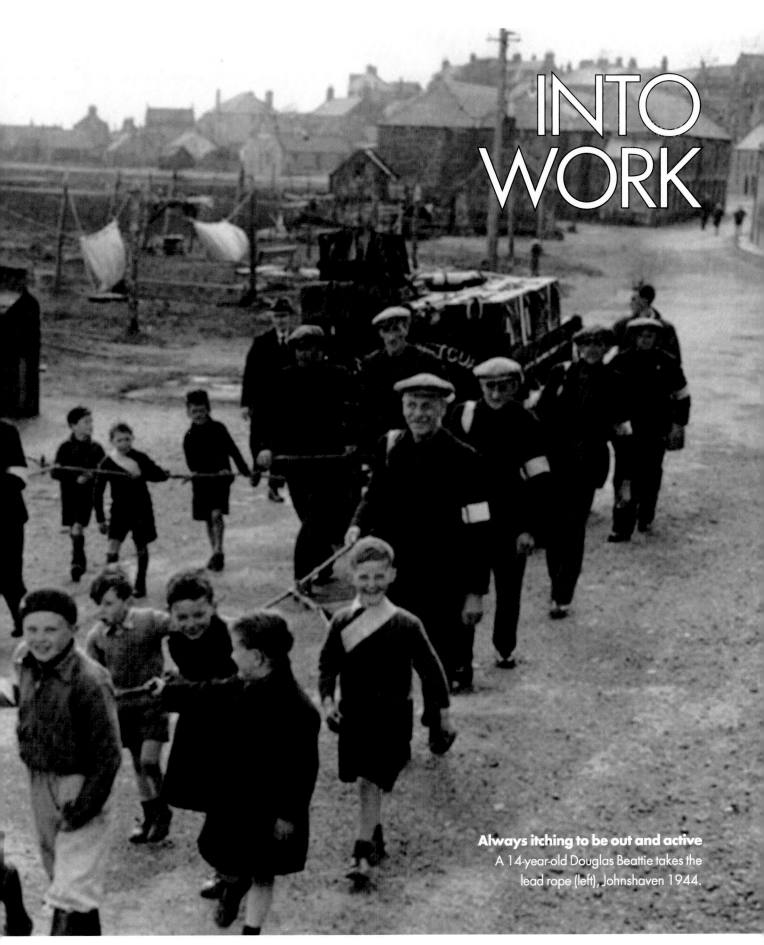

# INTO
# WORK

**Always itching to be out and active**
A 14-year-old Douglas Beattie takes the
lead rope (left), Johnshaven 1944.

**A high-achieving
trio**

A three-year old
Margaret Carmichael
flanked by brother and
sister at Oyne manse in
1918. Both she and her
brother lived into their
90s. He worked on the
development of radar in
the Second World War,
while her sister was part
of the Enigma team at
Bletchley.

# The young doctor

I started school at the local place in Oyne and then I did three years at Inverurie Academy. I then went on to the High School for Girls in Aberdeen. My brother was going to Robert Gordon's at the same time, so we stayed in digs and came home for the weekends. The plan was for me to go to university, but the school wouldn't let me sit my highers; they said I wasn't clever enough. I went off and sat the university entrance exams myself and got in. I was just sixteen.

I decided to go in for medicine. I did well, although there was a difficulty at the start. We had these anatomy classes which consisted of us studying the human body by cutting open actual corpses. They were imported from abroad. To begin with I found that quite distressing. There was this thought of cutting into someone who had recently been alive. I also found it difficult to get rid of the smell; I'd be at the meal table and the smell of those bodies was still clinging to my hands. My landlady noticed that my appetite had disappeared. 'Why, you're not eating anything,' she said. I told her what the problem was so she said, 'Here, have a drink of this just before you set off in the morning'. It was a glass of whisky. I knocked it back and then I sailed down to Marischal and into the dissecting room. I never had any more problems after that. Nowadays they use models for the anatomy classes.

Another problem I had was having to go to Woolmanhill late at night. We had to go in for 'receiving night', when they'd take in the patients for operations. Sometimes it would be midnight before I could start for home. I got my digs as near to Woolmanhill as I could, but I never did feel easy going through the streets in the dark. Nothing ever happened, but I still felt scared.

There were 90 in my medical class; 12 of us were female. From the start we were told that we were all equal; this seemed to mean that when we were seated round a patient in the hospital, the boys grabbed the chairs and left us to stand. Not all of them could find a place, however; there was this big lad from Buckie who had particularly heavy breathing. As I was the smallest in the class he would position himself directly behind me while we were all peering over at the bedside. I can hear those snorting noises in my ears even yet, 75 years later. I called it the North Wind.

I was the youngest in the class. I graduated when I was one month older than 21. I loved my medical training. Of course, it was all very formal in those days. We had to address our lecturers with a 'Sir'. There was none of the Christian names you get everywhere nowadays. But I feel comfortable with that. I suppose I'm old fashioned that way. We had to wear proper skirts at the university then, and even now I don't like to see a woman in trousers. My three daughters all wear them, of course. 'Don't you come to see me unless you're in a proper skirt', I tell them. I was watching a documentary on the Blair years on TV last night and it showed someone addressing him as 'Prime Minister'. 'Oh, just call me Tony,' he said. Imagine Winston Churchill inviting a member of the public to call him 'Winnie'. No, there was far more respect in my day and I think that was quite as it should be.

Some of the lecturers did carry things to an extreme, though. We had a biochemistry lecturer who demanded that we should stand up when he entered. The next day when he came in everyone stood up all right, and broke into the National Anthem. He refused to have anything more to do with us after that. So that was the end of our biochemistry for that term. Another one – the professor of surgery – held early morning lectures and he would lock the door fast at eight o'clock sharp.

I led a very serious undergraduate existence. My classes ran from eight to twelve-thirty; an hour-and-a-half for lunch, then lectures till five. The evenings would be spent going over it all and sorting out my notes. Money was short because we had to pay our own fees. My digs cost me 22/6 a week. They were in Hamilton Place and the tram fare to Marischal was two shillings. I would usually walk the two miles to save the money. I never went out drinking or dining. I was never in a pub; in fact I'm now 92 and I've never been in a bar yet.

**Margaret Carmichael,** born 1915: Oyne

> We had to wear proper skirts at the university then, and even now I don't like to see a woman in trousers.

# A lady writer's upbringing

I became a writer, but really it was just for fun. I started writing little pieces for the *Buchany*, the *Buchan Observer*. I called myself 'Ravenscraig', because we lived beside Ravenscraig Castle. My mother used to be a writer, a very good writer. She'd write these rubbishy stories for the *People's Friend*, just for a little bit extra for the family. She loved writing.

My sister was the clever one of the family, but she wasn't a writer. There were these heck of a scenes on a Sunday night when she had to do her composition for the school and mother would end up doing it for her. Then when it came to the exams she had to write for herself and the marks went right down. But she was good at arithmetic, at geometry and so on. I was completely the opposite. I was never good at figures.

I knew I could aye make up the marks with my writing. But we had no real freedom for our writing. It would be a matter of being given some topic like, 'Write a story about a dog'. But it was a damned good school. All of us left it able to read and to write. But as a child I didn't really read. I never read at all. I had these books as prizes and I never read any of them. I was too busy playing outside. My mother was a terrific reader. But I never read a book; none of us did. First thing in the morning, after breakfast, and we'd be outside, playing. I would only read the set books for school. Even then it would be mother who would read them and tell us the stories.

My mother was a teacher, you know. That was the only job for a young lady in her day. She went to the uni in the 1890s. There were only the six of them then, the females. They had to sit at the back of the room and if all the seats were taken, then they just had to miss out on their lecture. She had to give up her teacher's job when she got married. That's what had to happen then. It would have been seen as an insult to the husband if they hadn't.

**Like mother, like daughter**
Winnie Brown, centre front, with parents and brother and sister in front of their Inverugie home, 1929.

Suddenly here she was talking about her teaching career: 'I got good money, you know – but then I met this bloody idiot!' This was her husband – and this was the drink talking.

I remember once when the water baillie came in with a bottle, when he'd got this posting to Strathpeffer, and insisted that she have a drink. My mother never drank, so when she had her glass it went straight to her head. Suddenly here she was talking about her teaching career: 'I got good money, you know – but then I met this bloody idiot over there!' This was her husband – and this was the drink talking.

But, of course, I only ever wrote bits and pieces: my main career was the Civil Service. When I left school I attended night classes and then I became a typist in an office in Peterhead. For this I received £1 per calendar month. Riches! With my first pay packet I went right out and bought a jar of marmalade – as a Sunday breakfast treat for the whole family; I also gave ten shillings to my mother as keep.

One day a work colleague, Mae she was called, came in with this cutting from a newspaper: 'Sit the Civil Service typing examination. Very good rates of pay in London'. 'Fit aboot you an me haein a go?' Now quite what this 'Civil Service' could be I hadn't the foggiest, but I decided to give it a go.

Well, I passed and Mae failed. We used to get the typewriters seen to once a month; this loon would come and clean them and he was a bitty saft. We'd take the wag of him. At the exam the machine broke down and she said, 'That pit me reet aff!'. But she wasn't bothered; she just went off and married Walter Scrogie.

So that was me down to London all by myself. On the first day at the office, I had to present myself before a panel to see which department I should be assigned to. I put on my very best English voice, but as I was leaving, one of them took me aside and whispered in my ear, 'A small piece of advice. Never lose that accent of yours; it's wonderful; it'll take you anywhere'.

**Winnie Brown (Carnegie),** born 1916: Inverugie

## The smithy and the pupil teacher

My father was one of twelve – there was no TV to keep them occupied at night in those days, you see. It was a hard upbringing: Father can remember being thrashed by my grandfather's leather belt and being sent out on the coldest of winter days to pull neeps for the cattle and coming back with all feeling in his hands gone.

My father had served his time as a blacksmith near Methlick and then ran a business in Torphins with his brother-in-law, Frank Mitchell. They had horses, phaetons, carriages and then the first car in Torphins, an old grey Talbot purchased from Sir Henry Grey. They actually made quite a lot of money out of that: they would take the summer visitors up to the Lyn o' Dee for picnic runs. He also built bicycles; his most successful model was the 'Daisy Belle', a very reliable machine. Some of them were still in use right up to the Second World War.

Unfortunately his partner was a real drunkard, a bottle a day man, and I don't mean

**Ninety not out**
Jimmy Morrison on his 90th birthday, Inchmarlo, July 2008

beer! Father carried the business; he worked very hard and made a success of it. The Depression years were very hard, but the car hiring side kept him going. For a time they had the only one in the village – and he survived. In the First World War a conflagration had destroyed their stable and garage; some say it had been started by Mitchell for insurance purposes. But the disaster made my father concentrate on the car and bicycle side of the business and that proved to be where the real success lay.

My mother was a trained teacher; she taught near Tarland and then at Logie Coldstone. She then came to teach at Torphins and that's how she met my father.

She began life as Margaret Dey, the illegitimate daughter of Dey of Braehead, which is this side of Culter. The whole family worshipped education and my mother was encouraged to become a pupil teacher at her own school and then go on to the TC. My grandmother ran a laundry business in the Auld Hoose at Anguston. It's amazing to think she did all this with no running water, let alone electricity. They would pump the water in, every single drop, and press out the clothes with flat irons. They prided themselves on their ability to attain perfect results in the washing, starching and ironing of sheets, shirt collars, table clothes and so on.

Jean Dey was a slave driver, a perfectionist. I can still see her reprimanding my mother for her failure to fold a tablecloth in the correct manner while ironing. Two rooms were devoted to the task: a wash house and the ironing and starching room. The ironing had to be accomplished by flat irons that were heated on a large stove fuelled by coal and wood. They had to be very particular not to get any soot or smudges on all that white linen. After washing, the clothes would be hung in the Black Sheddie, a large barn-like structure with slatted walls and painted in black creosote, that was situated on the Braehead where they could catch all the winds that blew.

Education was seen as the escape from all that drudgery. Despite the illegitimacy, my grandmother Dey was a very holy woman. You weren't allowed so much as to breathe on a Sunday, but were expected to sit there pondering your Bible. Every night she would read her chapter from it, all annotated with the message for the day.

**Jimmy Morrison,** born 1918: Torphins

**The pupil teacher**
Jimmy Morrison's mother at Eddieston, 1897

**The young apprentice**
Jimmy Morrison's father with two fellow apprentice blacksmiths, Methlick, 1890s

# Casting the peats

The farm was mixed; we had corn and we kept cattle. We had a yellow and red tractor, a small Minneapolis Moline which I drove. But it was my brother who did the ploughing mostly. I did go out to the tatties for the howkin – that's where I got my slim figure from, I think! I also had to do the neeps and, oh, how cold it got out there in the fields with the frost on the neeps. I got paralysed with the cold.

But the farm was beside the Red Moss, which is an ancient peat bed, one of the best examples left. It goes deep, really deep. We used to dig up these jet black peats, heavy and oily and wet they were. The distilleries used them during the malting, because they gave the barley a nice flavour. Glenury Distillery in Stonehaven – well, I think we must have sold about 300 tons of the stuff to them each year.

But a peat bog's a very vulnerable place. When you cut the moss it'll never heal; no matter how many years pass, the wound will aye be there, gaping and open. No one really cuts peat nowadays, at least not round here. The know-how's gone and the peat bogs are usually under some kind of protection. But it was our livelihood.

It was a big job, the cutting of the peats. Then there was the business of storing them, so they would dry out properly. We used to wheel them away in a barrow; I was doing it when I was 14, straight from the school, and damn heavy work it was too, for a young quine like me. You'd cut them with a special spade; it had a long handle and a lug on it so you could slice them and take them out the right shape and size.

You'd work at an open bank, one that had already been established, but the peats were heavy wet things and while the men handled 18 at a time, 12 was all I could manage. The first thing you had to do was the 'terring'. At the bottom of the peat face it would be all wet – it sucks you in the peat does – so you'd cut a layer from the top, the ones that had loose dry earth and heather, and then you'd lay them on the bottom so as to make a nice dry surface and that's what you'd push your barrow along. If we hadn't done that we'd have just been slithering and sinking into raw peat and getting nowhere.

You'd wheel them off and make a stack so they could dry. The stack was like dominoes and it was quite an art getting them all neatly lined up together, leaning into each other so as not to collapse. You'd put them two-by-two into a kind of pyramid shape and then place another peat at each corner so there were eight to a rickle. You had to go back later to turn them round so each peat got the chance to dry out.

Do you ken the worst thing about working with the peats? Midges! They loved the

**Stack them up high**
William Wilson and Dorothy McDonald, both family friends
August, 1930

**With the Minneapolis Moline**
Hilda Brand standing in front of brother and future husband Bob (home on leave) and worker and child, 1943.

warm moisture. You'd be sorting out the peats and suddenly a great swarm would be at you, nipping all over your face. They'd get into your lugs and buzz away in there. It fair knocked you crazy. Some got away with only wee pinpricks to their faces, but they used to make me come up in lumps the next day.

**Hilda Brand,** born 1921: Cookney

## The cutting of the Fite Coo

My earliest memories are bound up with the West Lodge, in the district of the Forest of Deer. At the back of the house were the woods and the sawmill. I can recall the arrival of a donkey engine and the way it was pulled up the road by a team of horses, after it had arrived at Mintlaw by train. I can remember the foresters pulling the logs up to the sawmill and cursing their horses as they struggled along. I picked up their words and started to use them in the house. My father went to have a word with the foreman to ask his men to guard their tongues, only to be told, 'A cairter niver swears at his horses, niver'.

Some 15 years later I became a forester myself. When I left school in 1938, my first job was just across the way from Maud Junction with the Anglo-American Oil Company, now known as Esso, acting as attendant on a lorry which conveyed oil, in the form of kerosene, to farms and homes and businesses in the surrounding area, mostly for their lighting, though there was the odd tractor.

I got 16 bob a week for carrying out these duties. Then came the fateful day of third September 1939, my 16th birthday. We were all summoned to the Anglo-American Oil company at Maud where at 11 o'clock, on the wireless, we listened to Chamberlain telling us all that Great Britain was now at war. The boss then went to the safe and took out the sealed orders which had been deposited there to be opened in time of war. He read out to us all that the oil companies were now to be amalgamated under the direct control of the

**The Fite Coo team**
Stanley Rothney is the slim young man in 1941, grinning away in the centre. Allan Ross, the boss, is at the back left in paddy hat.

Within minutes the resulting conflagration could be seen all over Buchan. It was at that moment that a Heinkel decided to pay us a visit.

Government so as to form the Pool Petroleum Board. All permanent staff were to be transferred to its employ; I, being temporary, was paid off.

I then sought employment temporarily at a shoemaker's, where I learned how to drive tackets into the filthy boots of the local farm servants. This not having much appeal, after one miserable week I was delighted to follow the advice of one of our customers, Charlie Sim, who worked in the Forestry and who told me that I should 'git a job in the wid'. So I upped and got a job with the Forestry Commission, over in the Fite Coo Wood. I operated as sawmiller, a woodcutter and a carter of timber – an all-round timber hand in other words.

I was a willing worker, but just a bit green. Now defence legislation prohibited the burning of brushwood during the hours of darkness, for obvious wartime reasons. Consequently, when at the end of the working day we gathered brushwood together, it was to be left in a neat heap for burning the next day – never that night. But once, in a fit of over-enthusiasm, I piled a mammoth heap up and the next morning I lit it. Unfortunately, I hadn't actually waited for the daylight to appear and within minutes the resulting conflagration could be seen all over Buchan. It was at that moment that a Heinkel decided to pay us a visit. It came in so low that you could see the reflection of the flames along its fuselage. Fortunately it decided that we weren't worth a bomb and then flew off again.

At the time I found the whole incident extremely exciting, but that was far from how the boss, Allan Ross, felt about it. When he came on the scene in the afternoon he made straight for me and gave me absolute hell. I was left a shaking wretch, convinced that the Military Police were about to show up and cart me off to the Tower of London.

Fortunately, they never showed up and the whole matter just drifted off into oblivion. Not long after I was a soldier myself, off on my travels through India and Singapore to the jungles of Burma, and the eventful days when I was a working forester in the Fite Coo Wood just a happy memory.

**Stanley Rothney,** born 1923: White Cow Wood

# Joining the family business

Both my father and my grandfather were plumbers – the family business. I wasn't going to go into it; my career path was to stay on at the academy, get my highers, go to Scott Sutherland's and train as an architect. But the war came and father's journeymen were called up and he was left short-handed. By 1941 he was working night and day trying to satisfy his customers and he told me, 'Well, laddie, there's nothing for it – you'll jist hae to cam hame and take up the plumbing'.

I was brought up in an era when everything had to be absolutely perfect; if there was even the slightest thing wrong you had to rip it out and start all over again. Now, the attitude is, 'You just can't afford to do that; time is money'. For example, any pipes you put in had to be dead straight, even if they weren't visible and were going to be covered up anyway. You'd be expected to fix clips all the way down and they had to be precisely equidistant from each other. The job not only had to be right, it had to look right too. From a practical point of view it made no difference, but that wasn't the point. But then we were only paid in sweeties, so time was of little account.

I did a six-year apprenticeship. When I started out, I worked with my father, as a journeyman. We used to do all the big local estates: Pitcaple, Pittodrie, Keith Hall. The Countess of Kintore came up here and she would renovate all the cottages, put bathrooms in them, and do up the Home Farm, too. She was an American millionairess – her father had been a Chicago meatpacker – before she married the Earl. Money was no object. She brought in some really classy stuff, up from London; marble fitments, lion tap heads, the very best. It was a joy to work with, but very, very expensive. She would let nothing stand in her way and found it difficult to accept that what she wanted might not always be possible: 'Oh, Ja-aack, I'm sure you'll find a way to do it,' that's what she'd tell me.

She took a very close interest in everything we were doing; she was in at us every day. Everybody would be working away and you'd hear this 'Wuff! Wuff!' She'd go around the estate in a chauffeur-driven Bentley and her Alsation would run after, barking and yelping. That's when the journeyman working alongside me would say, 'Watch out, the auld bugger's comin'.

When she came to renovate the old farm byres she decided she just couldn't tolerate the usual arrangement where the cattle stood with their heads to the wall. That would mean that their backsides would be sticking out at her and – tutt-tutt! – that wouldn't do. So she got the blacksmith to make pens so the cattle could be backed into these cages and now look outwards. But, of course, the beasts were defecating all over the wall at the back and they got into one hell of a mess. So she got a firm in to line the walls with fine black Terrazzo marble, right up to the height of six feet six, so the mess would be easily hosed off.

The Countess was a very particular lady. You'd fit something in one day and the next she'd be saying, 'Oh, Jack, I don't like it there. You'll have to move it'. I was only the apprentice, but I got on well with her; she respected the job I was doing and I did my best to give her what she wanted. She always called me 'Ja-aack'; my father was 'Hendry'. She once told us, 'Hendry, people criticise me for throwing my money around on making the

By 1941 he was working night and day trying to satisfy his customers and he told me, 'Well, laddie, there's nothing for it – you'll jist hae to cam hame and take up the plumbing'.

estate as beautiful as I can, but, do you know, I could lay out £10,000 on a necklace, wear it once and then put it away in a safe in the bank, out of sight. Here I can spend the same amount of money on renovations and have the pleasure of watching masons and joiners and plumbers like you doing good work. That's what gives my satisfaction. I can see the estate improving every day and leave something behind me'.

But now she's long gone and Keith Hall's more or less poverty stricken – death duties. But I enjoyed working with people like her. They could be demanding, but they always appreciated what you were trying to do.

**Jack Hendry,** born 1925: Inverurie

## The young tailoress

My brother was now working at the garage and one day he came in and said, 'The tailor wis in the day an he wis sayin he widna min' if ma sister cam to werk fer him'. All this was out of the blue, over the tea table. Mother said, 'Well, d'ye wint tae think aboot it?' So I went.

I was now working for Mr Henderson; a five-year apprenticeship. He just had a front shop, with the workroom at the back. It was a little workroom, quite grotty really. A pokey and dirty place. There was a stove for heating the goose irons; the thinking at that time was that the weight of the irons did the pressing – really it's the heat – so we had these huge, heavy irons and all the year round there'd be a stove burning to heat them, so it got hot and uncomfortable in the summer. There was electric light, but this was just the single bulb and there was just the one window, so it was all quite dingy. We also had a sewing machine: a treadle machine that you worked with your feet. Then there were three tables for sewing on, plus a sleeve board and a pressing board.

A small, hot and crowded place to pass our working hours in. These were eight-thirty to six, and two mornings a week you had to come in at eight and take your turn in lighting the fire and sweeping the floor. So, all in all, a 48-hour week.

On my first day there I was handed my equipment. This was a thimble, a topless one because tailors, unlike dressmakers, use the side rather than the top to push the needle through the cloth, and my own pair of scissors, which the boss had bought for me, but which I had to pay for. I still have that same pair, 65 years on. You also had a small pair, with sharp points for cutting out buttonholes, and another tool with a sharp blade for unpicking. Then you had a bodkin, a small piece of bone like a pencil; we used it for picking out the basting stitches. We also had our needles in their various sizes. Chalk was a must: dressmakers use pins, but a tailor sticks to chalk for making out the pattern. You had to keep it nice and sharp by using the edge of your scissors. That completed our basic equipment. We wore overalls and we'd stick our needles into the lapels.

Mr Henderson was an excellent tailor with a good reputation locally. A lot of his customers had their suits made with him year after year; he would keep the pattern for

It was a little workroom, quite grotty really. A pokey and dirty place. There was a stove for heating the goose irons; the thinking at that time was that the weight of the irons did the pressing – really it's the heat

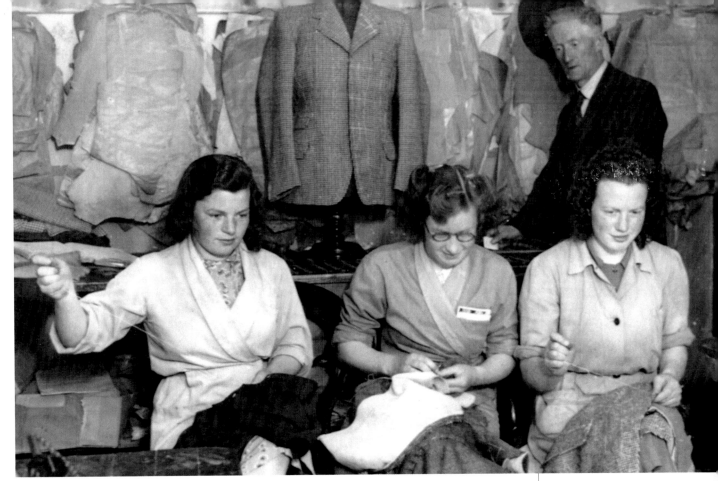

each customer and these would be hung along the wall from a piece of string. He was very skilled at adapting a suit to any particular shape; he'd cut the cloth in a way that disguised a hump or a large tummy and which hid any deformity like that. When somebody came in for a new suit, the boss would be the one to cut it out and then we would be given the basting to do.

The boss would do the final fitting on the customer. It would come back to us with lots of chalk marks on it showing that this bit should be let out a little, or that bit needed taking in a wee bit, that the shoulder could do with being lifted a half-inch, and so on. I can aye mind how a lot of the women would come in for a measurement and then decide to go away and slim down. This made him mad; 'They shid dae their slimmin afore, nat aifter!', he'd say. The boss would do the final 'cutting in'; the edges had to be absolutely right so that the facings could be sewn on properly. There's an awful lot of work in tailoring which is unseen: the inside of a jacket, for example, means masses and masses of sewing. And the great art is to do all this without the stitches showing on the finished product.

All this takes a lot of experience. The first jobs I was allowed to do was for the farm lads who came in for their work trousers to be made up. Then you moved on to boys' breeches, to skirts and waistcoats, then jackets and overcoats and kilts – I still love making kilts and recently did four for my two sons and two grandsons.

I was very innocent at the beginning. On my second day the boss told me he would be making up some moleskin trousers and that I was to go down to the garage to get the moleskin mail as it was being soldered. But when I got there, it was, 'Na, na, lassie, we hanna got it. Try the smithy.'. So I had to bike all the way to the smithy only to find they'd never heard of the order. So back to the workroom empty-handed. When I got there, Mr Henderson and the other girls were all falling about laughing. It was a trick they played on all the new apprentices.

**The boss keeping an eye on things**

Mr Henderson and his team of tailoresses, Torphins, 1946. Margaret Black, 'the Heid Ane', is extreme right, with Peggy Gibb and Evie Milne beside her. Margaret made the jacket hanging up, centre.

He'd promise a customer something, but not tell us and then he would come roaring into the workroom at ten o'clock, 'Gad Amichty quines, there's a fittin at twelve the day!'

I had to learn that if ever you were saying anything nasty about someone you immediately had to say 'barren'. You might be talking about Mrs So-and-so and remark, 'She's gettin real fat these days – barren'. If you forgot, everyone else would start whistling which meant you were 'gettin fat' as well. We called this 'being whistled in' and you had to be real quick to avoid it. It was a good friendly atmosphere in the workroom. We all got on well together. We were aye chatting away and Mr Henderson joined in, too. In my early days he'd be gossiping away and he'd turn to me and say, 'Oh, Merget, we'll be needin mair coal fer the fire. Ye'd better ging and get a fresh bucket in' – and while I was away he would get down to passing on some story that he deemed too much for my innocent young ears.

He was an excellent tailor and an excellent boss. I got a very good training under him. He was mean over money, though; often you had to ask him for your wages and I found that horrible. And he aye left everything to the very last minute. He'd promise a customer something, but not tell us and then he would come roaring into the workroom at ten o'clock, 'Gad Amichty quines, there's a fittin at twelve the day!'. We'd be thrown into it time and time again. We were constantly working against the clock like that – and it was a very busy tailor's anyway. There never seemed any chance to slack a bit. But one thing I did find restful and that was that he'd play classical music on the wireless through the house and we could hear it. The others complained that it was just a 'heap o noise', but I came to enjoy it and to listen out for it.

In those days folk didn't shop around when they wanted a new suit; they would just go to their regular tailor's. He had the same customers for years on end. He looked after them and had their trust. And he was awful fussy about the quality of the material we used; his clothes were built to last. Back in the '30s tailoring was a good trade for a young girl to enter, but after the war things were beginning to change. Younger folk were starting to buy off-the-peg.

The countryside once was full of tailors. They'd go out to the farms to measure you for a suit on the spot, then they'd come back with it for the fitting. Before that they would actually stay in the house and make the suit there; they'd arrive with their board, their iron and all the equipment. The tailor would hand sew everything, sewing with his board on his knee. But after the war ready-made came in and spread. The attitude towards clothes began to change: folk no longer wanted to wear the same suit year after year; they wanted to have a change of fashion every two years or so. The cost of labour rose and the hand-made suit became very expensive compared to what could be bought ready-made. My father had just the one wedding suit and it would last year on year. I doubt whether he had more than three different suits in the whole of his life. I'd go to the church at Torphins and I'd look around and see the same suits on the same people year after year. There was a farmer who'd come for communion and he was in a suit that was green with age and smelt to high heaven of mothballs.

**Margaret Black,** born 1927: Torphins

# Undertaker's apprentice

Johnshaven was dominated by two families: the Blues and the McBays. I'm descended from one of them, on my mother's side. My great grandfather, James McBay, had 25 children. He was first married to Ann Davidson, but she died and so he married her cousin. His children are now all scattered all over the world, but there are still plenty of McBays in Johnshaven and the chief fishing business is carried on within the family: Murray McBay

Looking back, I seemed to have spent most of my boyhood out on the rocks. Every night when I came in from the school I would put my bag into the house, grab my rod and then away. I'd use lugworms and go fishing, for cod, saith, or mackerel, or whatever. Later on me and my brother took out our own wee boat. In those days there seemed to be no end of fish off Johnshaven; you could pull them in nice and thick in the nets. Now there's none because of all the overfishing.

I didn't enjoy the school. We got a very efficient education, learned the basics and all that, but I just wanted to be out and away. I was always itching to be out on the rocks, or at sea in a boat, away off my backside, not sitting indoors at some book or other. I liked doing things with my hands, so when I got the chance of an apprenticeship with the

**The McBay dynasty**
The patriarch with the white beard is John Mearns McBay, father of 25 children. Douglas Beattie's grandmother, Jane Bell McBay, a daughter, is seated right in front and his grandfather, Douglas Duncan, is standing, left.

**The joiner's workshop**

Taken some years before Douglas entered it as an apprentice in 1945.

Issie was the village prostitute; she did good business. She was quite short and quite wide. No beauty, but she seemed to be in demand. She was some machine!

joiners' up the hill I jumped at it. After all, getting a trade was thought of as a good outcome for a young lad; work in the village was in short supply.

I started at five bob a week. You had to buy your own tools, too, hammer, saw, chisel – everything. I loved working with wood and dovetailing and shaping it; it was very satisfying to take a problem and work away till you got the right fit. I found myself scrambling over roofs and making up doors and windows and then fitting them. I was in action all the time and I loved it.

People would drop into the workshop for a chat and just to see what was going on. One of our regulars was Issie. She'd come by with her bag: 'Ony shavins?' We'd let her help herself. They were for her washing boiler. Issie was the village prostitute; she did good business. Many of her regular clients were outsiders who'd come down to the village in their cars for her services. She wasn't exactly a bonny woman either, quite short and quite wide. No beauty, but she seemed to be in demand. She was some machine!

**Joann:** Yes. She once told my father that she'd had as many cocks inside her as there are palin posts on the road between Johnshaven and Inverbervie – and there's' a good few of them! She wasn't at all ashamed of her trade; to her, prostitution was her job and she evidently did it well.

**Douglas:** One of my first jobs was to learn how to measure bodies for the coffins. There I was going around with the joiner to the houses where there had just been a death. The body would be lying out on the bed and he would take the head while I took the feet and we'd lower him into the coffin. The corpse had to be straightened out and then the head would be lifted up and the silk robes slipped on.

Coffins were a big part of the joiner's business. We'd make about one a week, steady. This was strange work for a young 14-year-old, but you just had to do it. In those days it was a question of get on with it; any complaint and you could expect your books.

His wife would always be on the lookout for any likely new customer. If she heard that someone was in a bad way, she'd go to the house, knock at the door and ask straight out, 'Is he ony waur?'. Always that, 'ony waur?', never, 'Is he getting better?'.

**Douglas and Joann Beattie,** born 1930 and 1946: Johnshaven

# Down at the mill

When I was 14 I left the school and went to the mill. It's what all the girls in Gourdon did then. You either went to the fish houses or the mill; there didn't seem to be any other choice. The work was very hard. You began at six in the morning and you had to go in on the Saturday forenoon as well. The gaffer kept us at it all the time. If you seemed to linger over a break, he would be in at us shouting to get back to our work. Once he actually hit me: by this time I was the whistle lady and while we were at our break, the frames had all filled up and I wasn't there to blow for a change about. He came in and swore at me; when I went to go back he raised his foot and gave me a boot up the backside. Imagine that happening nowadays? But none of us dared protest then; it was more than our jobs were worth.

I began on twelve-and six a week. I started off as a bobbin carrier. Conditions weren't good. The mill was a big, open kind of building and full of noise with machinery clattering away non-stop. We were making camouflage nets and there was little bits of stuff flying all over the place. We never even had anything to put over our nose and mouth – no health regulations in those days! It was a filthy place to work in.

It employed about eighty people, mostly from Gourdon, but some walked over each day from Bervie as well. As bobbin carrier my job was to take the new spools in boxes to the girls at the machines so as to keep them going. Then I got moved onto being a shifter; for this you had to shift the frames when they became full; you'd take off the full bobbins and fit on the new empty ones. Then I got made the whistle lady. All this was promotion, but I got no extra pay for this responsibility – though as a 15-year old my wages did rise to 15 shillings a week.

We did have our amusements. On Friday nights we'd all go off to the dances together and get back at two in the morning. But you still had to get up for a six o'clock start at the mill on the Saturday morning and I found it very difficult to cope with all the noise of the mill while the thump of the dance band was still running through my head. All the girls said the same: you'd be on the shop floor surrounded by all that machinery going full tilt and the accordions would still be booming away in your head.

On Wednesday we went to the pictures over at Bervie. You went whatever was on and it cost threepence for a wooden seat down at the front. A more plush seat further back would cost a full shilling, so we just sat pressed up against the screen, watching stuff like Flash Gordon or the latest cowboy film. The picture house was a bit of a fleapit; you reckoned that you'd come out of it with more than you went in.

**Margaret Duncan,** born 1928: Gourdon

> He came in and swore at me; when I went to go back he raised his foot and gave me a boot up the backside. Imagine that happening nowadays? But none of us dared protest then; it was more than our jobs were worth.

# A country joiner's workshop

When I left school I actually had my name down for an apprentice at the local garage in Maud, but Mr Taylor came to the house to see my mother about serving my time with his firm as a joiner. Well, at that time your parents' word

> I had to repair farm carts, make up hen houses, assemble grocer vans. A wee bit of everything. I did wallpapering; I cut glass; I was painter and plumber.

was law, so that's what I had to do.

So there I was at Nethermuir learning how to be a joiner. It was a small country shop and you had to do a bit of everything. In hindsight I couldn't say that it was the best place to serve your apprenticeship; a larger concern – Peterhead or Aberdeen – would have given me a more specialised training.

In a place like that you were really expected to turn your hand to whatever came along, and a lot of it wasn't really joinery. I had to repair farm carts, make up hen houses, assemble grocer vans. A wee bit of everything. I did wallpapering; I cut glass; I was painter and plumber. And Mr Taylor had some land, so I had to take in the cow, too. I've seen me having to go over to a job ten miles away on the other side of New Deer, with a pair of five-by-two planks and a set of tools tied onto my bike. You had to be with the job till five, then cycle all the way back – and that would be in your own time. And all for five bob a week.

Everything was haphazard. The workshop was well enough fitted out, but there was no machinery; everything had to be done by hand. I'd been there maybe a month and I had to carry in this ash plank – eighteen inch wide, four inch thick, it was – out of which I had to cut and shape a pair of shafts for a cart. All by hand. Hour after hour of drudgery. But I'll tell you: I can make a good barrow yet. I got the making of farm barrows down to a fine art: first two days, look out the materials, cut and dress; third day ready for painting. A two-and-a-half-day job – done!

I remember doing cartwheels. I'd see me taking off the ring and then working away on the spokes and the wheel itself. Now, the blacksmith was four miles away over at New Deer and the only way to get there was to hang the cartwheel and the ring on the pedal and walk beside your bike, pushing it along, the whole four miles. Then you had to stand and watch the ring being fitted again. If you hadn't done your job exactly right the ring and the wheel wouldn't grip together properly and that would be your responsibility. Then walk back, again pushing the bike. Wheelwright's work. Can you imagine a joiner's apprentice doing that today?

I once had to put new buckets in a water wheel. The trick was to do it and keep the wheel from turning at the same time. So I had to sit with my feet on the bucket below and jam myself up against the wall – and I had to do that for all fifteen buckets. You just had to improvise your way through.

After National Service I was working on a council house scheme at Boddam, on some dormer windows, alongside joiners from the town. We had to fit timber, cut angle-ways into the angle of the roof. The other boys came to a stop; they said they'd have to go off to the sawmill to get it cut. Now, in the town they could just nip along and get it done, but this was Boddam and the customer was waiting. I just set up two stools, took my ripsaw and set to work. 'Fat the hell are you daen?' they said. 'The customer wants his timber now,' I told them. That was the difference between the town and the country joiner; I would turn my hand to anything and just get on with it.

**William McRae,** born 1930: Nethermuir

# 'Not an ounce more, not an ounce less'

My first jobs after school were with licensed grocers. The second one was with Carry & Co. High class grocer; very smart business. The manager: white coat ex-Army man; very good training for me. Those were the days when everything came loose and had to be measured out – wooden tea boxes, weighing out the tea – split peas, whole peas, bacon, single eggs. Everything absolutely precise, not a fraction under, not a fraction over.

This poor old wifie came into the shop: 'Four ounces of cheese, please,'. 'Peer aul cratur,' I thought, 'Ah'll shave aff a wee bitty mair an slip it in'. But the boss was eyeing the needle on the weighing machine like some kind of enemy and he came in about and kicked my feet just like that. Then he raised his hand and clapped me round the lug – bang! – like a gun going off. 'See that mark on the machine?' he roared out. 'That's what the lady is paying for and that's what you will give her, not one iota more, not one iota less!'. He made me feel like dirt, doing that in front of the whole shop.

On a Monday morning kids would come in on their way to the school. 'Hey, mister, hae ye got ony broken biscuits fer us?'. They wouldn't have had any breakfast and some of the other grocers would oblige with a few bits, but not him. He'd come marching across the floor: 'Sorry son, I seem to have lost my hammer. Now get out of my shop!'

There were little things like that. Often I went home in tears. He wouldn't allow me to mix with the other grocer boys, especially the Co-op ones. We were exclusive, you see: white aprons, shining shoes, not a hair out of place. But there were compensations. Once a week I'd be put away over to Newmill with the horse lorry. This was a wagon pulled by the Clydesdale and piled with tomato boxes filled with different folks' messages. I had a float of four bob. Empty lemonade bottle, half-penny back. But most times it was, 'Ach, dinna heed the change, loon – jist keep it fer yersel'.

And old Mr Carry, a real gentleman, owner of the firm. He'd come to visit us; chauffeur-driven car, tour of inspection and then, just as he was leaving, to me, ten shilling note in his hand: 'Young man, I've noticed how clean you keep your bicycle. Please take this'.

It was all very strict. In the mornings I would have to get up early, go to his house, get the keys, open the shop. By the time he arrived I'd be expected to be out at the front, washing the windows, cleaning the pavement. Good training, but I was anxious to leave and become a painter. He took me aside: 'Young Ian, you're a fool. You're born to serve the public – you'll be wasted as a painter'.

As soon as I got to 16 and old enough to start my apprenticeship, I was for off. We left together. As I was lining up at the office ben the back for my last pay he came up to me: 'That's you leaving and that's me leaving the old firm. I've decided to accept the post of manager at an egg-packing plant. Mark my words, young Ian, there won't be a Carry's for very much longer'.

And he was right: under the new manager things got slack, the business went downhill and within a year or two it was finished. He'd been a hard taskmaster, but a master of his trade – and when I applied for jobs later, the reference he wrote for me was first class.

**Ian Stevenson,** born 1932: Keith

**How the life of work started**
Ian in his christening robe, which was his grandmother's wedding dress cut down, and mother at the door of his lifelong home in Fife Keith, 1932

**'You'll be wasted as a painter!'**
The young apprentice to Symon, Painters & Decorators, Keith 1948

**400 guineas worth**

The 15-year-old John Goodbrand heads for the Perth Sales with Ebric of Drumin.

# Selling the bull

When I left school I went to Drumin Farm as a cattleman. You had to grow up fast in those days and although only 14 I was expected to do a man's work and that included handling the bull. It was just after the war, the period when the Argentines were trying to improve their own herds and were buying the best of our breeding stock.

In February 1947 I was sent down to the Perth Bull Sales to sell our prize yearling 'Ebric of Drumin'. I cycled down to Ballindalloch Station to meet up with the cattleman from there and along with his son we took a special train which stopped all down Speyside to pick up other cattle and convey them down to Perth. It had these wagons where the bulls were arranged in partitions on either side, while we sat in the middle corridor.

Now, up to this point I had hardly left the glen at all – the biggest place I'd ever been to was Elgin – so to me the trip represented my first ever visit to the big city. We stayed in digs for the whole week and everything about Perth struck me as a revelation – the cars and the lorries, the shops, the people on the streets, the food we got at the market restaurant. I remember how, when I walked the bull to and from the market, a policeman stepped into the middle of the road and held up his hand to stop the traffic, so we cross safely. In fact, the whole of Perth seemed to be given over to the sale: the animals were paraded through the streets and the judges would carry out their inspections there.

For me a highlight was going to the cinema – another first. I can't recall what the picture was, but I do know that it was in the King's Cinema House.

For Drumin the sale was a great success: we sold Ebric for 400 guineas; our previous highest sale had been for no more than 100. He was a fine, docile beast, easy to handle. So at the end of the week I was able to return to Ballindalloch, pick up my bike and cycle back up to Glenlivet in triumph – and full of the sights and sounds from my great adventure.

**John Goodbrand,** born 1932: Glenlivet

**The young farm servant**

On the back of the tractor sowing grass seed with his future brother-in-law driving, Braes of Glenlivet, 1947

# EARLY CENTURY LIVES: 6
## Two Widow's Sons

**Back to his old school...**
but this time as Director of Education.
James Michie visits primary pupils
at Auchenblae School, 1991

> Oh, and the dentist. That was a terrible ordeal, the day he came. No fillings; if your teeth were just a wee bit rotten, out they'd come.

# The one who left school early

My father was a keeper on the estate, the Glenbuchat estate. He was moving up the ladder a wee bit, second keeper, but he caught bronchial pneumonia and that's what he died of. The kind of thing that would be cured nowadays, but then all you had was a couple of aspirins and a currant drink. So that was that. He was 36. My mother was a widow and she had all of us to bring up. There was six of a family; I was the oldest, fifteen just.

My childhood was filled with work and with jobs. It made you think you were somebody, out helping the men at their work. If there was sheep on the road which needed shifting, my brother and I would be out helping. In those days there'd be thousands of sheep out on the roads come springtime. They'd be driving the ewes and their lambs for the summer grazings, onto the hills, up from where they'd been wintering: Insch or Kinaldie – down that way. Now it's all done by lorry, but at that time they'd walk miles with them and there was always a chance the shepherd would be needing some help. For me the farming and the sheep were more important than the school.

For my primary schooling I went to the Glenbuchat school. We had a Miss Forgie and she would take you on her knee, whiles. A granny kind of lady. The two things I mind are cold feet and the cocoa. You'd be sweating in your tackety boots going and then you had to sit in this cold school room and your feet would cool right down. We'd get cocoa in an enamel mug, just a wee drop of milk going into it. That was something to look forward to – but I aye mind the cold feet.

Oh, and the dentist. That was a terrible ordeal, the day he came. You'd be last in the line and you'd hear all the bairns before you howling and yelling away. No fillings; if your teeth were just a wee bit rotten, out they'd come. I mind coming across him years later when I was with a flock of sheep on the road up Deeside and it was as much as I could do to stop myself from going up to his windscreen and putting my stick right through it.

**A good place to grow up**

Looking up Glenbuchat, including the castle. Bertie Grant was born at the Cottartons, which lie just beside it.

Really, it's the walk to the school that I mind more of than what went on inside it. Three miles of trudging each way. There was this big girl, Mary Thomson from the Dockington, out in front, and I was just a little chap then. I aye mind following the footsteps she made in the snow and I'd be trying to fit into each one. We had bad winters then and the snow would be piled up real high. Then on the way home you'd see what was going on in the fields. There was aye the chance that some help might be needed. There was once I looked over the dyke and saw this chap shovelling the neeps into a cart at the Mains. I had to have a shottie and I got into that field, but I had the terriblest job aiming the horse at the right drill and getting back up again. But it was something I just had to try. Being like the men, you see.

I enjoyed my growing up in the Glen. The thing that sticks in my mind is looking at each dyke end on the way to school; my father would set traps for weasels and I had to look out for them. We'd go ferreting for rabbits together. He kept bees and was reckoned to be something of an expert. He'd cycle down to Towie and give lectures on the subject. There was this firm in Aberdeen, Ogilvie's, and he would sell them hundredweights of pure sweet honey each season. At that time everyone in the Glen kept bees; the fields would be white with clover and the hills smothered in heather.

I did well enough at the Glenbuchat School. I got this prize for the pupil who had 'made most progress in the year'. Half-a-crown it was. I was bright enough, you see, and my parents were thinking I could go on and make something of myself, be a minister or a teacher, perhaps. But once my father died, the family needed the wages I could earn. That sorted that out and thank goodness for it. If I'd had to stay on and get a collar-and-tie job indoors I think I'd have just pined away.

I was the only one in my time to go on to Towie from the Glen and try for a proper secondary education. The rest stayed on at the Glen and left at fourteen. I'd been picked out at twelve when I passed the exam and was given money for a bike to get me back and forwards to the school down there: three pounds nineteen-and-six, it was. It was an eight-mile journey. Going wasn't so bad, but coming back, up all those braes and with the wind against you, well, that was murder. All I was fit for when I got back was my bed; the homework had to be put to one side.

The dominie at Towie knew the distance I had to travel and often when the afternoon was wearing on he would say, 'Grant, I've got these letters to post; you can go home now and catch the post on the way'. This was Dominie Smith. I liked him, even if he did have his methods. First thing in the morning, well, he knew how to waken you up. He'd fire off these ten questions of mental arithmetic at us, 'just to liven you up a bit', he said. He'd get us all out into this 'Line of Disgrace'. You'd be put in your place in the queue according to the number of answers you'd got wrong. Then he'd go down the line, belting us one by one as he went. Some of the girls would be greetin as soon as they saw him

**'At that time they'd walk miles with their sheep'**
Shepherd James Gray (see 'The Crack Shepherd': Patrick Scott) rests his flock overnight on the green at Aberlour church, en route from Grantown-on-Spey to Huntly.

He'd line us all up into this 'Line of Disgrace'. You'd be put in your place according to the number of answers you'd got wrong. Then he'd go down the line, belting us one by one'

reaching into the drawer for his strap, but it didn't concern me too much.

But then came the winter of '37 when we had a whole heap of snow and I couldn't get down the road to the school. I

### 'I was stuck there for eleven weeks'

In the 1930s, when Bertie Grant was at the school and when this shot was taken, the pupils of Glenbuchat School had to endure frequent spells of the harsh weather.

was stuck up there in the Glen for eleven weeks. It was after the Easter holidays when I got back and they thought I'd been away in a foreign country. I'd been out in the sun and the snow and my face was brown as a berry. All the rest, they were pale and white-faced, what with sitting inside the school all that time.

After that I think that the dominie and I came to a sort of agreement that I'd be giving up. In the end I was fed up with the whole school business. Couldn't get away quick enough. I didn't exactly hate the school, but I'd come to find it all a great irrelevance. My mother had this garden and she needed help with lifting the vegetables for her soup. That and the hens is what she got by on. I left and went home to help my mother and to get what work I could. I mind the big moment when my mother and I were out in the field at the croft and we could see Willy Ellison come striding up through the park towards us.

We stood there watching and my mother was saying, 'Noo, fit wad he be wantin?'. Well, he'd come to ask if I would be interested in going off to help the shepherd. That was right into my barrow. I was fifteen and away from the school. It was what I wanted to do – out in the fields, up in the hills, doing things, working towards something.

**Albert Grant,** born 1921: Glenbuchat

### Glenbuchat School, the final roll

The class at the school Bertie Grant attended, in 1960. The two adults are Rebecca Walker (right), teacher, and Mrs J. Thomson, school cook. When Bertie started school in 1927, the roll was still around 30.

# And the one who stayed on

**Where it all started**
Auchenblae School in the 1900s, a generation before James Michie enrolled there.

All my childhood and all my youth was spent in Kincardineshire, on the land. Father was a cattleman and because he was a cattleman he was a farm servant. The economics of the time were such that you were on a contract – a fee – and you were housed in a tied living and whether you stayed in employment or whether you would have to leave after six months, depended entirely on the whim of the farmer.

Consequently, after six months you might find yourself putting all the scanty furniture you had on board a box and cart pulled by a Clydesdale horse to go to live in yet another small cottar house in the hope that things might improve and that this time, you might have a longer time to stay to get some continuity and stability. The wages were extremely low and the working conditions were extremely harsh; you never left the work even under the most atrocious downpours and consequently a lot of farm workers died long before their time from conditions such as pneumonia or arthritis.

This is what happened to my father. We lost our father when I was nine; there were three below me, one sister and two brothers. My mother, she was Mother Courage; she had four of us and she did all the work. She had to go out and earn what she could, where she could. She worked in domestic work and also farm work, milking cows or working in the fields, at potato planting time, at hay time, at the hairst and the like. She was the anchor of the family and was its breadwinner. In those days you didn't have the Welfare State, nor did you have a National Health Service.

I went to Fordoun Public School till 1939 when I was thirteen. It was a six-teacher school: the primary classes and then the advanced divisions in charge of the headmaster. He was the only male teacher in the school; all the others were ladies, neatly dressed in twin sets, skirt and double row of pearls. Every one of them was a Miss, from the young infant mistress newly out of Training College, to the venerable and experienced ladies who were in charge of the older classes. Unmarried, because in those days if a woman married she had to leave teacher employment.

They were good folk and were a product of the time in the sense that the three Rs were paramount; we spoke when we were spoken to, we sat in serried rows, and we were summarily punished the moment we misbehaved. If you didn't do the work accurately and timeously you would be punished. That was quite normal, although as a bright pupil I usually escaped such measures. If the child could not do the work, it was attributed to some character deficiency. Lack of ability was not to be reckoned a mitigating factor. It was almost moral laziness, sloth, lack of conscientiousness.

At the end of the day, we all came out pretty well from it. At the age of twelve, the whole of us, for the most part, could read, we could write, we could count and we all of us knew right from wrong. It was a Biblical right, in other words an unqualified right.

There were wooden floors; the rooms were governed by tiers; we sat in pews. But I remember there was one teacher who loved her class and every Friday afternoon when the bell rang, this lady would go to her cupboard and take out a large bottle of sweeties, of boilings, and each and every one of us got one to suck. In the harsh days of the '30s these are the things you remember with gratitude.

I recall how I arrived in secondary education. In those days there were still fees for the secondary school. They were not high, but they were enough to be a deterrent for the working class. None of my siblings did; they went into the army, the navy; my sister went to a factory in Aberdeen. They stayed on at Fordoun and went into the advanced divisions there.

Very few, in fact, went on to an academic course. Most of the Auchenblae children left at fourteen to go into domestic service, to go on the land and become cattlemen or horsemen; some of the girls went to become shop assistants. Precious few went on and did the academic course at Mackie Academy; even fewer completed it. There were many who could have gone on, but lack of money stopped them; they had to help support the family. But, even sadder than that, there was the feeling of 'learnin's nae for the likes o us'. The fact was their family had always been in that situation and they just accepted it; there was a kind of fatalism. I had difficulty myself – there was a feeling that I might get too big for my boots, that I wasn't fitting into the mould that was meant for me.

My mother was surprised that I got on as well as I did. There were so many other things on her mind. She came from a working class family, from Kemnay, and in those days – well, all the sisters were in service, her brothers on the land. When I came to the age of twelve, it was automatically assumed that I should go on to the land. How else could it be? The times were such that it was quite out of the question to think otherwise.

But three teachers from my school came to see my mother and persuaded her to let me go on. And that is how I went to university and that is how I became a teacher of modern languages and Director of Education with responsibility for both Auchenblae and Mackie Academy, my two old schools.

You can have no idea what, at that time, all this meant. I was aware of a moral imperative, that I should not, dare not, fail. There was a huge responsibility weighing on me. Even more so when I went to university. I had to justify the sacrifice made. People talk blithely of the lad o' pairts and think what a wonderful thing it all was, but behind it

all, there were a large number who weren't able to go on. Quite a number who could have were denied, for various reasons, the main one being domestic economics. But the other reason was that they had never had anybody in the family who had gone. They had never had the tradition. Social determinism, that's what it was, social determinism.

**James Michie,** born 1926: Auchenblae

**' My mother was surprised at how well I got on'**
James Michie, Director of Education, takes his place in the fron row beside Chairman Maitland Mackie in this photograph of Aberdeenshire Education Committee, 1969.